THE GNOSTIC
DISCOVERIES

THE GNOSTIC DISCOVERIES

THE IMPACT OF
THE NAG HAMMADI LIBRARY

MARVIN MEYER

HarperSanFrancisco
A Division of HarperCollins*Publishers*

THE GNOSTIC DISCOVERIES: *The Impact of the Nag Hammadi Library.*
Copyright © 2005 by Marvin Meyer. All rights reserved. Printed in the United States of America. No part of this book may be used or reproduced in any manner whatsoever without written permission except in the case of brief quotations embodied in critical articles and reviews. For information address HarperCollins Publishers, 10 East 53rd Street, New York, NY 10022.

HarperCollins books may be purchased for educational, business, or sales promotional use. For information please write: Special Markets Department, HarperCollins Publishers, 10 East 53rd Street, New York, NY 10022.

HarperCollins Web site: http://www.harpercollins.com

HarperCollins®, ◆®, and HarperSanFrancisco™ are trademarks of HarperCollins Publishers.

FIRST HARPERCOLLINS PAPERBACK EDITION PUBLISHED IN 2006

Library of Congress Cataloging-in-Publication Data is available.
ISBN-10: 0–06–085832–x
ISBN-13: 978–0–06–085832–2

06 07 08 09 10   RRD(H)   10 9 8 7 6 5 4 3 2 1

CONTENTS

Acknowledgments

I WOULD LIKE TO EXPRESS my appreciation to Chapman University and the Griset Chair in Bible and Christian Studies for support of my research on this book. At Harper San Francisco Eric Brandt, Kris Ashley, and Lisa Zuniga have been particularly helpful in the production of this book, and the staff of the Institute for Antiquity and Christianity of Claremont Graduate University has assisted in locating photographs reproduced here. I offer special thanks to my wife and children, who have walked with me, literally and metaphorically, through the sands of Egypt for many years.

THE GNOSTIC
DISCOVERIES

INTRODUCTION

GNOSTIC WISDOM
ANCIENT AND MODERN

S INCE THE DISCOVERY of the ancient texts that comprise the Nag Hammadi library, the world of the historical Jesus, the schools of Judaism and Greco-Roman religion, and the varieties of Christianity has begun to look remarkably different than it did once upon a time.

In this book, *The Gnostic Discoveries*, I seek to assess the character of that world of Jesus, Judaism, Greco-Roman religion, and early Christianity in the light of the Gospel of Thomas, the Secret Book of John, the Gospel of Truth, and other texts unearthed in the discovery of the Nag Hammadi library and to suggest the extent to which a new understanding of that ancient world may impact our modern world.[1] Many of the texts found in the Nag Hammadi library and related collections, such as the Berlin Gnostic Codex, represent a mystical spirituality commonly called "gnosticism," a term derived from the Greek word *gnōsis*, "knowledge."[2] Hence the title of this book.

BEFORE THE NAG HAMMADI LIBRARY

Prior to the discovery of the Nag Hammadi library, "gnosticism" typically was considered to be an early and pernicious Christian heresy, and much of our knowledge of gnostic religion was gleaned from the writings of the Christian heresiologists, those authors who attempted to establish orthodoxy and expose heresy in the early church. The Christian heresiologists disagreed vehemently with Christian gnostics on matters of faith and life, and as a result they portrayed gnostic believers as vile heretics. Without a doubt the polemical intentions of the heresiologists influenced their understanding—or misunderstanding—of the gnostics. In the latter part of the second century, Irenaeus of Lyon composed a work entitled *Against Heresies* (*Adversus haereses*) in which he accuses those practicing gnostic religion of heresy and attempts to combat their "falsely so-called knowledge." In the early third century, Hippolytus of Rome wrote his *Refutation of All Heresies* (*Refutatio omnium haeresium*) to refute all those he considered to be followers of falsehood, giving special attention to gnostic heretics. Later, in the fourth century, Epiphanius of Salamis authored a particularly nasty piece, even by heresiological standards, entitled *Panarion*, or *Medicine Chest*, with an orthodox antidote for every gnostic malady.[3] From these and other heresiological writers, who were bristling with righteous wrath against their gnostic opponents, we can hardly expect to read a fair and balanced account of gnostic religion, and before the discovery of the Nag Hammadi library this heresiological bias permeated much of the discussion of gnosis.

Nevertheless, in the writings of the heresiologists and other early Christian authors, there are presentations of gnostic ideas and citations of gnostic texts that may provide at least some understanding of who the gnostics were, and scholarly commentators on gnostic life and thought prior to the Nag Hammadi discovery relied on these presentations and citations. Although the heresiological accounts are biased and apparently distort many features of gnostic religion, a careful and critical reading of these accounts may shed light on significant gnostic figures from the first and second centuries, such as Simon Magus, Helena, Marcellina, Basilides, Valentinus, and Marcus, and the gnostic movements they represent. Upon occasion the heresiologists quote from or paraphrase gnostic sources. Hippolytus cites two sayings that come from a version of the Gospel of Thomas as well as a text often referred to as the Naassene Sermon, and he quotes long passages from a work entitled the Book of Baruch said to be written by a gnostic teacher named Justin. (Hippolytus calls the Book of Baruch the most abominable book he has read; today, as a result of our modern sensibilities, we may have quite a different evaluation of the text.) Within the apocryphal Acts of Thomas is the "Hymn of the Pearl," and within the apocryphal Acts of John is the "Round Dance of the Cross." These texts, found in the heresiologists and early Christian writers, were used, before the discovery of the Nag Hammadi library, to gain as much insight as possible into gnostics and gnostic religion.[4]

Before the Nag Hammadi texts were known, there were also a few other gnostic sources that could be examined by those who wished to explore gnostic traditions. In the codex, or ancient book, called the Askew Codex is a sprawling work titled Pistis Sophia, and in the Bruce Codex are three difficult texts, two Books of Jeu and an untitled gnostic text.[5] To these may be added other texts, such as Hermetic works from the Corpus Hermeticum, Mandaean texts from the Middle East, and perhaps Manichaean texts from the Mediterranean region and throughout Asia.[6] A few scholars have also studied magical gems with possible gnostic motifs — figures with heads of roosters or donkeys and serpents for legs and feet, accompanied by engraved names, also known from gnostic texts, such as Yao Abrasax Sabaoth Adonaios.[7]

On the basis of these ancient sources, some biased, some obscure, some uncertain, scholars and authors studying gnostic religion before the Nag Hammadi discovery reflected upon the traditions and did their best to describe and evaluate the gnostics with what they had available. In spite of the limitations, some of the contributions have proved valuable and insightful. Of the books written about gnostics before the discovery of the Nag Hammadi library, by scholars and nonscholars alike, mention may be made of *The Four Zoas* by William Blake, *The Seven Sermons to the Dead* (*Septem Sermones ad Mortuos*) by Carl Jung, *History of Dogma* by Adolf von Harnack, *Orthodoxy and Heresy in Earliest Christianity* by Walter Bauer, *The Gospel of John* by Rudolf Bultmann, and *Gnosis und spätantiker Geist* and *The Gnostic Religion* by Hans Jonas.

The works of Hans Jonas have proved to be especially influential. In his scholarship on gnostic religion Jonas draws a distinction between the gnostic principle ("the spirit of late antiquity") and the gnostic movement. He maintains that gnostic religion is a religion of knowledge, with "a certain conception of the world, of man's alienness within it, and of the transmundane nature of the godhead."[8] This knowledge is expressed through a mythology that borrows from other religious traditions and employs an elaborate series of symbols. Jonas suggests that the result of gnostic reflection is the articulation of religious dualism, dislocation, and alienation, of "the existing rift between God and world, world and man, spirit and flesh."[9] Some gnostics (for example, Valentinians) sought to derive this dualism from a primordial oneness; others (for example, Manichaeans) founded their system upon two ultimate principles in opposition. For Jonas, the manifestations of gnostic dualism can be interpreted in terms of modern philosophical existentialism. The gnostic drama emphasizes the self-understanding of a human being as "thrownness," *Geworfenheit*, that is to say, the abandonment of the self in the world. At the same time, Jonas admits, "There is no overlooking one cardinal difference between the gnostic and the existentialist dualism: Gnostic man is thrown into an antagonistic, anti-divine, and therefore anti-human nature, modern man into an indifferent one. Only the latter case represents the absolute vacuum, the really bottomless pit."[10] Ancient gnostics and modern existentialists may both be nihilistic, but modern

The cliffs of Upper Egypt

people encounter the more profound abyss — the uncaring abyss. For gnostics, there is light in the darkness and hope in the abyss.

Hans Jonas wrote his books on gnostic thought just as word of the Nag Hammadi discovery was emerging. In *The Gnostic Religion* he was able to include a supplement to the second edition: "The Recent Discoveries in the Field of Gnosticism" (chapter 12).[11] We may question Jonas's preoccupation with dualism as the basic characteristic of gnostic religion, but his observations remain helpful. And although Jonas was able to include in his discussion last-minute thoughts about the texts that were becoming known, even he could hardly have imagined how these texts would revolutionize the way we now look at gnosis and the world from antiquity and late antiquity to modern times.

ANCIENT TEXTS FROM THE NILE VALLEY

Since the discovery of the Nag Hammadi library and related texts, the study of gnostic religion and its impact upon ancient and modern religion has been fundamentally transformed. When the Egyptian Muhammad Ali discovered the Nag Hammadi codices in late 1945, he uncovered a collection of thirteen codices with over fifty ancient texts, most of them previously unknown. A goodly number of these texts may be classified as gnostic texts — texts in the Thomas tradition, texts that are Sethian, Valentinian, Hermetic, and some texts that cannot be easily classified. Complementing the Nag Hammadi find are other discoveries of ancient texts, such as the texts in the Berlin Gnostic Codex, various documents found in a rubbish heap at ancient Oxyrhynchus, and, most recently, a newly available codex with more texts in it, including a Gospel of Judas.[12]

The availability of so many new religious texts has attracted the enthusiastic attention of scholars and others interested in gnostic religion from antiquity and late antiquity. Three major scholarly research teams were formed to undertake the arduous task of translating the Coptic texts of the Nag Hammadi library and the Berlin Gnostic Codex: an American team, constituting the Coptic Gnostic Library Project, based at the Institute for Antiquity and Christianity in Claremont, California; a German team, the Berliner Arbeitskreis für koptisch-gnostische Schriften; and a French-Canadian team, centered at Université Laval in Quebec and formed to produce the Bibliothèque copte de Nag Hammadi. In addition, individual scholars and students of ancient and late antique religions have turned their attention to these texts, and through their scholarly labors a large number of articles and books have appeared. David Scholer, a biblical scholar and professional bibliographer, has compiled two hefty volumes listing contributions in Nag Hammadi studies: *Nag Hammadi Bibliography 1948–1969* and *Nag Hammadi Bibliography 1970–*

1994. Between volumes he has published bibliographical installments annually in the periodical *Novum Testamentum*. In short, scholars and authors have been productive in the study of these texts from Egypt, and articles and books have been published in impressive quantities.

Of the contributions, some more scholarly, some more literary and artistic, created by those whose interest in Nag Hammadi has addressed a wider audience beyond the academy — *Gnosis* by Kurt Rudolph, a professor at Philipps Universität, Marburg; *The American Religion* by literary critic Harold Bloom; *Valis* by Philip K. Dick; the film *Stigmata*, directed by Rupert Wainwright; the Wachowski brothers' *Matrix* film trilogy; and so on — two authors have piqued the interest of readers in a special way: Elaine H. Pagels and Dan Brown.

Elaine Pagels is a distinguished scholar of gnostic and early Christian religion with a fine literary style and a rare ability to communicate difficult religious themes with clarity and grace. In her books *The Gnostic Gospels* and *Beyond Belief*, Pagels has invited readers into the exciting world of gnostic spirituality, Christianity, and ancient religions, and through her discussion of Nag Hammadi texts and other religious documents from the world of early Christianity these texts come alive. (For her efforts she was accused by one reviewer of engaging in the "greening of the gnostics" — a charge recalling the old heresiological perspective.)

In *The Gnostic Gospels* Pagels introduces the texts of the Nag Hammadi library by emphasizing the social and political concerns reflected in the texts. As the New Testament scholar Robert M. Grant has put it, "She has a genius for detecting social realities amid what look like the speculative fantasies of the gnostics."[13] Thus, when gnostic texts proclaim multiple manifestations of God as father and as mother, they affirm, Pagels observes, the authority of all people of knowledge, male and female, in opposition to the commitment of the emerging orthodox church to one God — a father in heaven — and one bishop — a male authority figure. Pagels concludes that these and similar concerns are still being addressed today:

> All the old questions — the original questions, sharply debated at the beginning of Christianity — are being reopened. How is one to understand the resurrection? What about women's participation in priestly and episcopal office? Who was Christ, and how does he relate to the believer? What are the similarities between Christianity and other world religions?[14]

In *Beyond Belief*, Pagels focuses attention on the Gospel of Thomas from the Nag Hammadi library. She identifies the differences between Judas Thomas, the twin brother of Jesus, in the Gospel of Thomas and doubting Thomas in the Gospel of John, and she contrasts the gospel of enlightenment proclaimed in the Gospel of Thomas with the gospel of belief in Jesus proclaimed in the Gospel of John. The Gospel of John won the day in the battle for legitimacy, Pagels admits, but the good news of enlightenment as found in the Gospel of Thomas, the Secret Book of John, and other gnostic texts remains a significant form of Christian proclamation. Pagels moves the discussion of Thomas and John beyond accusations of who is right and who is wrong: "What Christians have disparagingly called gnostic and heretical sometimes turn out to be forms of Christian teaching that are merely unfamiliar to us — unfamiliar precisely because of the active and successful opposition of Christians such as John."[15]

More recently, the novelist Dan Brown has published *The Da Vinci Code*, a volume that has attracted an unprecedented number of readers internationally to a tale developed from texts in the Nag Hammadi library and the Berlin Gnostic Codex, chiefly the Gospel of Mary and the Gospel of Philip. Brown's book is a novel, and it should be read as such, I would emphasize, in spite of the occasional historical claims of Brown and the comments — and complaints — of

some of his readers. *The Da Vinci Code* develops the sort of research
and wild speculation found in the book *Holy Blood, Holy Grail*,[16] yet
it is based upon ancient texts and authentic themes in those texts. In
the novel Brown has Sir Leigh Teabing show Sophie Neveu passages
from the Gospel of Philip and the Gospel of Mary, and then they discuss what is said about Mary Magdalene and Peter:

> *"The woman they are speaking of," Teabing explained, "is Mary
> Magdalene. Peter is jealous of her."*
>
> *"Because Jesus preferred Mary?"*
>
> *"Not only that. The stakes were far greater than mere affection.
> At this point in the gospels, Jesus suspects He will soon be cap-
> tured and crucified. So He gives Mary Magdalene instructions on
> how to carry on His Church after He is gone. As a result, Peter ex-
> presses his discontent over playing second fiddle to a woman. I
> daresay Peter was something of a sexist."*
>
> *Sophie was trying to keep up. "This is Saint Peter. The rock on
> which Jesus built His Church."*
>
> *"The same, except for one catch. According to these unaltered
> gospels, it was not Peter to whom Christ gave directions with which
> to establish the Christian Church. It was Mary Magdalene."*[17]

The issues of the roles of Mary and Peter, although presented in a
provocative fashion in *The Da Vinci Code*, are the issues of the Gospels
of Mary and Philip and other gnostic texts. As the reception of the
novel indicates, they remain powerful issues today.

THE IMPACT OF GNOSTIC WISDOM

The Gnostic Discoveries explores the impact of the gnostic wisdom in
the Nag Hammadi library, the Berlin Gnostic Codex, and related
texts. Chapter 1, "Fertilizer, Blood Vengeance, and Codices," recounts

the memorable stories of the discovery of the Nag Hammadi library and other texts, and notes how the archeological and codicological efforts that followed the discoveries provide a new perspective on the history of Christianity in the Nag Hammadi region, the nature of bookbinding, and the compilation of the Nag Hammadi codices. Chapter 2, "Coptic Texts from the Sands of Egypt," presents the documents from the ancient collections under consideration and evaluates their contents. Chapter 3, "They Will Not Taste Death," takes up the most famous text from the Nag Hammadi library, the Gospel of Thomas, along with other texts in the Thomas tradition, and suggests how these texts provide compelling ways of looking at Jesus of Nazareth. Chapter 4, "The Wisdom of Insight," discusses a classic among gnostic texts, the Secret Book of John, and other texts in the Sethian tradition, which proclaim salvation through insight, wisdom, and knowledge. Chapter 5, "Valentinus the Christian Mystic," discusses the Christian leader Valentinus and texts composed by him and his followers. The Valentinian texts include the Gospel of Truth, a sermon probably composed by Valentinus himself; this Christian sermon and the other Valentinian works from the Nag Hammadi library raise thought-provoking questions about the nature of Christian mysticism. Chapter 6, "Hermes, Derdekeas, Thunder, and Mary," presents figures, male and female, who aid in salvation in several additional Nag Hammadi texts. In the Appendix, "The Texts of the Nag Hammadi Library and the Berlin Gnostic Codex," all the texts in these collections are briefly described and characterized in order to provide an overview of the actual contents of all these extraordinary documents.

A goodly number of translations of Nag Hammadi texts and other works are included in this book. Unless otherwise indicated, the translations are my own. They are taken from *The Gospel of Thomas*, *The Gospels of Mary*, *The Gnostic Gospels of Jesus*, or a work in preparation, in collaboration with other scholars, *The Nag Hammadi Scrip-*

tures. Most of the translations of other scholars cited in this book will also appear in *The Nag Hammadi Scriptures*. Numerical references for Nag Hammadi texts and the texts in the Berlin Gnostic Codex refer to Coptic page numbers, except for the Gospel of Thomas, where the numbers refer to sayings. Square brackets indicate textual restorations and angle brackets indicate textual emendations. Notes and Bibliography are added to acknowledge the contributions of other scholars and to offer suggestions for further study.

1

FERTILIZER, BLOOD VENGEANCE, AND CODICES

THE DISCOVERY OF THE NAG HAMMADI LIBRARY

ABOUT 600 KILOMETERS south of Cairo and 125 kilometers north of Luxor, at the big bend in the Nile River in Upper Egypt, lies the city of Nag Hammadi. The Nile Valley is particularly scenic there, and the cliffs that flank the river loom large and are close to the river, giving an impressive definition to the inhabited valley. This valley, watered from ancient times by the Nile, is the "black land," in ancient Egyptian *Kemit* or *Kemi*, which was the name of the land of Egypt. The modern name, Egypt, derives from the Greek *Aigyptos*, as do the words "Coptic" and "Copt," so that by etymology Coptic means Egyptian and a Copt is an Egyptian person.

The fertile "black land" of Egypt was contrasted in ancient Egyptian mythological texts with the "red land," that is, the desert land beyond the waters of the Nile River. Before the Aswan High Dam was constructed to control the flow of the Nile, the river typically

The Jabal al-Tarif, at the foot of which the Nag Hammadi discovery took place

inundated each year, more or less on schedule. Water marks remaining on older mud-brick buildings in southern Egypt show how high
the water used to come during the season of inundation. The inundation of the Nile was judged to be a gift of the divine, since life-giving
water and nutrients borne by the water flooded over the land and
brought fertility to the soil. The red land extended beyond the reach
of the water into the desert that surrounds Egypt. In mythological
terms, the black land was the land of the god Osiris; the red land was
the land of his hostile brother Seth. As Osiris and Seth were rivals in
Egyptian mythology, so the black land, the rich, moist soil, struggled
with the red land, the dry desert sands, for the maintenance of life. It
was in the vicinity of the city of Nag Hammadi that the Coptic texts
of the Nag Hammadi library were discovered, buried in the dry sand
of the red land near the edge of the black land.

From early days the Nag Hammadi region was known for a Christian presence.[1] According to tradition, St. Mark brought the Christian gospel to Egypt when he arrived in Alexandria, in the Nile Delta, in the first century C.E. Christianity spread throughout Egypt and beyond, to Ethiopia and elsewhere in Africa, and Egyptian Christianity took a variety of forms and expressed itself with a variety of spiritualities: Jewish Christian, apocalyptic, Alexandrian, gnostic, Manichaean, monastic. The richness of Christianity in Egypt rests in large part in the diversity of its early manifestations. Some of this diversity is evident in the Nag Hammadi library and the related texts discovered along the banks of the Nile River.

THE DISCOVERY OF THE NAG HAMMADI CODICES

In about December of 1945, as Muhammad Ali of the al-Samman clan has told his story to James M. Robinson, several Egyptian fellahin, including Muhammad Ali himself, were riding their camels near the Jabal al-Tarif, a prominent cliff along the Nile River near Nag Hammadi.[2] Muhammad Ali recalled the date of this particular trip to the Jabal al-Tarif because he associated it with another event that had happened around this time. He had been collecting fertilizer a few weeks before the celebration of Coptic Christmas (January 6), but he remembered more clearly that his camel ride to the cliff had occurred shortly before the time of a dramatic act of blood vengeance on behalf of his father. We shall return to the act of blood vengeance soon.

As Robinson has reconstructed the story, Muhammad Ali was riding his camel, with his brothers Khalifah Ali and Abu al-Magd and others, to the cliff on the edge of the red land. The fellahin hobbled their camels at the foot of the Jabal al-Tarif and began to dig around a large boulder on the talus, or slope of debris, that had formed against the cliff face. They were gathering *sabakh*, natural fertilizer that accumulates in such places, but to their surprise they discovered a large storage jar buried by the boulder, with a bowl sealed on the mouth of the jar as a lid. Although it was the youngest brother, Abu al-Magd, who initially uncovered the jar, Muhammad Ali, as the oldest of the brothers, took over the operation. In his account, Muhammad Ali has suggested that he paused before removing the lid or breaking open the jar, since he was worried that the jar might contain a jinni, or spirit, that could cause grief if released from the jar. Muhammad Ali apparently also reflected upon stories of treasures hidden in the ground in that area of Egypt, and his love of gold overcame his fear of jinn. He smashed the jar with his mattock, and indeed something golden flew out of the jar and disappeared into the air. But when he peered into the broken jar to see what remained, he was disappointed to find nothing but old codices, or books.

The golden material that Muhammad Ali saw, we may conclude from his story, was not gold at all, but most likely fragments of papyrus, golden in color, that were released into the air from the jar and glistened like particles of gold in the sunlight. Muhammad Ali proceeded to take from the jar the codices that remained — the thirteen codices of the Nag Hammadi library. (The one intact tractate from Codex XIII, Three Forms of First Thought, was stuffed inside the front cover of Codex VI.) He tore up some of the codices in an offer to share them with the other fellahin, but they declined his offer, and so he removed the turban he was wearing and wrapped the codices in it in order to carry the old books back home to al-Qasr. James Robinson has observed that some of the damage done to the Nag Hammadi codices must have occurred when Muhammad Ali ripped them apart that day.

More damage was done when, upon reaching his home in al-Qasr, Muhammad Ali threw the codices unceremoniously into a courtyard reserved for the animals. A while later, the mother of Muhammad Ali took some of the dry papyrus leaves of the codices and used them along with straw to light a fire in the clay oven used by the family. Robinson has surmised that the papyrus leaves may have come from what we now call Nag Hammadi Codex XII, since that codex is very fragmentary, with only a few leaves remaining. On that day gnosis and wisdom of one sort or another went up in smoke and ash, lost forever.

As for the rest of the Nag Hammadi codices, the family of Muhammad Ali tried to sell the books for a few piastres each, and some were traded for cigarettes or pieces of fruit. The antiquities dealer Phokion J. Tano got involved in the dealings, and at last the codices were delivered to the Coptic Museum in Old Cairo, where they remain to the present day — though Codex I (now often referred to as the Jung Codex) was taken out of Egypt and purchased by the Jung Institute; it remained abroad for a time until it was returned to the Coptic Museum. The leather cover of the Jung Codex, and the bowl apparently used as the lid of the jar, found their way to the Institute for Antiquity and Christianity, until they became part of the Schøyen Collection.

The bloody event that Muhammad Ali associated with the discovery of the Nag Hammadi library was an act of revenge for the murder of his father. Muhammad Ali told Robinson that his father had been a night watchman at al-Qasr, where he had killed an intruder from Hamra Dum, a village at the foot of the Jabal al-Tarif. Within a day there was retaliation for what Muhammad Ali's father had done, and he himself was killed, shot through the head. A feud reminiscent of that of the Hatfields and the McCoys ensued. Muhammad Ali's mother, now widowed, told her sons to keep their mattocks sharp in preparation for their own act of vengeance against the murderer of their father. About half a year later, Muhammadi Ali recollected, the awaited day arrived. Muhammad Ali and his brothers were told that their father's killer, Ahmad Isma'il, was asleep by the roadside with a jar of sugarcane molasses next to him. The brothers, obeying their mother's wishes, grabbed their sharpened mattocks, found sleeping Ahmad, and chopped him to pieces. As the quintessential act of blood vengeance, they cut out Ahmad's heart, divided it among themselves, and consumed it then and there. It is no surprise that Muhammad Ali remembered the discovery of the Nag Hammadi codices to be a fairly coincidental occurrence shortly before those bloody days of life and death.

James Robinson notes he was informed that the local registry of deaths lists the date of the death of Muhammad Ali's father as May 7, 1945. If Muhammad Ali's memory is that the act of blood vengeance was about half a year later, and only a short time after the discovery of the Nag Hammadi codices, then the date of the discovery of the Nag Hammadi library may have been around the end of 1945.

In his account of these sordid affairs, Robinson reminisces about how he got Muhammad Ali to agree to return to the site of the discovery, so close to Hamra Dum, where Ahmad Isma'il had lived:

Muhammad Ali at al-Qasr, with the Jabal al-Tarif in the background

I had to go to Hamra Dum myself, find the son of Ahmad Isma'il,
the man Muhammad Ali had butchered, and get his assurance
that, since he had long since shot up a funeral cortège of Muham-
mad Ali's family, wounding Muhammad Ali and killing a num-
ber of his clan, he considered the score settled. Hence, he would
not feel honor-bound to attack Muhammad Ali if he returned to
the foot of the cliff. I took this good news back to Muhammad Ali,
who opened his shirt, showed me the scar on his chest, bragged
that he had been shot but not killed, yet emphasized that if he
ever laid eyes on the son of Ahmad Isma'il again, he would kill
him on the spot. As a result of this display of a braggadocio's fear-
lessness, he could be persuaded to go to the cliff, camouflaged in
my clothes, in a government jeep, with me sitting on the "bullets"
side facing the village and him on the safer cliff side, at dusk in
Ramadan, when all Muslims are at home eating their fill after
fasting throughout the daylight hours.[3]

The rest of the story of the disposition of the Nag Hammadi
codices is not as bloody, but it has its unpleasant moments. As in the
case of the Dead Sea Scrolls, a scholarly monopoly prevented scholarly accessibility to the texts and delayed their publication. Eventually a UNESCO committee was appointed, research projects were
organized, and the Nag Hammadi library was published in a facsimile (photographic) edition and in translation. The monopoly has been
broken, and the texts of the Nag Hammadi library are available for
study.[4]

THE BERLIN GNOSTIC CODEX AND OTHER TEXTS

A few decades before the discovery of the Nag Hammadi library, at the
end of the nineteenth century, a papyrus codex related in its contents
to the Nag Hammadi codices came to light in Egypt. The circumstances

surrounding the discovery remain obscure, but in January 1896 a dealer in manuscripts in Cairo offered the codex for sale to a German scholar, Carl Reinhardt. The dealer was from Akhmim, north of Nag Hammadi in central Egypt, and the codex may have come from there as well. The dealer claimed the codex had been discovered with feathers covering it in a recessed place in a wall, but that story may be a tall tale. Carl Schmidt, the editor of the codex, thought that it may have come from a cemetery or somewhere else near Akhmim. In any case, Reinhardt bought the codex in Cairo and brought it to Berlin, where it was housed in the Ägyptisches Museum. Today it is referred to as Codex Berolinensis Gnosticus 8502, or Berlin Gnostic Codex 8502.[5]

Carl Schmidt published the last text in the Berlin Gnostic Codex, the Act of Peter, in 1903, and he was preparing to publish the rest of the codex in 1912 when curses from the days of the pharaohs seemed to visit the publishing project. A water pipe in the print shop in Leipzig burst and destroyed the pages that were being prepared. World War I broke out and delayed publication. Carl Schmidt died. World War II again delayed publication. And — though this was hardly a curse — the discovery of the Nag Hammadi library in 1945 attracted the attention of scholars and distracted them from the work on the Berlin Gnostic Codex. At last, Walter C. Till, who had assumed editorial responsibility for the Berlin Gnostic Codex after the death of Carl Schmidt, was able to see the German edition of the first three texts in the codex through the press in 1955. Hans-Martin Schenke published a second, revised, edition of the Berlin Gnostic Codex in 1972: *Die gnostischen Schriften des koptischen Papyrus Berolinensis 8502*.

Berlin Gnostic Codex 8502 contains four texts written in Coptic like the texts of the Nag Hammadi library. The texts are the Gospel of Mary, preserved in an incomplete state; the Secret Book of John; the Wisdom of Jesus Christ; and the Act of Peter. Versions of the Secret Book of John and the Wisdom of Jesus Christ are also found in the Nag Hammadi library.

Other documents from the world of antiquity and late antiquity also include texts that bear a close relationship to works in the Nag Hammadi library. From an ancient accumulation of rubbish at the Egyptian site of Oxyrhynchus (modern Bahnasa, between Cairo and Akhmim) archeologists uncovered papyri that may add a great deal to our knowledge of the ancient world. The site of Oxyrhynchus has proved to be a treasure trove of texts of all sorts, and volumes of Oxyrhynchus papyri have been published, beginning in 1897, by Bernard P. Grenfell and Arthur S. Hunt and those succeeding them.[6] Among the texts are Greek fragments of versions of the Gospel of Thomas from the Nag Hammadi library (Papyrus Oxyrhynchus 1, 654, 655) and the Gospel of Mary from the Berlin Gnostic Codex (Papyrus Oxyrhynchus 3525; Papyrus Rylands 463), and a Greek fragment of the Wisdom of Jesus Christ known from both the Nag Hammadi library and the Berlin Gnostic Codex (Papyrus Oxyrhynchus 1081). Within the writings of the church fathers are additional testimonia regarding the Gospel of Thomas, and, in the *Refutation of All Heresies*, Hippolytus of Rome gives two quotations that originate in versions of the Gospel of Thomas (5.7.20; 5.8.32). Further, a fragmentary papyrus text from the British Library (British Library Oriental Manuscript 4926[1]) contains a portion of the Nag Hammadi text On the Origin of the World, and a fragment preserved in the Yale Beinecke Library (Yale Inventory 1784) has been identified by Stephen Emmel as a part of the papyrus text of the Nag Hammadi Dialogue of the Savior that made its way to New Haven, Connecticut.[7]

Additionally, a few texts in the Nag Hammadi library are Coptic versions of works previously known from other sources. The Coptic passage from Plato in Nag Hammadi Codex VI comes, ultimately, from *Republic* 588A–589B. The Hermetic Prayer of Thanksgiving and the Coptic selection from the Perfect Discourse are known from other Greek and Latin versions. The Sentences of Sextus, part of which is given in the fragmentary Nag Hammadi Codex XII, is a well-known ancient text also found in Greek, Latin, Syriac, Armenian, and Georgian versions. Mention should also be made of the poorly preserved tractate Zostrianos, which may now be partially restored from close parallels in Marius Victorinus's *Against Arius* (*Adversus Arium*).[8]

ARCHEOLOGY NEAR NAG HAMMADI

After the discovery of the Nag Hammadi library, archeologists and other scholars turned their attention to the physical context of the Nag Hammadi library, and the result has been archeological work done in the area around Nag Hammadi and codicological work on the codices themselves. This work has provided fresh glimpses into the history of Christianity in Egypt and the early history of bookbinding. The contributions of archeology and codicology may also help solve the mystery of who compiled the Nag Hammadi library and who buried it by the Jabal al-Tarif.

Archeological surveys and excavations in the region were undertaken in the 1970s and 1980s under the sponsorship of the Institute for Antiquity and Christianity, and Peter Grossmann of the German Archeological Institute brought this work to an appropriate — if penultimate — conclusion.[9] Prior to the archeological work in the area, it was recognized that during the early centuries there was a strong Christian presence in the Nag Hammadi region and that Christian monks and monasteries were especially prevalent in this part of Upper Egypt. In the fourth century, Apa Pachomius, often considered the father of cenobitic Christian monasticism, established monasteries all around this part of Egypt — including a monastery in a small village named Šeneset (in Greek, Chenoboskia), modern-day al-Qasr, the same village that was to become, much later, the home of the family of Muhammad Ali of the al-Samman clan.

The archeological site of the Pachomian monastic church at Faw Qibli,
with the Jabal al-Tarif in the distance

Archeological work at one of the most significant monasteries in
the area, at Pbow (or Pabau, modern Faw Qibli), located within sight
of the Jabal al-Tarif, has given a clear indication of how important and
impressive a Pachomian monastery and monastic church could be.
Pbow was the administrative center of the Pachomian monastic
movement, where monks from the surrounding monasteries could
come for special occasions. The site of Pbow is littered with the archi-
tectural and archeological remains of the monastic church in its
several stages of building and rebuilding: rose granite columns, lime-
stone foundation blocks, brick rubble, and countless potsherds. More
granite pieces — for example, an olive press for making olive oil used
for preparing food and in oil lamps — are scattered around the archeological site, and sometimes the remaining hieroglyphs and artistic
markings (such as stylized stars) seem to indicate that the granite used
in the church had been recycled from an older building, probably an
Egyptian temple.

The Pachomian church at Pbow went through at least three building stages. Gary Lease, who participated in the archeological excavations and collaborated with Peter Grossmann, has described the
church buildings uncovered at Pbow.[10] Each church had five aisles,
with a central nave and two aisles on each side, and each church was
built to be larger than the one before — an indication of the growth of
the Christian population in the area and the success of the monastic
movement. The first (and lowest) church may have been built during
the lifetime of Pachomius; the second was constructed somewhat
later; and the third, the great basilica, was completed in 459. That date
for the great basilica seems secure, since a text said to be a sermon of
Timothy II of Alexandria preached on the occasion of the dedication
of the Pachomian basilica at Pbow refers to that very date.[11]

Each of the church buildings at Pbow may have been quite a
stately ecclesiastical structure, but the great basilica must have been
especially impressive. The great basilica was an imposing church with
massive brick walls, huge granite columns, and attractively decorated
capitals for the columns. It might be hoped that the church buildings
were not too attractive. There is a legend that when Pachomius saw
the finished early church at Pbow, he was disturbed at its beauty, and
so he ordered the monks to twist the columns from their positions to
ensure that no one would be seduced and led astray by artistic beauty.

Archeological forays throughout the area, and especially around
the Jabal al-Tarif and up the Wadi Sheikh Ali, have illumined other
aspects of monastic life in the Nag Hammadi region. The evidence
indicates that Christian monks wandered from place to place all
around this area. In the cliff face of the Jabal al-Tarif, near the boulder next to which the Nag Hammadi codices were discovered, there
are caves that were used from the days of the Old Kingdom. On the
wall inside one of the caves (cave 8), dubbed the "Psalms cave," are
the opening lines, or incipits, of Psalms 51–93, painted in the red
paint — "monastic Rustoleum" — commonly used by Egyptian monks.[12]

We can speculate that in their holy wanderings the monks used this cave as a meditation chapel, in which they could focus pious attention upon the Psalms and be aided in their thoughts and prayers by the opening lines, painted on the cave wall, which would remind them of the sequence of the Psalms.

The same sorts of Christian monks also seem to have hiked up the Wadi Sheikh Ali, a narrow and rather inaccessible ravine leading into the mountainous desert of the red land, off the Dishna plain not too far from the Jabal al-Tarif.[13] Archeological investigation of the wadi indicates that Christian monks made their way up the wadi, past an unfinished obelisk abandoned by Egyptian stonecutters long ago, and stopped in the shade of an overhanging rock. There on the surface of the rock are incised hieroglyphs (including the word "gods" and a cartouche of Pharaoh Menkaure) and hunting graffiti, perhaps scratched onto the rock by the stonecutters and hunters accompanying them. Christian monks at the site apparently noticed the pagan

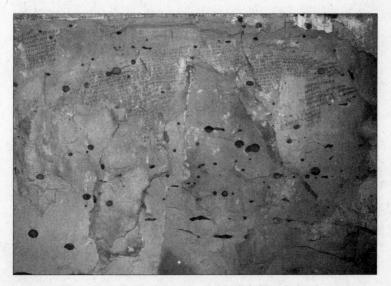

Inside the Psalms cave at the Jabal al-Tarif

inscriptions and consequently rededicated the place to Christ by adding Coptic Christian graffiti. Most of the Christian graffiti are painted onto the rock in the familiar red paint as simple prayers:

> *Pray for me. I am Phibamon.*
> *Pray for me in love. I am Pakim.*
> *Pray for me in love. I am the servant Pakire.*
>> *("the servant" is scratched out)*
> *Jesus Christ, help me.*
> *. . . in the name of God. . . . I am Solomon. Pray for me in love.*
> *Da + David +*
> *Remember me in love. I am Philothe the son of David.*
> *+ I am Chael the sinner. Observe love. Pray for me.*
> *Remember me in love. I am more of a sinner than any other*
>> *person.*
> *I am Stauros the son. . . .*[14]

A stone chip left at the site includes another painted graffito: "I am Archeleos. Remember me in love." (A similar pious plea — "Remember me also, my brothers, in your prayers" — is written in a scribal note at the conclusion of Nag Hammadi Codex II.) There is also a portrait of a monk named John incised onto the surface of the rock. Brother John is shown with beard and robe and hands raised in the praying position, and he identifies himself in rough Coptic: "I am faithful John" or "I, John, am faithful."[15]

At the same locale there are Byzantine bricks and potsherds, including some sherds that resemble fourth- and fifth-century red-painted slip ware found throughout the region. Ware like this has been found in the excavations of the Pachomian monastic church at Pbow — and at al-Qasr James Robinson acquired a similar bowl that likely was used as the lid of the jar within which the Nag Hammadi codices were buried.

CODICOLOGY AT THE COPTIC MUSEUM

Meanwhile, back at the Coptic Museum in the aftermath of the Nag Hammadi discovery, scholarly work on the physical remains of the Nag Hammadi codices has provided new codicological perspectives on the Nag Hammadi library.[16] Codicology is the study of the practice of making books, and the codices of the Nag Hammadi library represent some of the earliest books known. We now understand how these early books were put together. The Nag Hammadi codices stand at a point of transition from scrolls to codices, from the written word preserved on sheets that were rolled up to the written word preserved on sheets that were bound as pages within covers. That transition, aided by those who produced the Nag Hammadi codices, changed forever the way in which the written word could be communicated.

In many respects the Nag Hammadi bookbinding process resembles the process of bookbinding employed ever since. For the Nag Hammadi texts, like other Egyptian texts, papyrus reed was the source of the fibers used for the creation of the sheets on which the texts were written. Papyrus fibers have been made into sheets as a kind of paper in Egypt for millennia; the ancient process continues today at the Papyrus Institute in Egypt. It turns out that papyrus is an especially durable writing surface. If the Nag Hammadi codices had been manufactured using wood pulp instead of papyrus, the texts of the library would have disintegrated into dust long ago.

Traditionally papyrus was assembled into rolls, and at the time of the manufacture of the Nag Hammadi codices papyrus must have been obtained in that form. In the production of papyrus book pages from papyrus rolls, the rolls were cut into the proper width for sheets of a book (each sheet is two pages wide), and the sheets were stacked and folded to form a quire (a bundle of sheets). The use of papyrus fibers in the construction of Egyptian books allows scholars to identify and trace fibers in sheets and pages, and this has enabled scholars to position and place fragments and reassemble fragmentary pages of the Nag Hammadi codices.

After the quires of the Nag Hammadi library were put together, and apparently after the scribes had copied the texts onto the papyrus pages, the quires were bound in leather covers and secured with thongs. Leather covers could be decorated, and the cover of Nag Hammadi Codex II bears an attractive design. The portion of the leather that came from the tail of the animal could form part of the protective flap for the book, and a thong could be attached. Codices were valuable, and the covers and flaps protected such valuable possessions.

In order to convert the leather-bound codices from softbound to hardbound books, scrap papyrus from letters and documents was sometimes pasted inside the covers of the Nag Hammadi codices, and then a blank piece of papyrus could be glued over the unsightly used material. This scrap papyrus, called cartonnage, from the Nag Hammadi

The cover of Nag Hammadi Codex VII, with cartonnage inside

library has been carefully examined by scholars and published in a volume dedicated to ancient wastepaper: *Nag Hammadi Codices: Greek and Coptic Papyri from the Cartonnage of the Covers*, edited by John W. B. Barns, Gerald M. Browne, and John C. Shelton. The cartonnage contains names of people, places, and dates, and these bits of information provide clues to the time and place of the construction of the codices. In the cartonnage there are dates in the middle of the fourth century and just before, and names suggesting monks and locations around Pbow and Šeneset (Chenoboskia). Cartonnage from the cover of Nag Hammadi Codex VII mentions a monk named Sansnos who supervised the cattle of a monastery.[17] He would have had easy access to leather for codex covers. In other words, the evidence of the cartonnage may provide points of contact between the production of the Nag Hammadi codices and the Pachomian monastic movement.

THE PRODUCTION AND THE BURIAL OF THE NAG HAMMADI LIBRARY

The evidence remains circumstantial, but archeological and codicological work has provided tantalizing hints that may help resolve the mystery of who produced and who buried the Nag Hammadi codices. I suggest that the hints implicate Pachomian monks. On the basis of information from the pottery remains and the Wadi Sheikh Ali and the cartonnage from the codices themselves, we may conjecture that Pachomian monks most likely compiled the Nag Hammadi codices and later buried them by the cliff. The Nag Hammadi codices were put together around the middle of the fourth century, or a little later; their date of manufacture cannot precede the dates found in the cartonnage. The Nag Hammadi library may have functioned, formally or informally, as a part of a Pachomian monastic library in the area. In that regard the Nag Hammadi codices may be compared — and contrasted — with another collection of manuscripts discovered in the area, the Dishna Papers (sometimes referred to as the Bodmer Papyri).

James Robinson, the scholarly sleuth who pieced together the story of the discovery of the Nag Hammadi library, has also researched the story of the Dishna Papers, and he describes the discovery of these texts and their place within a Pachomian monastic library:

> *This discovery included archival copies of formal letters of abbots of the Pachomian Order. And the rest of the holdings are also what one would expect of a Pachomian library: biblical, apocryphal, martyriological, and other edifying material. To be sure, there are also some Greek (and Latin) classical texts, whose presence may be explained by the assumption that persons who joined the Pachomian movement gave their worldly possessions to the Order, which would thus have acquired non-Christian texts. Later they would have been taken to be venerable texts like the others in the archives, fragile and fragmentary relics to be preserved and no longer texts to be read.*[18]

In the case of the Nag Hammadi library, the texts finally were buried at the foot of the Jabal al-Tarif, to be discovered centuries later. The fact that they were buried and not burned or thrown into the Nile River indicates a desire to preserve and not destroy. Further, the scribal notes in the texts themselves are pious and not heresiological in their perspectives. What, then, could have prompted Pachomian monks to bury the Nag Hammadi codices there at the cliff?

A momentous event that happened in the year 367 may suggest an answer to this question. In that year the archbishop of Alexandria, Athanasius, soon to be acclaimed the champion of orthodox Christianity, wrote a festal letter to be read in the churches of Egypt. Among other things, the letter addresses the issue of the canon, of what books should be considered authoritative and inspired and thus included in the Bible. In his festal letter Athanasius lists what he as archbishop believes to be the canonical books of the Christian scriptures, and his list may be the first ever to include the twenty-seven books of the New Testament that eventually were used in most churches. Later Jerome opted for the same twenty-seven books in his Latin translation of the Bible, the Vulgate. Athanasius was deeply concerned about the canon, and that issue of canon is confronted anew in the discovery of the Nag Hammadi library with newly recovered Christian gospels, acts, letters, and apocalypses that also claim to be authoritative and inspired.

In his festal letter Athanasius raises another, related, issue that was dear to his heart: heresy. He condemns the heretics and warns the faithful to beware of the heretics and their despicable writings. Apocryphal texts, he maintains, "are a fabrication of the heretics, who write them down when it pleases them and generously assign to them an early date of composition in order that they may be able to draw upon them as supposedly ancient writings and have in them occasion to deceive the guileless."[19] These heresiological words of warning were translated into Coptic and, it is said, were adopted to serve as a rule and guide for Pachomian monks.

It is quite plausible, then, to conclude that one likely scenario for the time of and occasion for the burial of the Nag Hammadi codices may be related to Athanasius's festal letter of 367. When Pachomian monks heard the stern words of admonition of the holy archbishop, they may have thought of the books of spiritual wisdom in their possession, books that could be considered heretical, and they determined to dispose of them. Yet they simply could not destroy them, so they gathered them and hid them safely away, to be uncovered on another day.

What texts they buried by the boulder at the Jabal al-Tarif is the matter to which we now turn.

2

COPTIC TEXTS FROM THE SANDS OF EGYPT

THE NAG HAMMADI LIBRARY AND THE BERLIN GNOSTIC CODEX

THE COLLECTION OF CODICES discovered at the Jabal al-Tarif is usually called the Nag Hammadi library, after the city close to the spot of the discovery. But this collection has also been termed the "Coptic gnostic library," and that phrase or an approximation thereof has been used to name two of the research projects established to translate the texts (the Coptic Gnostic Library Project in the United States and the Berliner Arbeitskreis für koptisch-gnostische Schriften in Germany) as well as a set of volumes in the prestigious series of scholarly publications on the Nag Hammadi library (Coptic Gnostic Library, Nag Hammadi and Manichaean Studies, published by E. J. Brill in the Netherlands). But how is the library a Coptic library? Is the library gnostic? And to what extent is it a library?

A Coptic Library?

Coptic means Egyptian, as noted before, and the Nag Hammadi library may be called a Coptic library, but with qualifications. The most obvious way in which the Nag Hammadi library may be described as a Coptic library is in terms of the language of the texts. In general, the texts of the Nag Hammadi library do not represent the perspective of the Coptic Orthodox Church as that has developed over the years, but all the texts in the Nag Hammadi library are written in the Coptic language. Occasionally a title of a tractate or a textual annotation is written in Greek, and Greek loanwords abound in the Coptic texts. In one instance, at the conclusion of the text Zostrianos (Codex VIII), there is another curiosity of language: a cryptogram that may be comprehended only when the twenty-four letters of the Greek alphabet are divided into three groups of eight and the letters are reversed in each set (with modifications). Then the cryptogram may be understood to mean "Words of truth of Zostrianos. God of truth. Words of Zoroaster."[1]

Nonetheless, in spite of these issues of language, the texts of the Nag Hammadi library and the Berlin Gnostic Codex have been copied onto the pages of the codices in the Coptic language. The Coptic language is a form of Egyptian; it represents a stage in the history of the Egyptian language, which includes, in earlier periods, hieroglyphic, hieratic, and demotic. Coptic grammar is Egyptian grammar, but the main script employed in Coptic is Greek, to which have been added several letters from demotic for sounds not indicated by Greek letters. The Greek alphabet provided a fitting basis for the Coptic form of the Egyptian language, since from the days of Alexander the Great's entrance into Egypt and establishment of the city of Alexandria, the influence of Hellenistic culture and Greek language upon Egypt was significant.[2]

The Coptic texts of the Nag Hammadi library and the Berlin Gnostic Codex, along with other Coptic texts that have emerged from the sands of Egypt in recent years, are helping to increase our understanding of the Coptic language, including the various dialects of Coptic used in different times and places of Egypt.

Scholars generally concede, however, that none of the texts of the Nag Hammadi library and the Berlin Gnostic Codex were actually composed in Coptic. Rather, they were composed in Greek and translated into Coptic. Some scholars have tried to argue that the Gospel of Thomas, which most likely was composed in Syria, may have been written in Syriac, but there is limited evidence for a Syriac Gospel of Thomas. The cartonnage within the covers of the codices indicates that the books themselves were probably produced sometime around the middle of the fourth century, so that if the texts of the Nag Hammadi library were translated from Greek into Coptic and subsequently copied into thirteen codices, the actual translation of the texts into Coptic must have preceded that date. Precisely how long a time before then the work of translation took place is difficult to ascertain. If the texts of the Nag Hammadi library were translated into Coptic, in Egypt, sometime around or before the middle of the fourth century, the original documents must have been composed earlier, perhaps much earlier in some cases, and possibly in locales close by or far away from Upper Egypt.

The determination of the place and date of the composition of ancient texts — their provenance — is an inexact science at best, and the question of the origin of the texts in the Nag Hammadi library and the Berlin Gnostic Codex is no exception.[3] The Greek language was widely used as a literary language throughout the Mediterranean region and into the Middle East in Hellenistic and Roman times, and only occasionally are there clear indications in a text of the place of composition. A few Nag Hammadi texts — On the Origin of the World and the Hermetic texts Discourse on the Eighth and Ninth and the Perfect Discourse — allude to sites in Egypt and may have been composed there. The Nag Hammadi excerpt from Plato's *Republic* originated in the world of classical Athens. For most of the other texts in the Nag Hammadi library and the Berlin Gnostic Codex, we must resort to historical conjecture for matters of provenance. Because of the rich cultural and religious traditions, including gnostic traditions, of Syria and Egypt, and particularly Alexandria, these places are often suggested as possible regions where the Nag Hammadi and Berlin Gnostic texts may have been composed. Thomas was revered in Syria, and it is reasonable to suggest that Thomas texts were written there. Valentinus was an influential figure in Alexandria, and some Valentinian texts, including the Gospel of Truth, may have come from Alexandria. On the other hand, the Valentinian Gospel of Philip discusses the meaning of Syriac words, so that a place of composition in Syria is plausible.

The dating of the composition of the texts in the Nag Hammadi library and the Berlin Gnostic Codex is equally challenging, and sometimes contentious. Occasionally, as with Sethian texts exhibiting Platonizing characteristics, it may be possible to compare the Nag Hammadi texts with developments in the broader world of Middle Platonic and Neoplatonic philosophy. We may be able to relate these Sethian texts from Nag Hammadi — the Three Steles of Seth, Zostrianos, Marsanes, and Allogenes the Stranger — to the debates about gnostics and their texts going on in the Platonic school of Plotinus in Rome in the third century.[4] Gnostic texts mentioned in the Platonic literature include revelations of Zoroaster, Zostrianos, Nicotheos, Allogenes, Messos, and others, and most of these names are also to be found in the Nag Hammadi texts.

At other times the determination of what dates might be assigned to a given text in the Nag Hammadi library may be influenced by the

The codices of the Nag Hammadi library assembled together

historical and theological preferences of scholars and fought out on the battlefield of scholarly controversy. The dating of the composition of the Gospel of Thomas is the best example of such impassioned dispute over the date of a text. I believe that many of those who wish, for historical or theological reasons, to minimize the significance of the Gospel of Thomas and marginalize it in the discussion of who Jesus was and how the early church developed assign it a later date of composition for that reason. Conversely, many of those — and I am one of them — who wish to employ the Gospel of Thomas in the study of Jesus and Christian origins support their use of the text by arguing for an earlier date of composition. Points in support of either an earlier or a later date have been made by scholars, and the argument goes on. We shall revisit the argument in our discussion of the Gospel of Thomas in the next chapter.

All things considered, it is appropriate to describe the Nag Hammadi library as a Coptic library in the sense of a collection of texts all of which have been translated into Coptic.

A GNOSTIC LIBRARY?

It may not be quite as easy to call the Nag Hammadi library a gnostic library. Part of the reason is that the Nag Hammadi library incorporates texts that seem not to be gnostic by any standard of definition. Among the Nag Hammadi and Berlin Gnostic texts, non-gnostic works include the Acts of Peter and the Twelve Apostles, the Teachings of Silvanus, the Sentences of Sextus, the Act of Peter, and an excerpt from Plato's *Republic*. Opinions vary on other texts. Whether the Gospel of Thomas and the Book of Thomas should be termed gnostic is debated among scholars. I prefer to describe them, in a more qualified way, as gnosticizing texts, and I suggest that the Gospel of Thomas has an incipient gnostic perspective. The jury is still out on the Gospel of Mary, though I believe a case can be made for a gnosticizing point of view in this text too. The same may be true for Authoritative Discourse.

But the issue of whether the Nag Hammadi library may be called a gnostic library goes much deeper than the mere identification of texts that are not gnostic works. Recent discussions have questioned whether we can use the term "gnosticism" and related words in any meaningful way whatsoever. The two scholars who have been most prominent in formulating their arguments against the category "gnosticism" are Michael A. Williams and Karen L. King.

When Michael Williams, in his book *Rethinking "Gnosticism,"* proposes that we reconsider ancient gnosis and dismantle "a dubious category," the category he has in mind is "gnosticism" itself. "The term 'gnosticism,'" he posits, "has indeed ultimately brought more confusion than clarification,"[5] and he supports his claim by showing the multiplicity of ways — often contradictory — that scholars have tried, in vain, to define and describe "gnosticism." "Gnosticism" has been seen variously as a protest movement that overturned traditional values and textual interpretations; a religion of innovators who adopted and adapted ideas from other religions; a religion of spiritualists who despised the body and the life of the body; and a movement of ethical extremists who opted for either an ascetic or a libertine way of life. In the face of such scholarly obfuscation and with no scholarly consensus, Williams recommends that we replace the old, vague category of "gnosticism" with "biblical demiurgical traditions":

> By "demiurgical" traditions I mean all those that ascribe the creation and management of the cosmos to some lower entity or entities, distinct from the highest God. This would include most of ancient Platonism, of course. But if we add the adjective "biblical," to denote "demiurgical" traditions that also incorporate or adopt traditions from Jewish or Christian Scripture, the category is narrowed significantly.[6]

In her book *What Is Gnosticism?* Karen King also acknowledges problems with "gnosticism" as a term and category, but her approach is somewhat different and her arguments are directed at more fundamental issues. King sees difficulties with definitions in general, since definitions "tend to produce static and reified entities and hide the rhetorical and ideological interests of their fabricators."[7] How much more problematical, according to King, is the definition of "gnosticism," with rhetorical and ideological interests lurking at the very foundation of the term. From the times of the ancient heresiologists until today, King maintains, terms like "gnosticism" and "gnostic" have functioned as rhetorical constructs employed to designate the religion of those with whom one disagrees as "the other" and to name it "heresy." These designations have been tainted with anti-Catholic, anti-Jewish, colonialist, and evolutionary prejudices. As King states, "gnosticism" never really was any "thing" other than a rhetorical construct, and the term simply reflects "the reification of a rhetorical entity (heresy) into an actual phenomenon in its own right (Gnosticism)."[8]

The term "gnosticism" is so flawed, King concludes, that it may need to be rejected outright. In a pluralistic and postmodern setting, we need new and different discussions of what has been called "gnosticism." She states,

> The analysis I propose here aims to get at practice rather than at origins and essence. It offers no larger connected totality but rather a set of episodes no longer linked in any causal-linear frame of origins and development. . . . These twenty-first-century historical practices would without doubt result in more than one possible, legitimate narrative of Christianity, based as they would be not only in the different perspectives of scholars and the communities to which they are accountable, but also in different ethical orientations.[9]

We can learn a great deal from the thoughtful presentations of Michael Williams and Karen King, and their scholarly contributions should make us more cognizant of the polemical bias and subjective point of view that have permeated the discussion of "gnosticism" from antiquity to modernity. We might wonder whether, after Williams and King, there is any more life left in the term "gnosticism" and related terms.

I suggest that these terms may not be dead and buried just yet, and that we still might be able to make good use of them in our discussion of texts from the Nag Hammadi library and the Berlin Gnostic Codex.[10] To be sure, the word "gnosticism" was apparently coined in the seventeenth century by adding the suffix "-ism" to an ancient Greek root word; but that root word, *gnōsis*, "knowledge," and its derivative, *gnōstikos*, "knower," are well-known terms from the world of antiquity and late antiquity, and the word *gnōsis* in particular is commonly attested in ancient texts. In acknowledgment of these issues of terminology, we might wish, if we choose to be especially scrupulous, to be reticent in our use of the word "gnosticism." I choose to be scrupulous in this book, and I refrain from employing the word "gnosticism" in the discussion. The words *gnōsis* and *gnōstikos*, however, are found throughout the writings of the heresiologists, and when Irenaeus of Lyon mentions "falsely so-called knowledge" — taking the phrase from 1 Timothy 6:20 — it is clear that he is referring to claims and counterclaims among his friends and foes about whose *gnōsis* is true *gnōsis*.

In his heresiological work *Against Heresies*, Irenaeus admits that some of those whom he opposes, especially Sethians (or Barbelognostics) and followers of Marcellina, used "gnostic" as a self-referential term and called themselves gnostics. Clement also writes about those who refer to themselves as gnostics. To the present day the Mandaeans in the Middle East and throughout the world speak of themselves as *Mandaye*, or "knowers," that is, gnostics, possessors of *manda*, or gnosis. This use of "gnostic" as a term of self-designation functions as the groundwork for our appropriation of the same term. If these people call themselves gnostics and understand themselves to be gnostics, do they not deserve the benefit of the doubt? Since, according to Irenaeus, Sethians thought of themselves as gnostics, and since we now have the Secret Book of John, a central text of Sethian spirituality, readily available in the Nag Hammadi library and the Berlin Gnostic Codex, we may analyze the Secret Book of John in order to gain insight into what the main points of gnostic thought are according to the Sethians. Sethian texts appear to be connected to other texts — for example, Valentinian texts — historically, and they resemble still other texts phenomenologically — that is, with regard to themes and characteristics — so that the term "gnostic" may also be applied beyond Sethian texts to Valentinian and other texts that fit the description of gnostic religion.

On the basis of leading themes of the Secret Book of John, I propose this description of gnostic religion, which may be used to evaluate and classify other texts as gnostic:

> *Gnostic religion is a religious tradition that emphasizes the primary place of gnosis, or mystical knowledge, understood through aspects of wisdom, often personified wisdom, presented in creation stories, particularly stories based on the Genesis accounts, and interpreted by means of a variety of religious and philosophical traditions, including Platonism, in order to proclaim a radically enlightened way and life of knowledge.*[11]

Sethian texts, then, may be termed gnostic, as may Valentinian texts and any other texts that reflect these gnostic themes, while other texts may appear to be less than fully gnostic. Comparisons and classifications are like this; taxonomy is hardly a neat and precise enterprise. In *Drudgery Divine* Jonathan Z. Smith reminds us that comparisons and classifications are part of the imperfect and subjective world of scholarly research and creativity. Comparisons typically tell us more about the people doing the comparing than how things really are—recall Karen King's observations. Smith goes on to note that when items—or movements—are compared, there is always an implicit statement of the degree of comparison ("more than") as well as a reference to themes or traits being compared ("with respect to"). Comparison and classification are relative and contextual—yet that is what we as scholars do.

As a result, when we engage in careful and honest comparison and classification of Nag Hammadi and Berlin Gnostic texts, we may call many of them gnostic texts. Others may be described and qualified as more or less gnostic, and still others as not gnostic at all. Even among the gnostic texts there is considerable variation in perspective, as we shall see.

Thus the Nag Hammadi library is not gnostic in the sense that it contains a uniform set of gnostic texts. To be sure, all the texts in the Nag Hammadi library could have been read and interpreted from a given gnostic or gnosticizing vantage point, and it is also probable, as we have seen, that the Nag Hammadi library functioned in a Pachomian monastic community and could have been understood within that context. But for our purposes, the texts in the Nag Hammadi library are most significant for what they contribute to our appreciation of the diversity of approaches to gnosis.

A LIBRARY?

To what extent is the Nag Hammadi library even a library? The Nag Hammadi library is not a library in a modern sense of the term. It is a collection of codices that Pachomian monks apparently produced and eventually buried in a jar by the Jabal al-Tarif. The monks may have read the texts as a part of their own meditation and edification. If such a collection may be called a library, so be it. Within this collection of codices, however, there are clear indications of heterogeneity.

The differences to be observed within the Nag Hammadi library extend from the covers, the scribal hands, and the Coptic dialects represented to the contents of the codices. James Robinson has surveyed these covers, scribal hands, and dialects in the Nag Hammadi codices, and he judges that this collection of thirteen codices can be subdivided into several smaller groups or libraries that may have been merged to form the Nag Hammadi library as we know it.[12] Nag Hammadi Codices IV, V, and VIII have bargain-basement covers, with cheap papyrus and no flap (or, in the case of Codex V, with a flap that was added later). Codices II, VI, IX, and X have high-quality covers, with a leather reinforcement (called a mull) lining the spine for strength. Codices I, III, VII, and XI have undistinguished and even primitive covers. (Nag Hammadi Codex XII is poorly preserved and lacks a cover, and all that remains of Codex XIII is sixteen papyrus pages of a single text, Three Forms of First Thought, and the opening of On the Origin of the World, placed inside the cover of Codex VI.) The handwriting styles of the various scribes who copied the texts in the Nag Hammadi library can also be identified, and Robinson submits that the hands of the copyists "diverge most clearly just where the bookbinding divergences take place."[13] The presence of different Coptic dialects — most notably Sahidic and Subachmimic — and different stylistic preferences in the Nag Hammadi texts underscores the observation that different copyists with different language skills worked on the texts.

All this suggests that monks brought the codices together at the time of their burial or before that, even a considerable time before that, out of several smaller collections. In this sense the Nag Hammadi library may be called the Nag Hammadi libraries.

The duplicate copies of texts in the Nag Hammadi library confirm the likelihood that smaller libraries were brought together. No fewer than three copies of the Secret Book of John survive in the Nag Hammadi codices, with an additional copy in the Berlin Gnostic Codex, and several texts are preserved in two copies. That fact, together with the uncertain reason for the order and arrangement of texts within the codices, raises new questions about the contents of the books in the Nag Hammadi library.

Ingenious theories have been proposed to explain the sequence of texts in a given codex or in codices of the Nag Hammadi library. It has been suggested that Nag Hammadi Codex I may be a Valentinian codex, with texts that all may be taken as advocating a Valentinian point of view. In a more pedestrian way, I once suggested that the Letter of Peter to Philip may have been added after Zostrianos in Nag Hammadi Codex VIII simply because it filled the space available in the codex.[14]

Now several more interesting and creative theories to account for the arrangement of texts in the Nag Hammadi library are presented and discussed by Michael Williams in *Rethinking "Gnosticism."*[15] Three times in the Nag Hammadi library the Secret Book of John appears at the beginning of a codex (in the Berlin Gnostic Codex it comes second), and Yvonne Janssens has guessed that the same may have been true for Nag Hammadi Codex XIII, where only the one text and fragments remain and the intact text was not the first in the codex. Within the Nag Hammadi library, Williams proposes, the arrangement of texts within a codex may have been quite deliberate. Far from merely filling space, the texts may have been arranged to rehearse the history of revelation, as in Nag Hammadi Codices IV and VIII (grouped together in terms of covers and other considerations), from the story of Genesis reinterpreted (the Secret Book of John), to the story of Seth (the Holy Book of the Great Invisible Spirit) and other ancient testimony (Zostrianos), to the revelation of the risen Christ to his disciples (the Letter of Peter to Philip). Or the arrangement of texts may imitate the order of Christian texts in the emerging New Testament, as in Nag Hammadi Codex I, with an introductory prayer (the Prayer of the Apostle Paul), a gospel-like text (the Secret Book of James), a Christian exposition (the Gospel of Truth), and statements of eschatology (the Treatise on Resurrection and the Tripartite Tractate). Or the arrangement may follow a liturgical order, or the sequence of spiritual ascent to visionary knowledge of the end of all things.

Williams concludes,

In at least most of the codices, the way in which tractates are arranged may suggest that scribes perceived complete theological consistency within the volumes. Or to put it another way, the arrangement itself in most instances seems to be the scribal method of demonstrating or establishing *the theological coherence among the works.*

A few lines later, he adds,

> *In other words, the very repackaging and ordering of the material resolved, as it were, theological diversity among the writings. Each writing had its own function and could be interpreted in terms of that function in relation to the other works within the codex. Once this is seen, it is fair to ask whether there is really all that much more theological diversity within the Nag Hammadi library (or at least within its subcollections) than within, say, Codex Sinaiticus, or the Septuagint, or even the New Testament itself.*[16]

THE DIVERSITY AND UNITY OF THE NAG HAMMADI AND BERLIN GNOSTIC TEXTS

The forty-seven texts (plus fragments and duplicates) of the Nag Hammadi library and the Berlin Gnostic Codex make an extraordinary contribution to our knowledge of spirituality, and especially gnostic spirituality, in the world of antiquity and late antiquity. In the Appendix to this book I survey all the texts and attempt to characterize them by summarizing their contents and providing illustrative quotations. Here I give an overview of the texts and indicate some of the ways in which they differ from one another and — in the spirit of Michael Williams's comment — some of the ways in which they may be understood to resemble each other.

Initially when we encounter the Nag Hammadi library and the Berlin Gnostic Codex, we are impressed with the diversity of the texts. Most of the texts are Christian texts of one sort or another, but a number of texts exhibit few Christian features and some no Christian features at all. Those that are marginally Christian or non-Christian

Scholars at work on the Nag Hammadi codices in the library
of the Coptic Museum in Old Cairo

may show Jewish, Greco-Roman, Platonic, or Hermetic characteristics, often in fascinating combinations. The Christian texts include
gospels — the Gospel of Thomas, the Gospel of Philip, the Gospel of
Mary, the Gospel of Truth, and the Holy Book of the Great Invisible
Spirit (also entitled the Egyptian Gospel) — and texts that are like
gospels in certain respects — the Secret Book of John, the Secret
Book of James, the Book of Thomas, the Dialogue of the Savior, and
the Second Discourse of Great Seth. The Gospel of Thomas offers a
series of sayings of Jesus, and the Second Discourse of Great Seth is
ostensibly a discourse delivered by Jesus himself, something like a
"Gospel According to Jesus." There are other Christian texts: the Act
of Peter, the Acts of Peter and the Twelve Apostles, the Prayer of the
Apostle Paul, the Treatise on Resurrection, the Letter of Peter to Philip,

and revelations, or apocalypses, galore—one of Peter, one of Paul, two of James. Another revelation, the Revelation of Adam, is more fully Jewish in perspective. Besides Jewish and Christian texts about the apocalypse, many other texts interpret the genesis of things: the Secret Book of John, the Nature of the Rulers, On the Origin of the World, the Holy Book of the Great Invisible Spirit, the Paraphrase of Shem. Several texts, like the Three Steles of Seth, describe how to ascend to a mystical vision of the divine. Liturgical passages aid in the celebration of the divine.

Many of the texts in the Nag Hammadi library and the Berlin Gnostic Codex are gnostic or gnosticizing, but not all. Of the non-gnostic texts, the Acts of Peter and the Twelve Apostles describes the adventures of the apostles in a city far away across the water, the Teachings of Silvanus proclaims Christian wisdom with statements of advice, the Sentences of Sextus communicates words of wisdom in a text known for some time from other sources, and the Act of Peter tells a story of how Peter did—and undid—a miracle for his daughter. The fragment from Plato's *Republic* may have been edited in a tendentious fashion with gnostic concerns in mind, but it comes ultimately from Plato, and Plato was no gnostic.

Research on the Nag Hammadi library and the Berlin Gnostic Codex has disclosed a broad spectrum of perspectives among the texts that may be identified as gnostic or gnosticizing, and the texts seem to fall roughly into five groups. These five groups may reflect, for several of the groups, gnostic schools of thought embraced by teachers and students in communities.

The first group of gnostic texts in the Nag Hammadi library consists of the Thomas texts: the Gospel of Thomas, the Book of Thomas, and probably the Dialogue of the Savior.[17] The texts in the Thomas tradition—what Bentley Layton calls the school of St. Thomas—grew out of reflections upon sayings of Jesus and their relationship to the figure of Judas Thomas, thought to be the twin brother of Jesus. Devotion to Thomas was strong in Syria, particularly in Edessa, and the Thomas tradition seems to have developed in a Syrian milieu. Eventually interests in Jesus and Thomas come to expression in the Acts of Thomas with the "Hymn of the Pearl" and the story of Thomas's mission to India; a form of Thomas Christianity lives on to the present day in the church of St. Thomas in India. Within the texts of the Nag Hammadi library, the Gospel of Thomas consists of a collection of sayings of Jesus that may be compared with the sayings gospel Q.[18] The Book of Thomas incorporates some of the sayings, as it has Jesus talk with Thomas about passions and punishments. The Dialogue of the Savior works some of the sayings of Jesus into a dialogue of Jesus with his disciples Judas Thomas, Mary of Magdala, and Matthew.

The second group of texts derives from the Sethian school of thought. Sethian texts reflect traditions of Seth, son of Adam and Eve, as a paradigmatic human being.[19] In the book of Genesis, after the account of the family debacle with Cain and Abel, Seth was born as a new son for Adam and Eve, and it is said that then people began to call on the name of the Lord (4:25–26). Sethian texts build upon these traditions. Sethian texts frequently include a brilliant portrayal of the heavenly realm, with the *plērōma*, or fullness, of the divine displayed in all its glory and manifestations. The divine human being is a part of that heavenly realm. According to Sethian texts, the primordial fall from grace may be understood as the fall of the divine through the folly of Sophia, wisdom, and from this cosmic mistake come the creation, fall, and redemption of the world of humankind. Sethian texts give substantial attention to the opening chapters of the book of Genesis and interpret these chapters in a creative fashion, blending their revolutionary interpretation with Greek philosophical and mythological ideas. Hans-Martin Schenke and John D. Turner are the two scholars who have led the way in the scholarly examination of the variety of Sethian gnostic texts and the development of Sethian gnosis, and they have begun to reconstruct the history of the Sethian movement from its origins to its multiple manifestations.

The most noteworthy Sethian text in the Nag Hammadi library and the Berlin Gnostic Codex is the Secret Book of John, which is a Jewish gnostic text that has been Christianized. In the longer version of the Secret Book of John, divine forethought — or Jesus — reveals a threefold descent of the savior to the world below, and this threefold descent is described in detail in another, poetic, Sethian text, Three Forms of First Thought. Other Sethian texts, such as the Holy Book of the Great Invisible Spirit, are more fully Christian in their approach, and the Holy Book may also betray Hermetic elements. Platonizing Sethian texts, however, show fewer Christian themes, and they were among the works discussed in the school of the great Neoplatonic philosopher Plotinus.

The third group of gnostic texts represents the Valentinian school of thought.[20] Valentinus was a second-century Egyptian who became a Christian gnostic teacher and preacher in Alexandria and Rome. It is said that he aspired to be bishop of Rome. Blessed with a mystical and poetic eloquence, Valentinus may very well be the author of the Gospel of Truth. According to Irenaeus of Lyon, Valentinus took over leading ideas of Sethian thought and adapted them to fit his own spirituality. Such Nag Hammadi Valentinian texts as the Tripartite Tractate and the Valentinian Exposition demonstrate that Valentinians, like Sethians, made use of complex cosmological depictions of the *plērōma* of the divine, and these descriptions of God's world above were applied to our world below. Valentinus and Valentinian teachers and authors brought pleromatic speculation down to earth, to speak to the lives of Christians, as we can see in the Gospel of Truth, the Gospel of Philip, the Prayer of the Apostle Paul, and the Treatise on Resurrection. Two branches, or "denominations," of the Valentinian school of thought are commonly distinguished by scholars, the western (or Italian) branch and the eastern (or Anatolian) branch, and names of leading teachers of these two Valentinian denominations are known: Ptolemy and Heracleon in the western denomination, Theodotus and Marcus in the eastern denomination. The Valentinian texts from the Nag Hammadi library may now be added to the commentaries, epistles, and other literary contributions of this Christian movement.

The fourth group of gnostic texts in the Nag Hammadi library comes from the Hermetic heritage. The Hermetic tradition has been known for a long time, and Hermetic texts, collected in the Corpus Hermeticum, have assumed a prominent place in discussions of mystical religion in antiquity and late antiquity.[21] The Greek god Hermes, given the nickname "thrice greatest" in Hermetic literature, is the divine messenger and guide of souls; he is identified with the Egyptian god Thoth and assumes the role of teacher and mystagogue in Hermetic texts. Among these texts, the work entitled *Poimandres* (a name that may be compared with the reference to Poimael in the Holy Book of the Great Invisible Spirit) has been especially influential.[22] In this work, Poimandres (perhaps meaning "shepherd of men") discloses a vision of the nature of the universe and the fate of the soul that resembles other gnostic visions and employs Egyptian, Greco-Roman, Platonic, and Jewish themes.

The Hermetic literature comes from the cosmopolitan world of Hellenistic and Roman Egypt, perhaps from the city of Alexandria itself. In these texts Hermes the mystagogue refers to the student as "my child" or "my son" or by such names as Asclepius (who was identified with the deified Egyptian architect Imhotep) or Tat (from the god Thoth), and the student in turn calls the mystagogue "my father." Within the texts of the Nag Hammadi library there are three Hermetic texts, two previously known, an excerpt from the Perfect Discourse and the Prayer of Thanksgiving, and one new Hermetic text, the Discourse on the Eighth and Ninth.

The fifth group of gnostic texts in the Nag Hammadi library and the Berlin Gnostic Codex is hardly a definable group, but instead consists of those gnostic texts that defy classification. These texts seem to incorporate leading gnostic themes, as suggested above, and may show similarities to other gnostic texts and traditions, but they do not fit neatly into the other groups of gnostic texts. Such is the nature of the texts and traditions that we organize and classify into taxonomic systems. Our orderly systems may not always reflect the realities of a complex and disorderly world. Thus, On the Origin of the World resembles the Sethian text the Nature of the Rulers, but it also seems to include Valentinian and Manichaean concepts. The Exegesis on the Soul is an account of the myth of the soul (Psyche) with general gnostic overtones. Eugnostos the Blessed is a Jewish discourse, with Greek influences, on gnostic themes, and the Wisdom of Jesus Christ is a Christian expansion of Eugnostos. The Concept of Our Great Power uses terms dear to the first-century teacher and gnostic patriarch Simon Magus and his companion Helena, but the text may not really represent their thought and remains difficult to classify. The title of the Paraphrase of Shem recalls the title of another text, the Paraphrase of Seth, known from the heresiological literature, but the Paraphrase of Shem has little that is Sethian about it. Likewise, the Second Discourse of Great Seth refers to Seth — great Seth — in its title, but the title may be the most Sethian aspect of the work. And so on.

The contributions of these groups of gnostic texts will be discussed and assessed in the following chapters.

With this rich diversity, the texts of the Nag Hammadi library, both gnostic and non-gnostic, may still have certain themes in common. There may be certain ways in which the texts resemble each other or may be understood as parts of a collection. Some themes would have been valued by the monks who collected the texts: an esoteric interest in the soul and its destiny, an ascetic tendency to promote the life of the soul and regulate the life of the body, and a preoccupation with the beginning and the end of the world.

Here I propose that the themes of knowledge — mystical knowledge — and wisdom are particularly prominent in gnostic texts and can even be alluded to in some of the non-gnostic texts of the Nag Hammadi library and the Berlin Gnostic Codex. In a variety of ways — gnostic and non-gnostic — the term *gnōsis,* "knowledge" (and Coptic *sooun,* along with synonyms), is employed in a great many of these texts. In the Exegesis on the Soul it is said that salvation does not come from practical knowledge, technical skill, or book learning. In the Gospel of Thomas, the Gospel of Philip, the Second Discourse of Great Seth, and other texts it is said that saving knowledge is explicitly mystical. In such non-gnostic texts as the Teachings of Silvanus and the Sentences of Sextus there is also an emphasis upon knowledge. In the Teachings of Silvanus, as in many gnostic texts, knowledge is portrayed as self-knowledge, and the famous maxim from Delphi, Greece, *gnōthi sauton,* "Know yourself," is invoked. For ancient Greeks such self-knowledge originally meant that people should know that they are mortals and not gods. For philosophers, and especially for gnostics, as we see from Nag Hammadi and Berlin Gnostic texts, the meaning of self-knowledge is transformed, and it is said that people should know they are essentially divine in soul or spirit.

In the Nag Hammadi and Berlin Gnostic texts, a discussion of wisdom frequently accompanies the discussion of knowledge. In these texts wisdom is understood variously — as the general disposition of the insightful and judicious person, or as a divine attribute that is often personified in the divine mother named Sophia (the Greek word for "wisdom"). In the Teachings of Silvanus, Christ is the word and wisdom of God, and it is said, "God's wisdom — Sophia — took on a foolish shape for you, so that she (wisdom as Christ) might take you up, O foolish one, and make you wise" (107). In gnostic texts, Sophia is capable of falling from glory and may be in need of restoration, yet she is still mother and savior. In the Gospel of Philip, as in other Valentinian texts, there is a distinction between higher wisdom and lower wisdom: there is wisdom, Echamoth (cf. Hebrew *hokhmah*), and little wisdom, wisdom of death. The Gospel of Philip states, "Wisdom — Sophia — who is called barren, is the mother of the angels" (63). The final vindication of wisdom and of all is celebrated in a variety of gnostic texts, including the Wisdom of Jesus Christ, where the savior Jesus says to the disciples and the readers:

> I have come from places above, by the will of the bright light, and I have escaped from that fetter. I have smashed the work of those who are robbers. I have awakened the droplet sent from Sophia, that it may produce an abundance of fruit through me, and be made perfect and never again be defective. Then the droplet from the light may be <whole> through me, the great savior, and its glory may be revealed, and Sophia also may be vindicated of what was defective, and her children may never again be defective but may attain glory and honor and go up to their father and know the words of the light of maleness. (III, 107–8)

These themes of knowledge and wisdom, specifically gnostic knowledge and wisdom, will be traced through the texts discussed in the following chapters.

THE AUTHORITY OF GNOSTIC TEXTS

The story of the production and the burial of the texts of the Nag Hammadi library is caught up, as we have seen, in the issues of the day, issues having to do with the authority of sacred texts. When Athanasius addressed the canon of scripture in his festal letter of 367, he did so in the context of his discussion of orthodoxy and heresy, and when in heresiological fashion he condemned the books of the heretics — like the gnostic texts of the Nag Hammadi library — he used his authority as archbishop of Alexandria to define orthodoxy and heresy and to condemn what was heretical. The gnostic texts of the Nag Hammadi library were fated to be damned as heretical.

But what are orthodoxy and heresy? What is the source of the authority of the "orthodox" texts in the canon of scripture? From an historical point of view, orthodoxy and heresy may be understood as rhetorical constructs, as Karen King states, fashioned in the arena of political debate. Understood in this light, orthodoxy and heresy have little to do with truth and falsehood and everything to do with power and position. In a vote, the majority defines what is orthodox, and the minority is charged with being heretical. Among competing political factions, the dominant force dictates what is orthodox; those less powerful are designated as heretical. And the winners define the Bible. Athanasius of all people should have been aware of the political and rhetorical aspects and implications of the discussions of orthodoxy, heresy, and canon. In the course of the fourth century, Athanasius was exiled as a heretic and recalled from exile as a champion of orthodoxy five times, depending on the latest vote of a council or the latest political move of a ruler. As a result, Athanasius spent much of the century packing and unpacking his luggage, until finally he was declared the victor in the battle for orthodoxy. Such are the issues that determine what sacred texts are considered authoritative and canonical — and orthodox.

The gnostic texts of the Nag Hammadi library and the Berlin Gnostic Codex make claims to be authoritative and inspired, and their claims may be as compelling as the claims of biblical texts. No less than biblical texts, the Nag Hammadi and Berlin Gnostic texts lay claim to the heritage of Judeo-Christian apostles and other authoritative figures and patriarchs of the Jewish scriptures and the New Testament. No less than New Testament texts, the Nag Hammadi and Berlin Gnostic texts claim to be inspired with the words of Jesus, and they affirm that what Jesus says in these texts is authorized by apostles and siblings of Jesus. In a note at the end of the Holy Book of the Great Invisible Spirit, or the Egyptian Gospel, it is said, twice, to be written by God (in Coptic, *shai ᵉnnoute*; in Greek, *theographos*). The Revelation of Adam claims to be what Adam taught his son Seth, the Paraphrase of Shem what Derdekeas revealed to Shem, Zostrianos what is preserved through the person Zostrianos. At the end of Zostrianos the cryptogram refers not only to Zostrianos, but also to the Iranian prophet Zoroaster and "words of truth" and the "God of truth." At the conclusion of Three Forms of First Thought there is appended, in Greek, "Sacred scripture written by the father with perfect knowledge" (*agiagraphē patrographos en gnōsei teleia*).

Thus, the gnostic texts of the Nag Hammadi library and the Berlin Gnostic Codex provide an occasion to reflect upon the politics and rhetoric of orthodoxy and heresy and upon which ancient texts are judged worthy of study and appropriate for spiritual guidance. The scriptural canon is often considered closed in the Judeo-Christian-Islamic heritage, and these newly discovered texts, hidden for so long, raise serious questions about the canon of scripture. These texts, too, though excluded from the canon, contribute to our understanding of history and spirituality. When today the Gospel of Thomas from the Nag Hammadi library is sometimes referred to as the fifth gospel alongside the four canonical gospels of the New Testament, what was formerly hidden away is brought into the light of day. As Jesus asserts in the Gospel of Thomas, "Know what is in front of your face, and what is hidden from you will be disclosed to you. For there is nothing hidden that will not be revealed" (5).

3

"THEY WILL NOT TASTE DEATH"

THE WISDOM OF THE LIVING JESUS IN THE GOSPEL OF THOMAS AND THOMAS TEXTS

L ONG BEFORE THE TEXTS of the Nag Hammadi library and the Berlin Gnostic Codex were written, there was wisdom, *hokhmah*, Sophia. One of the earliest expressions of religion in the Mediterranean world and the Middle East was the way of wisdom, and wisdom has proved to be one of the most enduring. Throughout Egyptian, Mesopotamian, Jewish, Greco-Roman, Christian, and Islamic texts, wisdom has occupied a central place, and in the tradition of the Gospel of Thomas and Thomas texts Jesus is presented as a man of wisdom.

WISDOM IN THE ANCIENT WORLD

In Egypt and elsewhere in the Middle East, from the second and third millennia B.C.E., wisdom and knowledge were recognized as providing the key to success and happiness in life, and sagacious words of advice were collected for the instruction of children, students, and all those willing to address the issues of life in the world.[1] An Egyptian sage uses the name Ptahhotep to give wise instruction to his "son":

> Do not let your head be puffed up because of your knowledge. Do not be confident because you are wise. Take counsel with the ignorant as well as the wise. The full limits of skill cannot be attained, and there is no skilled person equipped to full advantage. Good speech is hidden more than the emerald, but it may be found with young women at the grindstones.[2]

A Mesopotamian sage praises Marduk, god of Babylon, as the embodiment of wisdom:

> I will praise ... Marduk, the lord of wisdom, the deliberate god, who lays hold of the night but frees the day, whose fury surrounds him like a storm wind, but whose breeze is as pleasant as a morning zephyr, whose anger is irresistible, whose rage is a devastating flood, but whose heart is merciful, whose mind forgiving ... whose hands the heavens cannot hold back, but whose gentle hand sustains the dying.[3]

In the book of Proverbs, a Hebrew author, writing under the name of King Solomon, composes proverbs for his "son" and describes wisdom as a gift of the god of Israel:

> My son, if you accept my words
> and store my commands within you,
> turning your ear to wisdom
> and inclining your heart to understanding,

yes, if you will call out for insight
and cry aloud for understanding,
if you seek it like silver
and search for it as for hidden treasure,
then you will understand the fear of the Lord
and find the knowledge of God.
For the Lord gives wisdom,
and from his mouth come knowledge and understanding.
He stores up victory for the upright
and is a shield for those who walk in truth.
For he guards the path of the just
and protects the way of his faithful ones. (2:1–8)

Such words of wisdom were collected throughout the Middle East in ancient books of wisdom, and this wisdom literature was published under the names of those reputed to be truly wise — not only Ptah-hotep and Solomon, but also Amenemhat, Amenemope, Shuruppak, Ahikar, Koheleth, ben Sirach, and others. Many books of wisdom were published anonymously.

In the Greco-Roman world, wisdom was the domain of the philosopher, the "lover of wisdom," and the philosopher dispensed wisdom and knowledge to those who would listen. One such philosopher, Diogenes of Sinope, lived a good but simple and sometimes unconventional life as a Cynic philosopher, and he and his fellow Cynics were given a prominent place in the *progymnasmata*, the rhetorical handbooks of the day, because of their astute observations. These handbooks were written with exercises intended to teach students how to fashion arguments for effective communication, and included in the exercises were memorable statements, called *chreiai*, "useful sayings," that were to be used as topics that could be expanded into rhetorical presentations.[4] *Chreiai* were characterized as sayings that were attributed appropriately to specific speakers such as Diogenes and other philosophers, including Cynic philosophers. As a result, many Greco-Roman *chreiai* have a Cynic bite:

> *Marcus Porcius Cato, when asked why he was studying Greek literature after his eightieth year, said, "Not that I may die learned but that I may not die unlearned."*

> *The Pythagorean philosopher Theano, when asked by someone how long it takes after having sex with a man for a woman to be pure to go to the Thesmophoria (the festival celebrated in honor of Demeter and Kore), said, "If it is with her own husband, at once, but if with someone else's, never."*

> *When Diogenes the Cynic philosopher saw a country boy scooping up water in his hand in order to drink, he threw away the cup he was carrying in his bag and said, "Now I can be this much lighter."*

Chreiai continued to be used into the Middle Ages and beyond by students of rhetoric and grammar, but eventually among Christian rhetoricians *chreiai* lost much of their Cynic cleverness and wit and became domesticated. They turned into the serious statements of those engaged in the business of Christian theology and ethics, where there may be little room for cleverness and wit.

When words of wisdom are attributed to Jesus in Christian texts, such as the Gospel of Thomas and other collections of sayings of Jesus, these may be classified as *chreiai* of Jesus. And if over the centuries *chreiai* in general lost much of their spark, so also sayings of Jesus often became domesticated in the Christian tradition.

The earliest known collection of sayings of Jesus — *chreiai* of Jesus — is the sayings gospel Q, a wisdom text that most scholars believe was composed in the middle of the first century. The text of Q no longer exists, but since it most likely was used, along with the Gospel of Mark, in the composition of the Gospels of Matthew and Luke, it can be reconstructed out of sayings of Jesus in Matthew and Luke. Such a reconstruction has now taken place, and the result is the restored text of Q, edited by an international team of scholars and published as *The Critical Edition of Q*.[5] Q may be called a gospel of wisdom, and in Q Jesus not only utters words of wisdom but is associated with the figure of wisdom. (Personified wisdom — Sophia — will occupy our attention in the next chapter.) Q is a remarkable text and the sayings of Jesus in Q are potent, but Q was destined to be taken over by Matthew and Luke and situated within a narrative leading to the crucifixion. In the New Testament the message of Q is overshadowed by the gospel of the cross, and Jesus the teacher of wisdom becomes Jesus the crucified one.

THE GOSPEL OF THOMAS

Like Q, the Gospel of Thomas is a gospel of wisdom, and Jesus in the Gospel of Thomas speaks forth to lead the hearers — and readers — to insight and knowledge.[6] The Jesus of Thomas and other Nag Hammadi texts of the Thomas tradition — Bentley Layton's school of St. Thomas — may not be quite a full-blown gnostic teacher, but there are gnostic tendencies in the Gospel of Thomas and the Book of Thomas and more of such themes in the Dialogue of the Savior. At the same time, we should be careful not to exaggerate the gnostic features of the Gospel of Thomas. The Jesus of Thomas is also somewhat different from the Jesus of the New Testament gospels, and it would appear that the Gospel of Thomas is not fundamentally dependent upon the New Testament gospels but is an independent gospel and a primary source for the Jesus tradition. Jesus in the Gospel of Thomas performs no physical miracles, reveals no fulfillment of prophecy, announces no apocalyptic kingdom about to disrupt the world order, and dies for no one's sins. I might add that Thomas's Jesus is "the living Jesus," but he does not rise from the dead and leave an empty tomb. If Jesus is called the living one in the Gospel of Thomas, so is God referred to as the living one, and the followers of Jesus are also living ones. In the Gospel of Thomas Jesus is proclaimed the living one, and he lives in his sayings.

Although Albert Schweitzer, the great medical doctor of Gabon and the author of *The Quest of the Historical Jesus*, seems not to have commented directly on the Gospel of Thomas, he did care very much about sayings of Jesus, and in a sermon he preached at St. Nicolai's Church in Strasbourg in 1905, he made the same connection between the living Jesus and his sayings:

> *What kind of living person is Jesus? Don't search for formulas to describe him, even if they be hallowed by centuries. I almost got angry the other day when a religious person said to me that only someone who believes in the resurrection of the body and in the glorified body of the risen Christ can believe in the living Jesus. . . . Let me explain it in my way. The glorified body of Jesus is to be found in his sayings.*[7]

The Gospel of Thomas is the second tractate of Nag Hammadi Codex II, and it is situated immediately after the Secret Book of John and just before the Gospel of Philip. Three Greek fragments of the Gospel of Thomas also survive as Papyrus Oxyrhynchus 1, 654, and 655, as do testimonia in early Christian literature, particularly in Hippolytus of Rome (*Refutation of All Heresies* 5.7.20; 5.8.32). The variations among the several texts make it clear that the Gospel of Thomas went through several editions, and changes could be made from one edition to another. Such fluidity in the written word was characteristic of the textual world of scribal activity prior to Gutenberg and the invention of the printing press. The Gospel of Thomas was probably

The cover of Nag Hammadi Codex II

composed in Greek, in Syria, perhaps at Edessa, where at least later on, it is said, the bones of Thomas could be seen and venerated.

As I intimated earlier, a very reasonable case can be made for a first-century date of composition for the Gospel of Thomas. The Coptic Gospel of Thomas from the Nag Hammadi library was translated no later than the middle of the fourth century, or more likely some time before then, but the Greek papyrus fragments have been dated much earlier, at the beginning of the third century or somewhat later. On the basis of such suggested dates, Grenfell and Hunt, the first editors of the Oxyrhynchus papyri, estimated that the original documents must have been composed at least half a century earlier, around 140 at the latest. More recently, Søren Giversen has revised these dates and has stated, on papyrological grounds, that the Oxyrhynchus papyrus fragments of the Gospel of Thomas may be assigned earlier dates, so that the date of composition may be pushed back even further, perhaps into the first century.[8] The textual evidence for an early date for the Gospel of Thomas thus may rival that of any of the New Testament gospels.

Further, the Gospel of Thomas illustrates concerns that are usually judged to belong to the first century: disagreements about apostleship, uncertainty about the role of James the righteous, interest in sayings of Jesus and sayings collections, and so forth. Sayings in the Gospel of Thomas also seem to be transmitted in a form that is earlier than the form we have in the canonical gospels. Such may be noted, for instance, in parables: Thomas preserves parables of Jesus simply as stories, but the New Testament gospels append allegorical interpretations to the parables in an effort to explain them and apply them to new situations. One saying in the Gospel of Thomas (17) offers words of Jesus — "I shall give you what no eye has seen, what no ear has heard, what no hand has touched, what has not arisen in the human heart" — that sound very much like what Paul cites in his description of wisdom Christians in Corinth (1 Cor. 2:9) in the middle of the first century. If the composition of the Gospel of Thomas may be given a date in the first century, then Thomas may take us back to a place that much closer to the historical Jesus, and the Gospel of Thomas together with the sayings gospel Q may provide strong evidence for Jesus as a teacher of wisdom.

In the Gospel of Thomas, Stephen Patterson has pointed out, Jesus is just Jesus.[9] Thomas's Jesus does not pull rank, and almost all Christological titles are absent. In the Gospel of Thomas Jesus is not addressed as Christ or Messiah, nor is he called master or lord, and when Jesus refers to himself, one time (86), as child of humankind or son of man, he does so in the general sense of any person — including himself—being a child of humankind: "[Foxes have] their dens and birds have their nests, but the child of humankind has no place to lay his head and rest." In the Gospel of Thomas Jesus is not the exalted apocalyptic son of man coming at the end of time to usher in a new world. There is, in fact, no new world to be ushered in, according to Jesus in Thomas. Jesus says that God's kingdom is already here:

> *His disciples said to him, "When will the kingdom come?"*
> *"It will not come by watching for it. It will not be said, 'Look, here it is,' or 'Look, there it is.' Rather, the father's kingdom is spread out upon the earth, and people do not see it." (113)*

If Jesus is a child of humankind in the Gospel of Thomas, other people are also called children of humankind. And Thomas's Jesus is not born miraculously of the virgin Mary and is not the unique or incarnate son of God.

In the Gospel of Thomas Jesus does not dwell on his titles but on his sayings, and the sayings of Jesus are the point of the Gospel of Thomas. The gospel's prologue, or incipit (opening phrase), identifies these sayings as hidden sayings: "These are the hidden sayings that the living Jesus spoke and Judas Thomas the Twin recorded." Here Judas Thomas, who is described as the twin of Jesus with words derived from Aramaic (Thomas) and Greek (Didymos), is presented as the recorder and guarantor of the sayings of Jesus. In this gospel Judas Thomas knows, and this portrayal contrasts sharply with that of the Gospel of John, in which Thomas neither knows nor believes and is depicted as "doubting Thomas" until the end of the gospel. Immediately after the prologue of the Gospel of Thomas it is said, "Whoever discovers the interpretation of these sayings will not taste death" (1), and then follow dozens of sayings of Jesus. The sayings are usually numbered at 114, and although the system of numeration is flawed, the convention has stuck. There is no narrative story line in the

Gospel of Thomas, but there are sayings to be heard and read, and these sayings, when understood, can save.

To encounter the sayings of Jesus, however, is a challenging task. Saying 2 lays out the epistemological process whereby a person comes to knowledge and understanding: "Let one who seeks not stop seeking until one finds. When one finds, one will be troubled. When one is troubled, one will marvel and will reign over all." According to saying 2, those who seek Jesus's sayings and do not stop seeking will find, but what they find may be disturbing. Yet if they persist in their quest for meaning and understanding, they will be amazed at what they discover, and they will be part of God's reign. That, according to the Gospel of Thomas, is God's kingdom, and that, the Greek Gospel of Thomas adds (Papyrus Oxyrhynchus 654), with a theme dear to gnostics, is "rest" — that is, rest and peace from all the unsettling aspects of life in the world.

The concern in the Gospel of Thomas for encountering the hidden sayings of Jesus assumes that the disciples and readers will interact with Jesus's sayings in a creative way, find an interpretation of his words, and think his thoughts after him. The sayings in the Gospel of Thomas all leave room for interpretation, and some are especially cryptic. Jesus says he is not even a teacher, in the conventional sense of someone who imparts information and truth. Rather, he declares, he tends the bubbling spring and offers wisdom from it, but those who seek must acquire the wisdom for themselves (13).

Richard Valantasis, in his book *The Gospel of Thomas*, is correct, I believe, when he calls the theology of the Gospel of Thomas "a performative theology." He says that "the theology emerges from the readers' and hearers' responses to the sayings and their sequence and their variety."[10] At the very end of his book Valantasis writes:

> *Knowledge emerges from an act of interpreting. The collection of*
> *sayings under the authorship of Jesus and editorship of Didymos*

Judas Thomas demands a performance to unlock their individual
and collected meaning. It requires work and toil to perform these
and to discover (note it is not to learn) the interpretation. . . . Whereas
a narrative defines carefully the actors and their actions, sayings
simply float meaning without careful definition or careful control.
This Gospel proclaims the priority of living voice over narrative, of
textualized presence over narrative definition. The Gospel remains
performative.[11]

This emphasis upon the living voice of Jesus in the Gospel of
Thomas may be corroborated not only by the identification of Jesus
as "the living Jesus," but also by a grammatical feature of the sayings
themselves. The sayings are introduced by the quotation formula
"Jesus said," "He said," or the like, and the Coptic for this formula is
peje i(ēsou)s or *pejaf* or something similar. The Greek fragments,
however, employ the present indicative, *legei i(ēsou)s* or simply *legei*,
and it may be that we should translate the Coptic with the English
present tense. (The German translation in *Nag Hammadi Deutsch*
and the German and English translations in *Synopsis Quattuor Evan-*
geliorum do in fact use the present tense.[12]) The sayings coming from
the living voice of Jesus are not what Jesus once said as much as they
are what Jesus continues to say.

What, then, does Jesus say in the Gospel of Thomas? As in other
gospels, including New Testament gospels, Jesus announces the kingdom or reign of God, and as in those gospels Jesus in the Gospel of
Thomas refers to God's kingdom in aphorisms and parables, but keeps
his references vague and metaphorical. In saying 3 Jesus uses humor
to explain that the kingdom is not up in heaven or down in the abyss,
but rather within and without:

If your leaders say to you, "Look, the kingdom is in heaven," then
the birds of heaven will precede you. If they say to you, "It is in the

sea," then the fish will precede you. Rather, the kingdom is inside
you and it is outside you.

Jesus follows this statement with a comment about knowing oneself
reminiscent of the Delphic maxim: "When you know yourselves,
then you will be known, and you will understand that you are children of the living father. But if you do not know yourselves, then you
dwell in poverty, and you are poverty." In saying 22 Jesus says that
those who are like nursing babies will enter the kingdom when they
are transformed and attain unity and wholeness:

> *When you make the two into one, and when you make the inner*
> *like the outer and the outer like the inner, and the upper like the*
> *lower, and when you make male and female into a single one, so*
> *that the male will not be male nor the female be female, when you*
> *make eyes in place of an eye, a hand in place of a hand, a foot in*
> *place of a foot, an image in place of an image, then you will enter*
> *[the kingdom].*

Children will enter the kingdom, but not businesspeople and mer-
chants. At the end of the Gospel of Thomas Jesus declares that fe-
males also will enter the kingdom — when they become male. We
shall return to that last saying of Jesus later.

In the Gospel of Thomas, Jesus is a Jewish storyteller who illustrates what the kingdom is like by telling stories taken from everyday
life. Most of the stories, or parables, are familiar; some are not.
Among the new stories of Jesus in the Gospel of Thomas are the parables of the jar of meal and the assassin (97–98):

> *Jesus said, "The [father's] kingdom is like a woman who was carry-*
> *ing a [jar] full of meal. While she was walking along [a] distant*

*road, the handle of the jar broke and the meal spilled behind her
[along] the road. She did not know it; she had not noticed a problem. When she reached her house, she put the jar down and discovered that it was empty."*

*Jesus said, "The father's kingdom is like a person who wanted to
put someone powerful to death. While at home he drew his sword
and thrust it into the wall to find out whether his hand would go
in. Then he killed the powerful one."*

The life Jesus advocates in the Gospel of Thomas is a radical,
countercultural life. In saying 42, noteworthy for its brevity, Jesus
says, "Be passersby," thereby apparently advocating a homeless life of
wandering — perhaps wandering from the things of this world.[13] This
saying is paralleled by a saying in the work of the medieval author
Petrus Alphonsi and a saying attributed to Jesus and inscribed on a
mosque at Fatehpur-Sikri, India: "This world is a bridge. Pass over it,
but do not build your dwelling there." Jesus also suggests that his disciples follow an itinerant life of wandering, and he recommends that
as they travel about they eat whatever people serve and show their
thanks through acts of healing:

*When you go into any region and walk through the countryside,
when people receive you, eat what they serve you and heal the
sick among them. For what goes into your mouth will not defile
you; rather, it is what comes out of your mouth that will defile
you. (14)*

Just prior to this, Jesus rejects outward acts of religious piety — fasting, prayer, giving to charity — and instead proclaims a more spiritual
observance: "If you do not fast from the world, you will not find the

kingdom. If you do not observe the sabbath as a sabbath, you will not see the father" (27). Physical circumcision too is useless, Jesus says, but spiritual circumcision is of great value:

> His disciples said to him, "Is circumcision useful or not?"
> He said to them, "If it were useful, children's fathers would produce them already circumcised from their mothers. Rather, the true circumcision in spirit has become valuable in every respect." (53)

Conventional family values are dismissed in the Gospel of Thomas, and, Jesus says, earthly fathers and mothers are to be despised:

> Whoever does not hate [father] and mother as I do cannot be a [disciple] of me, and whoever does [not] love [father and] mother as I do cannot be a [disciple of] me. For my mother [gave me falsehood], but my true [mother] gave me life. (101)

Jesus turns away from his siblings and his own mother and advocates a new order of family:

> The disciples said to him, "Your brothers and your mother are standing outside."
> He said to them, "Those here who do the will of my father are my brothers and my mother. They are the ones who will enter my father's kingdom." (99)

And those coming to dinner in Jesus's parable of the feast in the Gospel of Thomas are people off the street (64).

The disciples of Jesus, and the readers of the Gospel of Thomas, are urged to engage Jesus and his sayings in the gospel. According to the Gospel of Thomas, Jesus is like a wise bartender: as saying 13 states, Jesus serves the spiritual brew, but those with him must drink for themselves in order to become spiritually intoxicated. Later Jesus says, "I disclose my mysteries to those [who are worthy] of [my] mysteries" (62), and those mysteries are the wisdom Jesus pours out and the words that come from his mouth. As Jewish wisdom literature can recommend that people drink of wisdom, so also Jesus in the Gospel of Thomas can invite people to drink of him. When people drink from the mouth of Jesus, they will become one with Jesus, mystically united with him, and come to knowledge and understanding. Jesus says, "Whoever drinks from my mouth will become like me; I myself shall become that person, and the hidden things will be revealed to that person" (108).

Nag Hammadi Codex II, open to the Gospel of Thomas
and the Gospel of Philip, pages 50–51

The wise words of Jesus in the Gospel of Thomas constitute a diverse series of sayings. Some sayings resemble sayings of Jesus in the New Testament gospels, especially the synoptic gospels, and some echo Q. Other sayings are quite different from anything in the New Testament or Q. Some reflect the interests of Jewish wisdom literature; others recall Greek wisdom sayings, the fables of Aesop, for instance. Some seem fairly clear in meaning; others are much more obscure and riddlelike, as in the case of saying 11:

> Jesus said, "This heaven will pass away, and the one above it will pass away.
> "The dead are not alive, and the living will not die.
> "During the days when you ate what is dead, you made it alive. When you are in the light, what will you do?
> "On the day when you were one, you became two. But when you become two, what will you do?"

Some sayings of Jesus in the Gospel of Thomas were destined to have a textual life beyond the gospel itself in other sources, including Islamic sources.[14] Abu Hamid Muhammad al-Ghazali preserves wise sayings of prophet 'Isa—Jesus—in his *Revival of the Religious Sciences*, and some of these sayings closely resemble those in Thomas. One such saying of 'Isa in al-Ghazali is reminiscent of sayings 39 and 102 of the Gospel of Thomas:

> Jesus said, "Evil scholars are like a rock that has fallen at the mouth of a brook: it does not drink the water, nor does it let the water flow to the plants. And evil scholars are like the drainpipe of a latrine that is plastered outside but filthy inside, or like graves that are decorated outside but contain dead people's bones inside."[15]

The wisdom of Jesus lives on in Islamic texts.

What all of these wise sayings of Jesus have in common in the Gospel of Thomas is the fact that they are hidden sayings that need to be interpreted to be understood. As Bentley Layton states in *The Gnostic Scriptures*, "Without recognition of their hidden meaning, Jesus' sayings are merely 'obscure.' "[16] When the meaning of these sayings is discovered, however, the obscurity is removed, insight is realized, and life is found.

The final saying in the Gospel of Thomas is infamous for its formulation, and Pachomian monks who read this saying may have reached their own strongly ascetic conclusion about the nature of women and sexuality:

> Simon Peter said to them, "Mary should leave us, for females are not worthy of life."
>
> Jesus said, "Look, I shall guide her to make her male, so that she too may become a living spirit resembling you males. For every female who makes herself male will enter heaven's kingdom." (114)

I suggest that an authentic interpretation of this saying takes its meaning to be symbolic.[17] In the ancient world the transformation of the female into the male was widely discussed, and although a few ancient authors like Ovid and Phlegon of Tralles tell colorful stories about women sprouting male genitals and becoming male, most of the accounts discuss gender categories in a symbolic sense. In ancient texts the female is frequently thought to stand for all that is earthly, perishable, passive, and sense-perceptible, and the male all that is heavenly, imperishable, active, and rational. The transformation of the female into the male, as mandated by Jesus in the Gospel of Thomas, may then be interpreted as the transformation of what is perishable into what is imperishable, and that transformation is necessary for all people, both men and women. Further, according to some ancient gynecological theories, only one gender, the male, is complete, and a female is an incomplete male, without a penis, so that a female may be restored to wholeness by growing a penis and becoming a male — a type of androgyne. This gender symbolism may be offensive to us, but many ancient thinkers found it convincing. So when Jesus in the Gospel of Thomas is made to affirm, in opposition to the position of Peter, that Mary can be saved when she and all that is female become male, I believe this saying is intended as a statement of liberation.

THE BOOK OF THOMAS AND
THE DIALOGUE OF THE SAVIOR

The Book of Thomas, also given the secondary title the Contender Writing to the Perfect, is the seventh tractate in Nag Hammadi Codex II, and the Dialogue of the Savior is the fifth tractate in Codex III. Both of these texts seem to make use of sayings from the Gospel of Thomas, and the Book of Thomas in particular presents itself as a part of the Thomas tradition. Among the disciples singled out for special attention in the Dialogue of the Savior are Mary of Magdala, Matthew, and Judas — most likely Judas Thomas.

The Book of Thomas utilizes sayings of Jesus from the Gospel of Thomas along with themes from Jewish wisdom and Greek philosophy, especially Platonic philosophy, to proclaim a message about the fire of passion and the fire of judgment.[18] Like the Gospel of Thomas, the Book of Thomas's incipit refers to hidden sayings of Jesus: "The hidden sayings that the savior spoke to Judas Thomas, which I, Mathaias, in turn recorded. I was walking, listening to them speak with each other." Also like the Gospel of Thomas, the Book of Thomas has Jesus go on to highlight the centrality of knowledge, especially self-knowledge. Jesus says to his twin brother Judas Thomas:

Since it is said that you are my twin and true friend, examine yourself and understand who you are, how you exist, and how you

will come to be. Since you are to be called my brother, it is not fit-
ting for you to be ignorant of yourself. And I know that you have
understood, for already you have understood that I am the knowl-
edge of truth. So while you are walking with me, though you do
lack understanding, already you have obtained knowledge and
you will be called one who knows oneself. For those who have not
known themselves have known nothing, but those who have
known themselves already have acquired knowledge about the
depth of the universe. So then, my brother Thomas, you have seen
what is hidden from people, what they stumble against in their ig-
norance. (138)

The Book of Thomas has a primary title and a secondary title, and
it is in the form of a dialogue between Jesus and Judas Thomas at the
beginning and a monologue by Jesus at the end. These features observed in the Book of Thomas have led to different theories of composition. John D. Turner has suggested that the Book of Thomas is
based on two sources, a dialogue between Jesus and Thomas and a
collection of sayings of Jesus.[19] Hans-Martin Schenke, alternatively,
proposes that originally the Book of Thomas was not a Christian text
at all, but rather a Hellenistic Jewish text, and that the secondary
title — the Contender Writing to the Perfect — indicates the character
of that Jewish text: it was a letter on wisdom and virtue, said to be sent
to those called the perfect by the contender par excellence in the
Jewish tradition, the patriarch Jacob, who wrestled with God. This
Jewish text then was Christianized, according to Schenke, and became the Book of Thomas, the brother of Jesus.[20]

The Gospel of Thomas has Jesus utter strong words about the body
and the life of the body, but the Book of Thomas is much more ascetic in its harsh condemnation of passion and its grim premonition of
the fire of hell. The Book of Thomas is a text Pachomian monks
could enjoy. In it Jesus observes that "everyone who seeks truth from

true wisdom — Sophia — will fashion wings to fly, fleeing from the passion that inflames human spirits" (140). Jesus is made to add, in terms close to those of Plato's *Phaedo*, that the fire driving people on in their passion imprisons them, blinds them, and constrains them like a stake in the heart or a bit in the mouth. Jesus also employs phrases that anticipate Dante's *Inferno* to warn that the lot of those who are wicked and oppress the righteous will be horrific, for they will be cast down into the abyss of fire and handed over to the angel Tartarouchos, who controls Tartaros with fiery whips spewing forth sparks. The wicked person is pursued and punished in hell, and Jesus says that such a person has nowhere to turn:

> If he flees to the west, he finds fire. If he turns south, he finds it there as well. If he turns north, the threat of erupting fire meets him again. Nor can he find the way to the east, to flee there and be saved, for he did not find it while embodied so as to find it on the day of judgment. (143)

At the conclusion of the Book of Thomas Jesus utters words of shame and blessing — shame for the godless and blessing for those who understand — again with Platonic themes about the body as the prison of the soul:

> Shame on you who hope in the flesh and in the prison that will perish. How long will you sleep, and think that what is imperishable will also perish? Your hope is based upon the world, and your god is this present life. You are destroying your souls. (143)

> Blessings on you who understand beforehand the temptations and flee from things that are alien. (145)

The text comes to an end as Jesus addresses the readers and urges them to be vigilant, and in his words of counsel he picks up terms and concepts that also are important in the Gospel of Thomas — "watch," "reign," "rest." Jesus says that those who watch and pray and leave bodily passions behind will find rest, and he assures them, "You will reign with the king, you united with him and he with you, from now on and forever. Amen" (145).

The Dialogue of the Savior also employs sayings of Jesus that may derive from the Gospel of Thomas, and it incorporates these sayings into a dialogue of Jesus with his disciples.[21] The dialogical form of the text allows for more freedom of expression and more expansion upon themes, as sayings of Jesus and other materials are worked into the text. In their analysis of the Dialogue of the Savior, Helmut Koester and Elaine Pagels identify as many as five sources that may have been

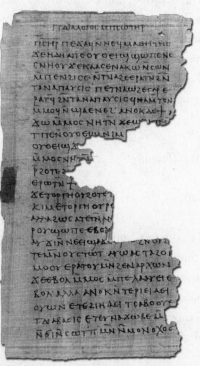

Nag Hammadi Codex III, 120: the opening of the Dialogue of the Savior, with title

consulted in the composition of the present text, and they suggest that cosmological, apocalyptic, and other sources were used in addition to sayings of Jesus.[22]

The text of the Dialogue of the Savior opens with Jesus saying to his disciples, "Now the time has come, brothers and sisters, for us to leave our labor behind and stand at rest, for whoever stands at rest will rest forever" (120). Jesus proceeds to teach the disciples a prayer — another Lord's Prayer — and he goes on, as far as we can tell in the fragmentary text, to teach about the end of all things. He speaks words of comfort and reassurance to his disciples, and, as in Gospel of Thomas 22, he advises, "Make what is [inside] you and what is [outside you a single one]" (123). A dialogue ensues, and Jesus and his disciples discuss the inner life, spirit, body, light, darkness, creation, the word, fire, water, the world, the rulers of the world, fullness, deficiency, life, and death — themes typical of gnostic texts. In the middle of the dialogue Jesus reiterates what he says in the Gospel of Thomas: "And I say to you, let one [who has] power renounce [it and] repent, and let one who [knows] seek and find and rejoice" (129). Mary of Magdala herself speaks three wisdom sayings that usually are pronounced by Jesus:

> The wickedness of each day <is sufficient>.
> Workers deserve their food.
> Disciples resemble their teachers.

For her insight Mary is praised in the text, and it is said, "She spoke this utterance as a woman who understood everything" (139).[23]

According to Jesus in the Dialogue of the Savior, the goal of this inquiry into knowledge and understanding — this seeking and finding — is salvation. Jesus says, once again in terms recalling the Gospel of Thomas, that what is to be sought is within, and it is of spirit: "I tell you [the truth], look, what you seek and inquire about [is] within you, and it [has] the power and mystery [of the] spirit, for [it is] from [the spirit]" (128).

JESUS, THE GOSPEL OF THE CROSS, AND THE GOSPEL OF WISDOM

Throughout the history of the Christian church, the proclamation of the crucifixion of Christ has been a central preoccupation and the gospel of the cross a dominant theme. In Christian soteriology (the interpretation of the nature of salvation), the crucifixion is commonly understood in a sacrificial context, and it is often maintained that Christ died to save people from their sins. With vividness and violence, Mel Gibson's film *The Passion of the Christ* proclaims the gospel of the cross as a salvific bloodbath, and when in the film Gibson himself takes the hammer in hand in the crucifixion scene, he confesses that he crucified Jesus and Jesus died for him.

There is no doubt that the story of the crucifixion of Jesus is not only an account based on an historical event, but also a story of pathos and power. In fact, the historical Jesus was executed by the Romans as a Jewish agitator who announced a subversive empire — God's kingdom — and acted on the basis of this announcement. The story of the death of Jesus has all the drama of other stories of men and women who died before their time for a just cause and had the courage of their convictions. Socrates drank the hemlock; Ali, Hasan, and Husayn died as Muslim martyrs; Joan of Arc was burned at the stake; John F. Kennedy, Robert F. Kennedy, and Martin Luther King were killed in the prime of life — and Jesus died on a cross. So when the Gospel of Mark proclaims that Jesus is recognized as the son of God on the cross and that strength may be found in weakness and life in death, the message resonates among us powerfully to the present day.

The gospel of the cross, however, is not the only proclamation of the good news of Jesus, and it is not the good news of the Gospel of Thomas and the Thomas tradition. The Gospel of Thomas proclaims another gospel, a gospel of wisdom. In the Gospel of Thomas the cross is mentioned only once, and there the image of bearing the cross is used in the general sense of bearing a burden (55). There is no sense of a cross with saving significance in the Gospel of Thomas, and if Jesus bears his cross, so must his followers bear their crosses.

Elsewhere in the Nag Hammadi library, particularly in Valentinian texts, there are references to the crucifixion of Jesus, but there is no doctrine of atonement through the death of Jesus on the cross. Valentinian texts understand that the real meaning of the cross is the disclosure of the will of God the father and the revelation of the incorruptible nature of the savior, as in the Gospel of Truth:

> Jesus appeared,
> put on that book,
> was nailed to a tree,
> and published the father's edict on the cross.
> Oh, what a great teaching!
> He humbled himself even unto death,
> though clothed in eternal life.
> He stripped off the perishable rags
> and clothed himself in incorruptibility,
> which no one can take from him. (20)

This is so, according to the Gospel of Truth, because Jesus "encompasses knowledge and perfection."

The Second Discourse of Great Seth goes further in its rejection of a gospel of the cross, and the text right after it in Nag Hammadi Codex VII, the Revelation of Peter, provides a similar perspective. In the Second Discourse of Great Seth, Jesus discusses his own crucifixion, and he opposes those who "proclaim the doctrine of a dead man" (60) — that is, those who preach a gospel of the cross. Jesus in this text says that he has come to his own and has united with them, so that they might come to knowledge of God and oneness with each other. When people understand what Jesus says, then they realize true salvation. Jesus states,

> They have come to know fully and completely that the one who is is one, and all are one. They have been taught about the One and the assembly — the church — and the members of the assembly. For the father of all is immeasurable and immutable, mind, word, division, jealousy, fire, yet he is simply one, all in all in a single principle, because all are from a single spirit. (68)

In the Gospel of Thomas and the Thomas tradition, it is what Jesus says and not how Jesus dies that is important, and the words and wisdom of the living Jesus bring insight, light, and life. The Gospel of Thomas proclaims a gospel of wisdom by inviting readers to encounter Jesus and his sayings and find an interpretation of the sayings that will enlighten their lives. Then they "will not taste death." Jesus in the Gospel of Thomas is not unlike the Buddha in Theravada Buddhism. Jesus and the Buddha point the way, but it is up to those who follow to labor at the task of understanding and living.

Jesus in the Gospel of Thomas also sheds light on aspects of the life and work of the historical Jesus. Before church dogma, before the formulations of Christology and soteriology, before the honorific titles bestowed upon Jesus, there was Jesus the Jewish man of wisdom, walking the roads of Galilee with his friends, speaking in aphorisms, stories, and other utterances about God's presence and God's reign, and showing God's presence and power through acts of faith healing and exorcism. The presentation in the Gospel of Thomas of the good news of wisdom, I am convinced, contributes a great deal to our understanding of the history and significance of Jesus, and this understanding provides another viable way of articulating the gospel of Jesus.

4

THE WISDOM OF INSIGHT

THE FALL AND RESTORATION OF
SOPHIA IN THE SECRET BOOK OF JOHN
AND SETHIAN TEXTS

A MONG SETHIANS and other gnostics, wisdom came to expression not only in the disposition of the wise and the instruction of the sage, but also in personified wisdom. Wisdom, Hokhmah, and Sophia were understood as female manifestations of the divine who reveal the wisdom of God and accomplish God's will. In gnostic traditions, Sophia is radicalized, and she becomes entangled in a cosmic drama with profound implications for both divine and human life. Her fortunes — and misfortunes — are a focal point of the gnostic story of the creation, fall, and salvation of the world as told in Sethian texts.

PERSONIFIED WISDOM IN ANTIQUITY

In the world of antiquity, everyday wisdom became the person of wisdom, Hokhmah, or Sophia, personified as a divine female figure who incorporates various features of divinity in her being. Already in ancient Egypt and Mesopotamia, goddesses like Maat and Ishtar disclose aspects of divine wisdom, but it is in Jewish, Greco-Roman, and Christian sources that we observe divine wisdom truly embodied.

In the book of Proverbs in the Jewish scriptures, wisdom raises her voice in revelation and explains her role in creation and history:

> O people, to you I call,
> and I cry out to the children of humankind.
> You who are simple, learn prudence,
> and you who are foolish, learn understanding.
> Listen, for I have good things to say,
> and from my lips will come what is right.
>
> Choose my instruction instead of silver,
> knowledge rather than choice gold.
> Wisdom is more precious than jewels,
> and nothing you desire compares with her.
> I, wisdom, dwell with prudence,
> and I possess knowledge and discretion.
>
> The Lord brought me forth
> as the first of his works,
> before his acts of old.
> Ages ago I was established,
> at the beginning, before the world began.
>
> I was at his side like a craftsman,
> and every day I was filled with delight,
> rejoicing before him always,
> rejoicing in his whole world,
> delighting in the children of humankind.
> (8:4–6, 10–12, 22–23, 30–31)

In the writings of the Jewish scriptures and beyond, wisdom assumes her place with God, and she as mother complements God as father in the divine realm. According to 1 Enoch 42, however, she finds no place among people, and instead iniquity is with them:

> *Wisdom could not find a place in which she could dwell;*
> *but a place was found for her in the heavens.*
> *Then wisdom went out to dwell with the children of the people,*
> *but she found no dwelling place.*
> *So wisdom returned to her place*
> *and she settled permanently among the angels.*
> *Then iniquity went out of her rooms,*
> *and found whom she did not expect.*
> *And she dwelt with them,*
> *like rain in a desert,*
> *like dew on a thirsty land.*[1]

In Greco-Roman mythological texts, wisdom also is portrayed with characteristics of the divine. Athena is often depicted as a goddess of wisdom. The daughter of Metis, who is intelligence or skill, Athena becomes the matron goddess of Athens and the guardian of Athenian civilization. Athena is associated with the owl and the olive tree, and in poetry she is praised for her wisdom and virtue. According to Hesiod's *Theogony*, Zeus produces Athena directly from his head, by the River or Lake Triton, in order to ensure that his first wife, Metis, would not give birth to a child who would surpass him in power, and Hera, jealous of what Zeus did, also brings forth a child by herself — Hephaistos, the smith and artisan of the gods and goddesses, whom Hera evicts from Olympus and casts down, hurt and lame, to the world below.

Hesiod writes,

> *Now king of the gods, Zeus made Metis his first wife,*
> *Wiser than any other god, or any mortal man.*

> But when she was about to deliver the owl-eyed goddess
> Athena, Zeus tricked her, gulled her with crafty words,
> And stuffed her in his stomach, taking the advice
> Of Earth and starry Heaven. They told him to do this
> So that no one but Zeus would hold the title of King
> Among the eternal gods, for it was predestined
> That very wise children would be born from Metis,
> First the grey-eyed girl, Tritogeneia,
> Equal to her father in strength and wisdom,
> But then a son with an arrogant heart
> Who would one day be king of gods and men.
> But Zeus stuffed the goddess into his stomach first
> So she would devise with him good and evil both. (891–905)

> From his own head he gave birth to owl-eyed Athena,
> The awesome, battle-rousing, army-leading, untiring
> Lady, whose pleasure is fighting and the metallic din of war.
> And Hera, furious at her husband, bore a child
> Without making love, glorious Hephaistos,
> The finest artisan of all the Ouranians. (929–34)[2]

Elsewhere, in the Homeric *Hymn to Pythian Apollo*, it is said that the child Hera bears is the monster Typhaon.

As we shall see, the Sethian story told in the Secret Book of John has many of the same features of this mythological account in Hesiod — the father's independent procreation and mental production of divine wisdom at a site by the water, followed by the mother's imitation and the birth of a child, a divine but malformed artisan, with the threat of a son who has an arrogant heart.

In the sayings gospel Q, as we have seen, Jesus is a teacher of wisdom, but Q also reflects the Jewish tradition of personified wisdom. In Q, personified wisdom, Sophia, is closely associated with Jesus, though the evidence is subtle. According to the Lukan version of Q 11:49 (Luke 11:49), the wisdom of God announces that she will send prophets and apostles. In the parallel Matthean version (Matt. 23:34), Jesus himself says this, and he maintains that he will do the job that Sophia claims she will do in the Lukan version of Q. Again, according to the Lukan version of Q 7:35 (Luke 7:35), Jesus states that wisdom is justified by her children — John the Baptizer and Jesus. In the parallel Matthean version (Matt. 11:19), Jesus says that wisdom is justified by her deeds. In all these texts, wisdom and Jesus are linked to each other; but the emphasis varies, and the Lukan versions of the sayings in Q stress the way wisdom speaks and acts in the ministry of Jesus and functions as mother of Jesus.

The role of wisdom, Sophia, is open to debate and discussion in some early Christian texts. In 1 Corinthians Paul argues with wisdom Christians in Corinth about which wisdom is true wisdom — their wisdom, which is Sophia among the rulers, or archons, of this age, or his. As noted above, in his argument Paul quotes a text (1 Cor. 2:9) that these Christian enthusiasts themselves may have used, and the text is now known as a saying of Jesus in the Gospel of Thomas: "I shall give you what no eye has seen, what no ear has heard, what no hand has touched, what has not arisen in the human heart" (17).

The place of Sophia — including Sophia among the archons of this age — becomes more prominent, more tragic, and more dramatic in the gnostic texts of the Nag Hammadi library, particularly the Sethian texts, but these gnostic texts may possibly have been preceded by the teaching of Simon Magus and Helena. In the New Testament Acts of the Apostles 8:9–25, Simon Magus (or Simon the magician) is introduced as nothing but a cheap wonder-worker from Samaria who wants to buy the gift of the holy spirit from Peter and John in order to strengthen his own spiritual arsenal. From this account comes the term "simony," the practice of buying an ecclesiastical position.

In the writings of the heresiologists, however, Simon is considered a much more important figure, and he is connected to the suggested beginnings of gnostic thought. (Vague hints of his importance may also be found in the New Testament Acts, where it is said that Simon is the "power of God called great.") According to Irenaeus of Lyon, Simon was the great power of God who traveled about with his companion Helena, who, although formerly a prostitute in Tyre, became his first thought (*ennoia*). Helena was, says Irenaeus, mother of all; she had descended and produced powers and angels, and they fashioned the world. But they turned on her and caused her much grief, and she fell into numerous bodies, being incarnated, for example, as Helen of Troy, before being rescued from her sorry state in Tyre.

If Irenaeus is to be believed, the career of Simon's Helena anticipates that of divine thought and personified wisdom in gnostic texts. Simon Magus is ridiculed in a particularly brutal way in the Acts of Peter, and that story has been made into the film *The Silver Chalice*, with Jack Palance playing the part of Simon. Although Simon and Helena do not play any overt role in Nag Hammadi texts, the Three Steles of Seth makes mention of Dositheos, the predecessor of Simon Magus, and the Concept of Our Great Power uses terminology—"great power," "thought"—that may provide a faint echo of Simon and Helena. Kurt Rudolph also suggests, in his book *Gnosis*, that the Exegesis on the Soul, with its story of the fall of the soul into prostitution (the soul is thought to be female, Psyche, in ancient texts) and her restoration to heavenly love, may reflect the thinking of Simon and Helena.[3]

THE SECRET BOOK OF JOHN

The Secret Book of John is a Sethian text in which Sophia nearly steals the show.[4] The Secret Book of John, also known as the Apocryphon of John, is a classic Sethian account of the origin of the cosmos and its ultimate destiny, and Sophia stands at the center of the text as the divine being who falls and is restored, thus bringing about the salvation and restoration of God and humankind. Like Hera in the *Theogony* of Hesiod, Sophia in the Secret Book of John tries to do what the father of all was able to do, to reproduce independently, and like Eve in the book of Genesis, Sophia is the mother who falls into error. In a number of respects the mythic story of mother Sophia recalls the mythic story of mother Eve, and the story of the primordial fall of Sophia in the heavenly realm of fullness resembles the account of the fall of Adam and Eve in the garden of Eden. By the end of the story in the Secret Book of John, the text promises that Sophia will be vindicated and the realm of God will attain its fullness once again. The Secret Book of John thus proclaims the good news of hope and assurance that through wisdom and insight salvation will be realized for the world.

The Secret Book of John is preserved in four copies, three in the Nag Hammadi library and one in the Berlin Gnostic Codex. The text survives as the opening tractate of Nag Hammadi Codices II, III, and IV, and as the second tractate of the Berlin Gnostic Codex. In his work *Against Heresies* (1.29.1–4), Irenaeus of Lyon also summarizes ideas from the gnostics (the Barbelognostics — named after Barbelo, the divine mother — or the Sethians), and his summary compares well with the main points in the first part of the Secret Book of John. The four copies of the Secret Book of John represent two basic versions, a longer version and a shorter version. There are variations among all four copies of the text, but in particular the two versions differ from one another. The Secret Book of John was almost certainly composed in Greek in the second century C.E., but there may also have been an earlier version, or the work may have been based on earlier Sethian sources. The place of composition is unknown, but Syria and Egypt, especially Alexandria, are good possibilities.

Nag Hammadi Codex II, open to the Secret Book of John, pages 28–29

In its present form the Secret Book of John is a Christian text of the Sethian school of gnostic thought. The text is framed with a story of John son of Zebedee at the Jewish temple in Jerusalem, where a Pharisee named Arimanios — the name calls to mind Ahriman, the evil Zoroastrian deity — confronts him and expresses doubt about the validity of what Jesus spoke about. Distressed, John leaves the temple and goes to a mountainous, barren place to meditate, and there he has a vision. In the vision a figure appears to John, and this figure, the savior, discloses the revelatory contents of the Secret Book of John. In the present, Christianized form of the text, the savior giving revelation is Christ, and the role of Christ is confirmed in the closing narrative of the text.

Before the Secret Book of John was Christianized, however, the text seems to have been a Jewish gnostic text that combined innovative and revisionist interpretations of the Jewish scriptures with Greco-Roman philosophical and mythological themes in order to proclaim a gnostic view of the world and the place of God and humankind in the world. In the longer version of the Secret Book of John, Pronoia, divine forethought, is given a significant role as revealer, alongside Epinoia, insight. At the end of the revelation in the longer version there is a hymn of the savior that is attributed to forethought, and even though Christ takes the credit for the hymn in the Christianized form of the text, it is forethought who speaks in aretalogical self-predications ("I am" statements) to describe her multiple appearances in the world:

> Now I, *the perfect forethought of all, transformed myself into my offspring. I existed first and went down every path.*
>
> *I am the abundance of light,*
> *I am the remembrance of fullness.* (II, 30)

Three times, forethought says, she has descended to this world, this underworld, until finally she awakens a sleeper from the ignorance of deep sleep to the remembrance of knowledge.

A similar threefold descent of the divine to this world is recounted, also in large part in self-predications, in another Sethian text, Three Forms of First Thought (Trimorphic Protennoia), where first thought reveals herself as voice, speech, and word. When Protennoia, or first thought, appears as *logos* (word), the word is said to come to expression in Christ, and the account resembles portions of the hymn to the word in John 1. In various ways Three Forms of First Thought is reminiscent of the hymn to the savior in the longer version of the Secret Book of John, which also moves toward a Christian understanding of Jesus as savior and revealer.[5]

The body of the revelation in the Secret Book of John opens with a description of the divine One, the Monad, the origin of all. With a sophisticated series of theological statements, the text explores the limitations of "God-talk" in the affirmation of divine transcendence. A number of very similar statements are found in another Sethian text, Allogenes the Stranger. The Secret Book of John acknowledges the finite character of language, which cannot transcend this world and embrace infinity, and the text suggests that, if we are to be precise in our language, it is inappropriate to describe the One as "God" or even to suggest that the divine "exists":

> The One is the invisible spirit. We should not think of it as a god or like a god. For it is greater than a god, because it has nothing over it and no lord above it. It does not [exist] within anything inferior [to it, since everything] exists within it, [for it established] itself. (II, 2–3)

> The One is not among the things that exist, but it is much greater. Not that it is greater. Rather, as it is in itself, it is not a part of the eternal realms or time. (II, 3)

Another Sethian text, the Three Steles of Seth, also includes hymns that address the divine, paradoxically, as "nonexistent being."

As has been said in modern philosophical and theological discussions and in the death-of-God movement, it may be impossible to assert, with any meaning, that "God exists." For the Secret Book of John and other gnostic texts, the One indeed does not "exist," but the One is greater than existence. Hence, the Secret Book of John resorts to the *via negativa*, the negative way, and offers a series of negations to suggest what the One is not:

> The One is
> illimitable, since there is nothing before it to limit it,

unfathomable, since there is nothing before it to fathom it,
immeasurable, since there was nothing before it to measure it,
invisible, since nothing has seen it,
eternal, since it exists eternally,
unutterable, since nothing could comprehend it to utter it,
unnameable, since there is nothing before it to give it a name.
(II, 3)

The Secret Book concedes that it is not accurate to describe the One as perfect or blessed or even divine, and the text presents statements somewhat reminiscent of what is found, for instance, in the Hindu Upanishads, where it is declared that the ultimate is *neti, neti,* "Not this, not that." The Secret Book of John goes beyond a simple use of the *via negativa* when it insists that the One is neither of two opposite categories, so that it is impossible to speak of the One in any quantitative or qualitative terms:

The One is not corporeal and it is not incorporeal.
The One is not large and it is not small.
It is impossible to say,
How much is it?
What [kind is it]?
For no one can understand it. (II, 3)

If the One, finally, cannot be understood, what can be said of it? The text maintains what other mystics have also stated: the One is silence. The revealer says of the One, "What shall I tell you about it? Its eternal realm is incorruptible, at peace, dwelling in silence, at rest, before everything" (II, 4). Because the silence of the One is ineffable, we would know nothing of it were it not for the revelation of the One. In the Secret Book of John, everything, good or bad, comes ultimately from the One.

The revelation of the Secret Book of John continues with a portrayal, in mythological terms, of how the One becomes the many, that is, how the *plērōma* of the divine is realized. The One, called the invisible spirit or the invisible virgin spirit, is depicted as the divine mind, and with an apparent mythological allusion to Narcissus, who falls in love with his reflection in the water in Greek mythology, the One as father is described as becoming enamored of his own image in the spiritual water of light and generating a thought, forethought, called Barbelo. The overall similarity between this gnostic account and the story of Zeus producing Athena from his head is striking. There are also other accounts in ancient mythology of male deities reproducing independently, for example, in the Egyptian story of the god Atum, who mates with his hand and spits, that is, he produces the seed of life through masturbation.

In the Secret Book of John, the father, the invisible spirit, and the mother, forethought or Barbelo, unite in spiritual intercourse — in the longer version the father gazes into Barbelo, in the shorter version Barbelo gazes into the father — and as a result of this union Barbelo conceives and gives birth to a spiritual child. One divine emanation leads to another, conception follows conception, and aeon follows aeon, until the entire divine realm is filled with mental attributes and aeons of light. Heavenly Adam — Pigeradamas ("holy Adam," "Adam the stranger," or "old Adam"[6]) — and heavenly Seth are also there. This process is the unfolding of the mind of God, and the text identifies aspects of the divine mind by retaining Greek loanwords to describe expressions of the divine mind (in Greek, *nous*). The One meditates and has a thought (*ennoia*), which is a forethought (*pronoia*), and this leads to insight (*epinoia*) and wisdom (*sophia*), though through a lapse in wisdom there emerges mindlessness (*aponoia*). This mythological story, with obvious psychological overtones, relates what happens to God, but it also relates what happens to human beings.

According to the Secret Book of John, Sophia, who is the wisdom of insight and who inhabits the suburbs of the divine fullness some metaphysical distance away from the One, also has a thought, but an inappropriate and unwise thought. The text narrates the indiscretion of Sophia in a vivid manner:

> *Now Sophia, who is the wisdom of insight and who constitutes an eternal realm, conceived of a thought from herself, with the conception of the invisible spirit and foreknowledge. She wanted to bring forth something like herself, without the consent of the spirit, who had not given approval, without her partner and without his consideration. The male did not give approval. She did not find her partner, and she considered this without the spirit's consent and without the knowledge of her partner. Nonetheless, she gave birth. And because of the invincible power within her, her thought was not an idle thought. Something came out of her that was imperfect and different in appearance from her, for she had produced it without her partner. It did not resemble its mother, and was misshapen. (II, 9–10)*

This imperfectly formed child of Sophia may recall Hephaistos and Typhaon. It also seems to reflect ancient gynecological theories about gender and sexual reproduction, according to which human conception without heterosexual intercourse and male semen can produce a malformed product. Virgin birth and independent procreation can bring unfortunate results. In the case of Sophia's child, he looks like a serpent with the face of a lion; there are carved gems and magical amulets from antiquity with figures that look rather like this.[7] Sophia is ashamed at what she has produced, and she removes her child away from the divine realm of fullness:

> *She cast it away from her, outside that realm so that none of the immortals would see it. She had produced it ignorantly. She*

surrounded it with a bright cloud and put a throne in the middle
of the cloud so that no one would see it except the holy spirit,
who is called the mother of the living. She named her offspring
Yaldabaoth. (II, 10)

The account of the fall of Sophia in the Secret Book of John, like
the account of the fall of Eve (and Adam) in Genesis, addresses the
question of the origin of evil. If God is all goodness, how do we account for evil in the world and in our lives? This is the question of
theodicy, and it remains one of the most profound questions in religion and human life. In the Sethian account of the Secret Book of
John, the evil that is experienced in life can somehow be traced back
to the failure and folly of the divine. Sophia errs, God errs, and for
that reason there is error in the world.

A Valentinian text that we shall examine in the next chapter, the
Gospel of Truth, addresses the same issue of theodicy. In this sermon
the preacher, probably Valentinus himself, describes how error in the
world has come from ignorance of the father:

Ignorance of the father brought terror and fear, and terror grew
dense like a fog, so that no one could see. Thus error grew power-
ful. She worked on her material substance in vain. Since she did
not know the truth, she assumed a fashioned figure and prepared,
with power and in beauty, a substitute for truth. (17)

The Gospel of Truth points out that the appearance of error was not
an embarrassment for God, since error and all that accompanies error
"were as nothing, whereas established truth is unchanging, unper-
turbed, and beyond beauty" (17). So error may be despised, as well as
the forgetfulness of error, for in the end the knowledge of God will be
triumphant: "Forgetfulness came into being because the father was

not known, so as soon as the father comes to be known, forgetfulness will cease to be" (18).

The Secret Book of John indicates that divine Sophia has erred, yet the innocence of Sophia is also maintained in this text and other texts. A tension remains between the indiscretion of Sophia and her innocence, which may also be affirmed, and her conception takes place, it is said, "with the conception of the invisible spirit and fore-knowledge." In the Second Discourse of Great Seth, Jesus also speaks of "our sister Sophia, whose indiscretion was without guile" (50), and in the Sethian Holy Book of the Great Invisible Spirit Sophia is termed "incorruptible Sophia" (III, 69). The Holy Book of the Great Invisible Spirit also refers to "Sophia of matter" (III, 57), and this may introduce a distinction between two Sophias, including one that may remain "incorruptible." Such Valentinian texts as the Gospel of Philip and the accounts about Valentinians also discuss two wisdoms, a higher wisdom and a lower wisdom. Later in the Secret Book of John Sophia can be described in glowing terms, and she is related to Eve and the divine expressions of forethought and insight:

> *Our sister Sophia is the one who descended in an innocent man-*
> *ner to restore what she lacked. For this reason she was called life*
> *(Zoe, Greek for Eve) — that is, the mother of the living — by the*
> *forethought of the sovereignty of heaven and by [the insight that*
> *appeared] to Adam. Through her have the living tasted perfect*
> *knowledge. (II, 23)*

Sophia in the Secret Book of John repents of her indiscretion, and the divine realm of fullness hears her prayer of repentance and offers praise on her behalf. Her partner joins her, at last, as she awaits the restoration of the divine spirit she lost — and God lost — through the birth of her child.

The Secret Book of John, like other gnostic texts, takes evil very seriously — too seriously, some critics have said. In his essay *Against the Gnostics*, Plotinus faults the gnostics for being too hard on the world and the demiurge, or creator of the world.[8] In his *Confessions*, Augustine reflects upon his background as a Manichaean and offers a similar complaint, adding that the Manichaeans were overly concerned about the origin of evil.[9] Kurt Rudolph quotes a scholarly evaluation

Nag Hammadi Codex II, 32: the end of the Secret Book of John, with title, and the opening of the Gospel of Thomas

of the gnostic view of evil and the reaction of Augustine and others: "It was the principal concern, from Augustine to high scholasticism, to rehabilitate the world as creation from the negative position of its demiurgical origin and to save the cosmos-dignity of antiquity for the Christian system."[10]

To be sure, the position of Augustine, informed by Platonizing Christianity, carried the day. Nonetheless, the urgent concern in gnostic thought to be aware of the place of evil in the world and the spiritual means by which gnostic texts suggest evil is to be opposed and defeated — through self-examination, insight, and knowledge — provides a thoughtful response to the problem of evil in the world.

The child of Sophia in the Secret Book of John is assigned names that define his nature: Yaldabaoth (probably "child of chaos"), Sakla ("fool"), and Samael ("blind god"). And he grows up to become the demiurge, or creator of this world. (Birger Pearson points out that Samael is known as the chief accusing angel, the devil, and the angel of death in other Jewish sources.[11]) Yaldabaoth is an arrogant megalomaniac, and he has within him some of the divine spirit he inherited from his mother. He also has mindlessness, and he mates with that part of himself — perhaps he masturbates — and produces a world order with a host of archons, authorities, rulers, powers, and angels in spheres and realms of the sky. The divine power within him from his mother prompts him to make a world in imitation of the divine world above, but he is mindless and does not know what he is doing. Consequently Yaldabaoth brags, "I am God and there is no other god beside me" (II, 11), as in Isaiah 45:5–6 and 46:9. Ignorant of where he came from, he does not know about the divine fullness, and he has no idea that the *plērōma* of God above is filled with divine entities. He only knows his mother.

According to the Secret Book of John, a divine voice, outraged at the arrogant claim of Yaldabaoth, responds to answer and refute him. The voice calls out from above, "Humankind exists, and the child of

humankind" (II, 14). Both humankind and the child of humankind
are from the divine realm, and precisely who they are appears to vary
in the gnostic texts. These may be the father of all and his child, divine
forethought and her child, or heavenly Adam—Pigeradamas—and
Seth. The most appropriate option is probably heavenly Adam and
Seth. The divine announcer also peeks out from heaven and appears
in human form. Yaldabaoth and his fellow archons look up to see
whose voice it was that called out, and they see the reflection of the
divine in human form—the image of God—on the water of the fir-
mament. Yaldabaoth says to those with him, "Come, let us create a
human being after the image of God and with a likeness to ourselves,
so that this human image may give us light" (II, 15; cf. Gen. 1:26), and
they create the first earthly human and name it Adam. This is psychical Adam, a soul man, made after the image of God and with a likeness to Yaldabaoth and his authorities and powers. The psychical
body of Adam is created by a committee of archons, and each of them
contributes a body part to shape Adam, but when they are finished,
Adam is immobile, lying on the ground and unable to stand.

According to the Secret Book of John, a plan is formulated to trick
Yaldabaoth and retrieve the divine light Sophia lost—or Yaldabaoth
stole—when Yaldabaoth was born. Emissaries from above tell Yaldabaoth, "Breathe some of your spirit into the face of Adam, and the
body will arise" (II, 19). Naively, Yaldabaoth agrees, but when he
breathes into Adam (cf. Gen. 2:7), he sends the divine spirit he got
from his mother into Adam. Adam inhales the spirit of God, arises,
and becomes enlightened. From now on Adam and the descendants
of Adam—human beings—will have the divine spirit within, and
they will be more enlightened and intelligent than the rulers of this
world, who are spiritless. The Secret Book of John explains, "The
human being Adam was revealed through the bright shadow within.
And Adam's ability to think was greater than that of all the creators"
(II, 20).

In desperation Yaldabaoth and the archons do all they can do dis-tract and confine Adam, and details from the Genesis account are in-terpreted in such a way as to show how the powers of the world get their job done: they forge physical bodies, entice humankind with food, separate humankind into male and female, tease people with sexual desire, and try to make the human mind forgetful of the gnosis and the enlightenment that have been given. Yaldabaoth tries to seize divine insight, which is within Adam, but, in the words of the text, "enlightened insight cannot be apprehended" (II, 22).

In the Nature of the Rulers and On the Origin of the World a story is told that is hinted at here in the Secret Book of John. The powers of the world attempt to seize and rape the divine female force within Adam, it is said, but, like Daphne in Greek mythology, she turns into a tree, in the case of Daphne, a laurel tree, and in the case of the di-vine female force (identified as insight in the Secret Book of John), the tree of the knowledge of good and evil. The world powers, the Na-ture of the Rulers reports, then defile the tree sexually. In the Secret Book of John, Yaldabaoth defiles Eve and she bears two sons, who are given the names Cain and Abel but actually are Elohim and Yahweh. Before Eve was violated, however, insight escaped. The world of Yal-dabaoth and the powers is harsh and cruel, and human history offers ample confirmation of the rapacious ways of this world and its rulers.

Divine forethought and the heavenly realm of fullness respond to the plots and ploys of Yaldabaoth by sending enlightened insight to assist Adam. The Secret Book of John states,

So with its benevolent and most merciful spirit the mother-father sent a helper to Adam—enlightened insight, who is from the mother-father and who was called life. She helped the whole crea-ture, laboring with it, restoring it to its fullness, teaching it about the descent of the seed, teaching it about the way of ascent, which is the way of descent. (II, 20)

Here insight is referred to as life, Zoe, the name of Eve in the Greek version of Genesis. Insight is in Adam, in his mind, rejuvenating and teaching and enlightening. She also takes the form of the tree of the knowledge of good and evil, and she constitutes its gnosis. Yaldabaoth sees that insight within humankind is a threat to his authority, and he tries, in vain, to eradicate insight from Adam, but insight continues to work with Adam and Eve and all human beings to awaken human minds.

Elaine Pagels, in her book *Beyond Belief,* discusses the role of insight, *epinoia,* in the Secret Book of John and other texts, and she emphasizes the centrality of this concept in gnostic thought. She notes that "the Secret Book says that human beings have an innate capacity to know God but one that offers only hints and glimpses of divine reality." Commenting on the identification of insight with Eve, she observes, "Eve symbolizes the gift of spiritual understanding, which enables us to reflect — however imperfectly — upon divine reality." Pagels alludes to the story about enlightened insight as life being sent to Adam, and she concludes, "The Secret Book intends this story to show that we have a latent capacity within our hearts and minds that links us to the divine — not in our ordinary state of mind but when this hidden capacity awakens."[12]

This is the message of hope in the Secret Book of John. In spite of all the evil, error, and ignorance in this world, people may still come to salvation through insight and awaken to creative thought. It is this human — and divine — capacity for thought that allows human beings to realize the wholeness of enlightened life and to embrace the knowledge and wisdom of God.

The remarkable and revolutionary story of the salvation of God and humankind in the Secret Book of John seems to have had a considerable influence upon Valentinus and his followers, and Valentinian thought is also interested in pleromatic speculation, but the influence of the Secret Book of John extends further. A textual fragment from Deir al-Bala'izah in Upper Egypt, published by Walter E. Crum and Paul E. Kahle and dated to the fourth century, also resembles parts of the Secret Book of John;[13] and Theodore bar Konai, writing in the eighth century, states that a certain Audius refers to a Revelation (or Apocalypse) of John that shows how various powers create the human body, part by part, as in the Secret Book of John.[14]

Even in an Islamic text, the *Umm al-kitab*, the Mother of Books, a text of the *ghulat* ("exaggerators" or "extremists") from the party (Shi'a) of Ali, there are motifs that recall the Secret Book of John.[15] The numbers seven and twelve occur frequently, as in the Secret Book of John and other gnostic texts, and the description of a primal sea of a thousand colors and another of godliness is reminiscent of the luminous spring of living water near the beginning of the Secret Book of John. As in the Secret Book, a realm of five is depicted in the *Umm al-kitab*, but in the Islamic text the five are the members of the family of prophet Muhammad: Muhammad, his son-in-law Ali, his daughter Fatima, and his grandsons Hasan and Husayn. The arrogant creator Azazi'il (developed from Azazel, chief of the fallen angels in Jewish lore) fashions the world with the same bad attitude that Yaldabaoth has in Sethian texts. Near the end of the *Umm al-kitab*, the text considers what secret knowledge is and where it comes from, and the words of the teacher Baqir, though envisioning the colorful qualities of the divine realm, remind us of what is said about divine insight in the Secret Book of John:

> *Then the almighty's spirit descends from*
> *the emerald green curtain and enters thought.*
> *The student's heart floats overhead, and in*
> *his limbs he clearly sees the holy realm.*
> *These words are clear but are not from the curtain*
> *until the will of one who knows the light*
> *of spirit and of wisdom descends from*

the agate-colored realm and joins the spirit
of the high lord. This spirit is gifted with language,
and light of knowledge speaks before the one
who knows. It is not perfect yet, and one
who knows has not approved it. Then intellect
comes down from the realm, the color of fire,
and enters knowledge. Finally the student
understands clearly, and hears the words
of one who knows. He cannot yet transcend
his sensual soul, the spirit of desire, and the rebuked Adam,
until the holy spirit appears from the dome
of red ruby and enters his spirit.[16]

THE HOLY BOOK OF THE GREAT INVISIBLE SPIRIT
AND THE THREE STELES OF SETH

Two other Sethian texts from the Nag Hammadi library, the Holy
Book of the Great Invisible Spirit and the Three Steles of Seth, provide more insights into Sethian spirituality. Both are texts that have a
ritual function. The Holy Book of the Great Invisible Spirit is a Christian Sethian text that offers ritual elements for a gnostic baptismal
ceremony. With its reference to Poimael, which recalls Hermetic
Poimandres, the Holy Book of the Great Invisible Spirit may also incorporate Hermetic notions, as Régine Charron suggests.[17] The Three
Steles of Seth is a Platonizing Sethian text, with no Christian elements at all, composed of hymns or prayers for a service in which
gnostics may ascend to a mystical vision of the divine.

The Holy Book of the Great Invisible Spirit, also entitled the Egyptian Gospel, is preserved as the second tractate of Nag Hammadi
Codex III and the second tractate of Nag Hammadi Codex IV.[18] The
Holy Book is a Sethian baptismal handbook that includes liturgical
materials for a baptismal ceremony, and the presentation of the cere-

mony is prefaced with an account of the origin of the cosmos and the history of the world given in Sethian cosmological and historical terms. According to the conclusion of the text, the handbook was composed by great Seth, heavenly Seth, and left in high mountains. Similar scenarios of texts and steles preserved in the mountains are provided in two other Nag Hammadi texts, the Three Steles of Seth and the Hermetic Discourse on the Eighth and Ninth. The same sort of story is told by the Jewish historian Josephus, who recounts how the descendants of Seth kept the wisdom of Adam, Eve, and Seth on two

Nag Hammadi Codex III, 69: the end of the Holy Book of the Great Invisible Spirit, or the Egyptian Gospel, with title

steles of brick and stone, so that the steles would survive, come hell or high water.[19] In the note of a copyist at the very end of the Holy Book of the Great Invisible Spirit, the name of the scribe is given — Gongessos, Concessus in Latin — and his spiritual nickname is Eugnostos, "well versed in knowledge." The same spiritual name is in the title of another text from the Nag Hammadi library, Eugnostos the Blessed.

The Holy Book of the Great Invisible Spirit gives an account, in glorious detail, of the heavenly realm and the history of the gnostic descendants of Seth, after which it presents the Sethian baptismal ceremony. The account of Sethian history states that the followers of Seth come in the spirit of Seth, but gnostic life in this world is a difficult business. The world is not a congenial place for the descendants of Seth, as the Secret Book of John also shows, but the seed of Seth endures through the hostile acts of the world rulers — flood, conflagration, judgment — and great Seth acts on behalf of his people. The Holy Book of the Great Invisible Spirit gives considerable attention to the career of Seth, and as it turns to the baptismal ceremony established by Seth, the text proclaims that Seth has been clothed with or has become incarnate in Jesus, "the living Jesus," as he is also called in the Gospel of Thomas. Jesus, then, is the manifestation of Seth.

Sethian texts are replete with references to gnostic baptism, but the precise nature of such baptism is unclear and the extent to which it was spiritualized remains uncertain. The Secret Book of John, for example, concludes with Jesus raising and sealing a person "in luminous water with five seals" (II, 31). John Turner, in his book *Sethian Gnosticism and the Platonic Tradition*, examines the baptismal language in Sethian texts and lists some of the ritual elements that may play a role in the baptismal liturgy, according to the Holy Book of the Great Invisible Spirit and Three Forms of First Thought:

> *In both these treatises, there are a series of references to certain gestures and verbal performances capable of ritual enactment: re-*

nunciation, stripping, invocation and naming of holy powers,
doxological prayer to the living water, anointing, enthronement,
investiture, baptismal immersion, and certain other manual ges-
tures, such as extending the arms in a circle. Whether any of these
acts, and if so, which ones, comprise the Five Seals is difficult to
tell; certainly all these were frequently part of the baptismal rite in
the wider church as well.[20]

The Sethian ritual of baptism may derive from the lustrations and immersions of Jewish groups during the centuries just before and during the common era; and the practices of the covenanters of Qumran, John the Baptizer, and others may have given rise to the baptismal ceremony presented in the Holy Book of the Great Invisible Spirit. Other gnostic and gnosticizing groups also claimed to have developed from these Jewish baptizing traditions. The Mandaeans announce the good news of John the Baptizer and celebrate their baptisms in the living water of what they refer to as "Jordans." Mani, founder of Manichaeism, claims that his father belonged to an Elkesaite community of Jewish-Christian baptizers, and Mani himself joined the baptismal group at an early age but left to preach a new universal message of light and darkness, with its ritual and dietary implications.[21]

In the Holy Book of the Great Invisible Spirit, the Sethian baptismal ceremony is enacted in the company of heavenly beings and exalted entities, and the baptismal hymn that is presented incorporates their names and epithets as well as chanted vowels, glossolalia, and other ecstatic words of praise and power. The one being baptized sings a hymn in which he or she has a vision of Jesus, assumes the name of Jesus, and unites mystically with him:

Yesseus
ĒŌ OU ĒŌ ŌUA
in truth truly

Yesseus Mazareus Yessedekeus
living water
child of the child
glorious name
in truth truly
eternal being
I I I I
Ē Ē Ē Ē
EEEE
OOOO
YYYY
Ō Ō Ō Ō
AAAA
in truth truly
ĒI AAAA ŌŌŌŌ
being who sees the eternal realms
in truth truly
A
EE
Ē Ē Ē
IIII
YYYYYY
Ō Ō Ō Ō Ō Ō Ō Ō
being who exists forever
in truth truly
IĒA AIŌ
in the heart
being who exists
U
forever and ever
you are what you are
you are who you are.

This great name of yours is upon me,
you who lack nothing
you self-conceived one,
who are close to me.
I see you,
you who are invisible to all.
Who can comprehend you? (III, 66)

The hymn closes with an affirmation that through the baptismal celebration life has been realized and oneness with the divine achieved:

So the sweet smell of life is within me.
I have mixed it with water as a model for all the rulers,
that I may live with you in the peace of the saints,
you who exist forever,
in truth truly. (III, 67)

In the Three Steles of Seth, the fifth tractate of Nag Hammadi
Codex VII, the incipit mentions the name of Dositheos, who sometimes is described, like Jesus, as a disciple of John the Baptizer, and
also as the teacher who appears prior to Simon Magus.[22] In the incipit
the Three Steles of Seth refers to itself as the revelation of Dositheos:

Dositheos's revelation of the three steles of Seth, father of the liv-
ing and unshakable generation. Dositheos remembered what he
saw, understood, and read, and gave it to the chosen, just as it was
written there. (118).

The remaining three sections, or steles, of the text present hymns
or prayers for a ritual of spiritual ascent to a vision of the divine. The
text is one of the Platonizing Sethian documents, and throughout the

text the divine is addressed as existence, life, and mind. At the conclusion of the three hymns, instructions for the proper use of the liturgy are appended to the hymns, and the instructions explain how to praise, when to sing, and when to be silent. The hymns seem to allow for a soloist and a chorus. Apparently the service involves both an ascent to the divine and a return to the mundane world:

> Whoever remembers these things and always glorifies will be perfect among the perfect and free of suffering beyond all things. They all praise these, individually and collectively, and afterward they will be silent.
>
> As it has been ordained for them, they ascend. After silence, they descend from the third. They praise the second, and afterward the first. The way of ascent is the way of descent.
>
> So understand as those who are alive that you have succeeded. You have taught yourselves about things infinite. Marvel at the truth within them, and at the revelation. (127)

The hymns of the Three Steles of Seth employ Sethian terminology nuanced with Platonic themes in the ritual of ascent. Three stages of ascent are indicated by the three hymns. In the first hymn, a Sethian worshiper identifies with Seth and offers praise to the father, Pigeradamas, heavenly Adam. In the second hymn, the chorus joins in and utters a hymn to Barbelo, divine forethought. In the third hymn, the worshipers glorify the supreme One with words and names of power and cries of thanksgiving:

> Truly we are saved.
> We have seen you through mind.
> You are all these
> and save them all,

you who will not be saved
nor have been saved by them.
You have commanded us.
You are One,
you are One,
let it be declared,
you are One.
You are a single, living spirit.
How shall we give you a name?
We have none.
You are the existence of all these,
you are their life,
you are their mind.
In you they all rejoice. (125)

After this, the text says, there is silence, for those joining in the liturgy of worship and ascent have seen and have been enlightened in mind. Their mind, now awakened, is one with the mind of God, and their insight and understanding are restored. Now they truly know.

INSIGHT IN THE SECRET BOOK OF JOHN AND OTHER TEXTS

If for the Gospel of Thomas those who find the meaning of sayings of wisdom — who gain insight into the interpretation of words — will not taste death, then for the Secret Book of John and other Sethian texts the role of insight is formally established and confirmed. In the Secret Book of John, Epinoia, insight, becomes a mythic character in a divine story of salvation. Insight functions as a manifestation of God and contributes to human thought and understanding; she helps to dispel ignorance and bring clarity of thought and restoration of wisdom.

In the Secret Book of John and throughout gnostic literature, sin is not the fundamental problem in human life that needs to be addressed. An original sin of human parents in the garden of Eden is not what causes our problems. If anyone fell, gnostic texts state, divine Sophia fell, and her indiscretion brought about a world of problems, but human sin is not really the issue. In the Gospel of Mary from the Berlin Gnostic Codex, Jesus declares bluntly, "There is no such thing as sin; rather you yourselves produce sin when you mingle as in adul-

Nag Hammadi Codex VIII, 132: the end of Zostrianos, with title and cryptogram, and the opening of the Letter of Peter to Philip, with title

tery, which is called sin" (7). In gnostic texts God is not angry at the unrighteousness of people, so that God needs to be pacified by means of sacrifice and the shedding of blood. In Christian gnostic texts, we noted in the previous chapter, Jesus does not need to die as a sacrifice on the cross for the forgiveness of sins, and people do not need to believe, through faith, in the efficacy of the cross of Christ to be saved. In Valentinian practice, ordinary baptism is for the forgiveness of sins, but the spiritual baptismal observance is for the gnostic transformation to the fullness of the divine. The place of faith in the traditional Christian sense is limited in gnostic texts, and more often than not *pistis*, faith, is personified as a spiritual entity, sometimes as an exalted form of wisdom, Pistis Sophia.

The Secret Book of John and other gnostic texts are more interested in knowledge than faith. Gnostic religion is, we reiterate, a religion of knowledge, mystical knowledge. In the Secret Book of John and throughout gnostic literature, the fundamental problem in human life is ignorance, forgetfulness, lack of insight. Countless forces oppose us, distract us, and beguile us, gnostic texts suggest, so that we lose track of who we are and where we have come from. For people who are rooted in the divine and have the light of God within, we can be surprisingly ignorant and dim-witted. We need insight.

The Secret Book of John provides an impressive and startling gnostic vision of how insight and knowledge may be restored, and the Holy Book of the Great Invisible Spirit and the Three Steles of Seth provide glimpses of gnostic rituals that may bring about the transcendent experience of insight, understanding, and oneness with God. The call to insight and knowledge is often alluded to in gnostic texts, and in the hymn of the savior in the Secret Book of John it is given by divine forethought — or Jesus — to anyone who will hear. The call is a summons to wake up and come to knowledge, and the words are memorable:

I am the forethought of pure light,
I am the thought of the virgin spirit,
who raises you to a place of honor.
Arise, remember that you have heard
and trace your root,
which is I, the compassionate.
Guard yourself against the angels of misery,
the demons of chaos, and all who entrap you,
and beware of deep sleep
and the trap in the bowels of the underworld. (II, 31)

The final words on insight and the restoration of wisdom may be provided by another Sethian text, Zostrianos. Like other Sethian texts, Zostrianos offers a vision of the divine world above, although in this case the text is badly damaged, and at the end of the text Zostrianos delivers a sermon to rouse an erring multitude. With fervor and conviction Zostrianos urges people to awaken the divine within them, save themselves, and become enlightened. The gnostic call has been given, Zostrianos says, and, making use of a number of the themes we have been exploring, Zostrianos emphasizes that now is the time to listen, respond, and live:

You who are alive, holy offspring of Seth,
understand this. Do not turn a deaf ear to me.
Awaken your divinity to divinity,
and strengthen your undefiled chosen souls.
Observe the constant change that is here
and seek the unchanging state of being unborn.
The father of all these beings invites you.
When you are being rebuked and maltreated,
he will not forsake you.
Do not baptize yourselves with death,

nor rely on those who are inferior
as if they were superior.
Flee from the madness and the fetter of femaleness
and choose the salvation of maleness.
You have not come to suffer,
but to break your fetters.
Break free, and what has bound you will be broken.
Save yourselves so that part may be saved.
The good father has sent you the savior
and has strengthened you.
Why are you waiting? Seek when you are sought.
When you are invited, listen, for the time is short.
Do not be led astray.
Great is the eternal realm of the eternal realms
of the living,
but great also is the punishment of those unconvinced.
Many fetters and punishers surround you.
Get away quickly before destruction overtakes you.
Look to the light, fly from the darkness.
Do not be led astray to destruction. (130–32)

5

VALENTINUS
THE CHRISTIAN MYSTIC

SALVATION THROUGH KNOWLEDGE
IN THE GOSPEL OF TRUTH AND
VALENTINIAN TEXTS

ACCORDING TO IRENAEUS OF LYON, "Valentinus adapted the fundamental principles of the so-called gnostic school of thought—that is, the Barbelognostics or Sethians—to his own kind of system."[1] The gnostic system of Valentinus and the Valentinians resembles the Sethian school of thought to a considerable extent, but Valentinian thought has its own distinctive features. Valentinian gnosis is specifically Christian, and Valentinian Christians were thoroughly involved in the life of the church. Very likely they did not refer to themselves as Valentinians, but rather as devoted Christians. In their way of understanding people, Valentinians employed a three-fold division of humankind: they thought of themselves as uncommon Christians and spiritual people—"the spiritual" (*pneumatikoi*) or "the perfect" (*teleioi*); they considered ordinary Christians psychical people (people with a soul, *psychikoi*); and unbelievers were judged to be material people (*hylikoi*, or people of flesh, *sarkikoi*).

Typically, Valentinian Christians seem to have attended worship services with other Christians, read the Christian scriptures, and participated in the sacraments. Valentinian scholars studied the writings of the apostles John and Paul, and they produced their own letters, commentaries, sermons, and other learned and pious Christian works. Among these works are Ptolemy's *Letter to Flora*, Heracleon's *Commentary on the Gospel of John*, and a number of texts preserved in the Nag Hammadi library, including the sermon entitled the Gospel of Truth.[2]

Valentinians also convened their own meetings in addition to the services of the churches they attended, and at their meetings they carried their Christian thought and practice beyond those of the great church to a deeper knowledge and a more mystical form of piety. Valentinian spirituality included an understanding of mystical sacraments, called "mysteries" in the Gospel of Philip. With the heightened concern for a clear differentiation between orthodox and heretical Christians from the fourth century on, however, Valentinian Christians eventually were subjected to a series of edicts and attacks, and late in the fourth century a mob of angry Christians burned down a Valentinian chapel on the banks of the Euphrates River. Nonetheless, the mystical Christianity of Valentinus and his followers made an impact upon the church and the world during these early centuries and beyond, and Valentinians produced some of the most beautiful Christian mystical literature of any era of church history.

VALENTINUS AND THE GOSPEL OF TRUTH

Valentinus was an African church leader born in Egypt, in a city in the Delta not far from Alexandria, around the beginning of the second century, and he lived to be about seventy-five years old.[3] Destined to become one of the most brilliant and eloquent Christian leaders of the second century, Valentinus received a sound Hellenistic education in Alexandria, where he must have become acquainted with the work of leading philosophers and religious thinkers. He learned about Platonic philosophy, and Bentley Layton speculates that he may have been familiar with the great Jewish thinker Philo of Alexandria, the Christian gnostic Basilides, and perhaps even the Gospel of Thomas, which was available in Egypt during the second century, as the Greek fragments from Oxyrhynchus prove.[4] Some early writers suggest that Valentinus may have been taught by a person named Theudas, who, it was claimed, had been a student of Paul, which may have allowed Valentinus to be granted Pauline or apostolic authority. A decade or so before the middle of the century, Valentinus moved to Rome, and there he became a well-known man about town and leader in the Roman church. According to Tertullian, he was considered for the position of bishop of Rome — the ancient equivalent of the pope — but he lost out in his quest for that position.[5] Had he been appointed bishop of Rome, the subsequent history of the church might have been altogether different. Valentinus, and perhaps all of us, lost on that day.

Valentinus continued to work as a Christian teacher and leader, and some of his literary achievements have survived, most in fragmentary form. Short selections from Valentinus are preserved as quotations in the church fathers, in Clement of Alexandria and elsewhere, and a passage from Valentinus cited in Hippolytus of Rome shows his poetic gifts:

Through spirit I see that all are suspended,
through spirit I know that all are conveyed,
flesh suspended from soul,
soul depending on air,
air suspended from atmosphere.
From the depth come crops,
from the womb comes a child.[6]

This poem by Valentinus deals with cosmological themes reminiscent of Sethian formulations regarding the *plērōma* of the divine. For Valentinus and his followers, the fullness of the divine is based in the depth of God, and all the emanations, or "crops," come from the depth, including the first emanation, the womb or mother, and the child. For Valentinus, the child may have been understood to be the word, the *logos* or Christ. The aeons or eternal realms are suspended, set in the fullness of the divine, and the constituent parts of this world too — flesh, soul, air, atmosphere — are set in their proper order. This vision of the universe, Valentinus says, he sees and knows "through spirit." It is quite possible that the poem was entitled "Summer Harvest," an allusion to the spiritual harvest of the cosmos.

The Gospel of Truth from the Nag Hammadi library is often also attributed to Valentinus.[7] The Gospel of Truth is the third tractate in Nag Hammadi Codex I (fragments of the Gospel of Truth are also known from Codex XII), and although no separate title is given, the text is named the Gospel of Truth in the incipit. The title is also mentioned by Irenaeus of Lyon, who states that a text called the Gospel of Truth was read by Valentinian Christians. No author is named for the Gospel of Truth, but a good argument can be made for attributing the authorship to Valentinus. In *The Gnostic Scriptures*, Bentley Layton gives three reasons to support the likelihood that Valentinus composed the Gospel of Truth: (1) the style of the Gospel of Truth resembles the style of the fragments of Valentinus; (2) the eloquent and poetic Valentinus would have been the sort of person who would have been able to author a eloquent gospel like the Gospel of Truth; and (3) features of the Gospel of Truth suggest an early date of composition, before the development of the later complexities of Valentinian thought.[8]

The Gospel of Truth is written in the form of a Christian sermon on salvation through knowledge of God. The progression of thought through the sermon is poetic, with image after image arising as the

Nag Hammadi Codex I, 16:
the end of the Secret Book of
James and the opening of the
Gospel of Truth

preacher addresses what it means to know God and to be loved by
God. The basic message of the sermon is given in the opening lines:

> *The gospel of truth is joy for people who have received grace from*
> *the father of truth, that they might know him through the power*
> *of the word. The word has come from the fullness in the father's*
> *thought and mind. The word is called "savior," a term that refers*
> *to the work he is to do to redeem those who had not known the*
> *father. And the term "gospel" refers to the revelation of hope, since*
> *it is the means of discovery for those who seek him. (16–17)*

Since this is a Christian text, Jesus figures prominently through-out, and he is shown to be a guide and teacher of wisdom who shows the way to God:

Jesus became a guide, a person of rest who was busy in places of instruction. He came forward and spoke the word as a teacher. Those wise in their own eyes came to test him, but he refuted them, for they were foolish, and they hated him because they were not really wise.

After them came the little children, who have knowledge of the father. When they gained strength and learned about the expressions of the father, they knew, they were known, they were glorified, they gave glory. (19)

The cross of Jesus is proclaimed in the sermon, but it is interpreted metaphorically as a source of life and a revelation of incorruptibility. Error, which comes from ignorance, persecutes Jesus and has him crucified, yet the outcome is not death but life, in mystical union with Jesus:

For this reason error was angry with him and persecuted him, but she was restrained by him and made powerless. He was nailed to a tree, and he became fruit of the knowledge of the father. This fruit of the tree, however, did not bring destruction when it was eaten, but rather it caused those who ate of it to come into being. They were joyful in this discovery, and he found them within himself and they found him within themselves. (18)

This is Jesus, called "Jesus of infinite sweetness" (24) in the sermon, who as the word of the father and the name of the father announces the mind and will of the father.

Within the Gospel of Truth the preacher employs parables and figures of speech to proclaim the points being made. The transformation from deficiency to completeness and from multiplicity to unity is illustrated by means of the parable of the broken jars:

This is like people who moved from one house to another. They had jars around that were not good, and they broke, but the owner suffered no loss. Rather, the owner was glad because instead of these defective jars there were full jars that were perfect.

This is the judgment that has come from above and has judged every person, a drawn two-edged sword cutting on this side and that, since the word that is in the heart of those who speak the word appeared. It is not merely a sound but it was embodied.

A great disturbance occurred among the jars, for some were empty and others were filled, some were ample and others were depleted, some were purified and others were broken.

All the realms were shaken and disturbed, for they had no order or stability. Error was agitated, and she did not know what to do. She was troubled, she lamented, she attacked herself, because she knew nothing. For knowledge, which leads to the destruction of error and all her expressions, approached. Error is empty; there is nothing within her. (25–26)

Ignorance in life is like a nightmare in sleep, filled with the terror and confusion of flight and falling and killing and being killed:

So it is with those who cast off ignorance from themselves like sleep. They do not consider it to be anything, nor do they regard its features as real, but they put them aside like a dream in the night and understand the father's knowledge to be the dawn. This is how each person acts while in ignorance, as if asleep, and this is

*how a person comes to knowledge, as if awakened. Good for one
who comes to himself and awakens. And blessings on one who has
opened the eyes of the blind. (29–30)*[9]

And once again, the savior is like the shepherd in search of the single lost sheep:

*He is the shepherd who left behind the ninety-nine sheep that had
not strayed and went in search of the one that was lost. He re-
joiced when he found it.*[10] *For ninety-nine is a number expressed
with the left hand, but when another one is found, the numerical
sum is transferred to the right hand. In this way what needs one
more—that is, the whole right hand—attracts what it needs, takes
it from the left and brings it to the right, and so the number becomes one hundred. This is the meaning of the pronunciation of
these numbers.*

    *The father is like that. He labored even on the sabbath for the
sheep that he found fallen into the pit. He saved the life of the
sheep and brought it up from the pit. (31–32)*

After recounting this set of parables of sheep, the preacher offers
an allegorical understanding of the parables. Such use of allegorical
interpretation was common among Valentinians, and in this instance
the preacher discloses an "inner meaning" of the stories:

*Understand the inner meaning, for you are children of inner mean-
ing. What is the sabbath? It is a day on which salvation should
not be idle. Speak of the heavenly day that has no night and of
the light that does not set because it is perfect. Speak from the
heart, for you are the perfect day and within you dwells the light
that does not fail. Speak of truth with those who seek it and of
knowledge with those who have sinned in their error. (32)*[11]

The sermon closes with tender and intimate images of mystical union with God. Those who recognize that they are from God and possess something of God within come to rest in the divine fullness, and they embrace God:

> *They embrace his head, which is rest for them, and they hold him close so that, in a manner of speaking, they have caressed his face with kisses. But they do not make this obvious. For they neither exalt themselves nor diminish the father's glory. And they do not think of the father as insignificant or bitter or angry, but as free of evil, unperturbed, sweet, knowing all the heavenly places before they came into being, and having no need of instruction.* (41–42)

They are one with the father, rooted in the divine:

> *They are truth. The father is in them and they are in the father, perfect, inseparable from him who is truly good. They lack nothing at all but are at rest, fresh in spirit. They will hearken to their root and be involved with concerns in which they may find their root and do no harm to their souls.* (42)

The preacher concludes, "Children like this the father loves."

The sermon in the Gospel of Truth incorporates many of the technical terms known from Valentinian discussions of the *plērōma* of the divine, and it employs these terms in a creative manner. Valentinian cosmological presentations typically affirm that everything in the universe comes from the divine depth, *bathos* or *bythos*, and the fullness of divinity emanates from depth and is organized as fifteen (or more) pairs of aeons, or divine couples, for a total of thirty (or more) aeons, or eternal realms. Valentinus's poem "Summer Harvest" alludes to these pleromatic emanations. Most important among the aeons are the first two groups of four (called tetrads), which together constitute a realm of

Nag Hammadi Codex I, 43: the end of
the Gospel of Truth and the opening
of the Treatise on Resurrection

eight (called an ogdoad). According to Irenaeus of Lyon, the Valentinian ogdoad consists of these divine couples: depth and thought (or
grace or silence); mind (or only child) and truth; word and life; human
being and church.[12]

In Valentinian discussion, Sophia, or wisdom, falls through ignorance and error, causing a disturbance in the divine order, so that two
other aeons, Christ and holy spirit, come forth to quiet the disturbance. Christ assists with the restoration of Sophia, but her desire is

thrown out of the divine realm of fullness, and it becomes Achamoth, a lower wisdom, from whose passions our world here below is created. Jesus the savior, here distinguished from Christ, emerges as the fruit of the fullness, and he comes to the aid of wisdom and the world. Through it all, Jesus Christ and wisdom are brought together in a number of significant ways. Heresiological sources, commenting on Valentinian thought, can reflect upon Christ as the son of Sophia, as in other Christian wisdom texts, and in another Valentinian formulation the sources can refer to Jesus being filled with the word, or *logos*, of Sophia at baptism. The Valentinian Exposition from the Nag Hammadi library also seems to suggest, according to Einar Thomassen, that Sophia's perfect half was separated off and became her son Christ.[13] The Valentinian Exposition ends with a vision of the resolution of the cosmic drama and the final restoration of Sophia and of all:

> *When Sophia, then, receives her partner, and Jesus receives Christ, and the seeds are united with the angels, then the fullness will receive Sophia in joy, and all will be joined together and restored. For then the eternal realms will have received their abundance, for they will have understood that even if they change, they remain unchanging.* (39)

The Gospel of Truth does not engage in such cosmological discussion, but it does use some of the same terms. The preacher of the Gospel of Truth — probably Valentinus — also refers to fullness, depth, thought, grace, mind, truth, word, life, wisdom, fruit, and error, but the preacher incorporates these terms into a sermon that invites people to come to experience the knowledge and love of God. Terms with metaphysical possibilities are brought into the lives of Valentinian Christians, and the glory of God's fullness is proclaimed to be within them.

THE GOSPEL OF PHILIP

The Gospel of Philip is a Valentinian anthology of meditations on a variety of gnostic themes.[14] Philip is referred to by name once in the text, and that may be the reason the text is attributed to him. The arrangement of meditations in the Gospel of Philip seems to be more or less random, though it is possible that sometimes they may be connected to one another by catchwords or the sequence of similar themes. We do not know where these meditations originated, but presumably they come from different sources. Layton guesses, "It is possible that some of the excerpts are by Valentinus himself."[15]

The Gospel of Philip is preserved as the third tractate in Nag Hammadi Codex II, where it is located immediately after the Gospel of Thomas. The text opens, somewhat abruptly, with a meditation on Hebrews and proselytes: "A Hebrew makes a Hebrew, and such a person is called a convert. A convert does not make a convert. [Some people] are as they [are] and make others [like them], while others simply are" (51–52). Many of the meditations in the Gospel of Philip recall themes in the Gospel of Truth, but the style of presentation is quite different. The Gospel of Philip is as abrupt throughout as it is at the beginning, and the overall impact of the individual meditations of the Gospel of Philip is not unlike that of the individual sayings of the Gospel of Thomas. Some scholars assign numbers to the meditations of the Gospel of Philip comparable to the numbers assigned to the sayings of the Gospel of Thomas, although these scholars cannot seem to agree on a numbering system. Layton refers to the individual meditations of the Gospel of Philip as excerpts. Still, through the juxtaposition of ideas and the repetition of themes, this anthology of meditations is able to communicate a Valentinian message of mystical oneness and sacramental joy.

Jesus is explicitly described as the one presenting several of the meditations in the Gospel of Philip, and his presence is sensed throughout the text, sometimes in the company of Mary of Magdala. The text ridicules a conventional view of the virgin Mary, the mother of Jesus, becoming pregnant by the holy spirit by asking, rhetorically, "When did a woman — Mary — ever get pregnant by a woman — the holy spirit?" (55). Philip the apostle narrates a tale about Joseph, the father of Jesus:

> *Joseph the carpenter planted a garden, for he needed wood for his trade. He is the one who made the cross from the trees he planted, and his own offspring hung on what he planted. His offspring was Jesus and what he planted was the cross. (73)*

The text describes how Jesus went into the dye works of Levi and threw seventy-two colored cloths into a vat, and when he took them out, they all were white. Jesus then says, "So the child of humankind has come as a dyer" (63). One of the most memorable meditations in the Gospel of Philip is a saying of Jesus that compares well with Gospel of Thomas 19. In the Gospel of Philip Jesus says, "Blessings on one who is before coming into being. For whoever is, was and will be" (64).

Mary of Magdala, or Mary Magdalene, is described as the companion of the savior in the Gospel of Philip. The text states, "The [savior loved] her more than [all] the disciples, [and he] kissed her often on her [mouth]" (63). (The word restored as "mouth" is in a lacuna in the manuscript, and other restorations might suggest additional options for the precise place on Mary where Jesus, according to the Gospel of Philip, chooses to plant his kisses.) This special love between Jesus and Mary of Magdala, which inspired Dan Brown in *The Da Vinci Code*, is also attested in the Gospel of Mary, to be discussed in the next chapter.

In the Gospel of Philip the crucifixion is mentioned in a meditation that quotes a form of the traditional words of Jesus on the cross — "My God, my God, why, lord, have you forsaken me?" — and then observes, "He spoke these words on the cross, for he had left that place" (68).[16] The meditation suggests that the divine person within Jesus of Nazareth left the crucified body behind and escaped death.

Just before the meditation on Mary of Magdala and Jesus, the Gospel of Philip mentions wisdom. The text reads, "Wisdom — Sophia — who is called barren, is the mother of the angels" (63). Elsewhere in the Gospel of Philip wisdom also comes up for discussion, and a distinction is made, typical of Valentinian texts, between two figures of wisdom, including a form of wisdom named Echamoth (cf. Achamoth), from the Hebrew *hokhmah*. The text plays with two names of wisdom: "There is Echamoth and there is Echmoth. Echamoth is simply wisdom, but Echmoth is the wisdom of death — that is, the wisdom that knows death, that is called little wisdom" (60). Layton notes, Echmoth is from the Hebrew and Aramaic for "like death."[17]

Several meditations in the Gospel of Philip proclaim the ultimate value of oneness, especially mystical oneness, and sometimes the themes of separation and union are traced back to the story of Adam and Eve. Like many other texts, including gnostic texts, that interpret the story of Adam and Eve in Genesis, the Gospel of Philip understands that originally humankind — Adam — was created as an androgyne, both male and female together in one body, and a removal of a side from Adam, as recounted in Genesis 2:21–24, entailed the division of humankind into separate male and female genders. The Gospel of Philip thus maintains that the original androgynous union of Adam and Eve in paradise was violated by the separation into male and female, and from this separation death came. "Christ came," the meditation continues, "to heal the separation that was from the beginning and reunite the two, in order to give life to those who died through separation and unite them." Such union happens in the bridal chamber, understood not only as the place of sexual union, but also as a sacrament for salvific union. The text states, "A woman is united with

Nag Hammadi Codex II, 51: the
end of the Gospel of Thomas,
with title, and the opening of
the Gospel of Philip

her husband in the bridal chamber, and those united in the bridal
chamber will not be separated again" (70).

Throughout the Gospel of Philip sacraments play a major role,
and five sacraments, or "mysteries," are enumerated: baptism, chrism,
eucharist, redemption, and bridal chamber. By participating in the
sacraments, people are brought closer to God and an understanding
of God. The sacrament of the bridal chamber is emphasized in the
Gospel of Philip, and although the bridal chamber is mentioned

elsewhere in Nag Hammadi literature — in the Gospel of Thomas, for instance — in the Gospel of Philip it has special sacramental value. The bridal chamber in this world is considered to be a mystery, but the pure sacramental bridal chamber is thought to be even greater. In April D. DeConick's interpretation, the importance of sexual intercourse is presupposed in Valentinian sources, and sex assisted in the passing on of the seed — the semen of light — of the spirit. She writes, "Sexual intercourse between Valentinian spouses was to continue until the last spiritual seed was embodied and harvested."[18] At the same time, the Gospel of Philip maintains that the sacramental bridal chamber is not of the flesh and desire but of the will, and the union that is realized in the sacramental bridal chamber restores the unity and oneness of humankind. The sacramental bridal chamber has a transcendent dimension, and through participation in the bridal chamber one is raised to a higher level of understanding. Ultimately the sacrament of the bridal chamber may unite a person with the divine, so that we, as images of the divine, may be joined with angels, heavenly beings who are our divine alter egos. A prayerful meditation in the Gospel of Philip states,

> You who have united perfect light with holy spirit,
> unite the angels also with us, as images. (58)

In a way that is somewhat comparable to tenets of other religious traditions, for example, Tantric Buddhism, Valentinian gnosis thus can employ sexual themes and understand sexual practices in such a way as to proclaim the reunion of male and female and the attainment of the oneness of salvation.

The mystical union thus achieved through sacrament and knowledge, the Gospel of Philip states, entails oneness with Christ and finally oneness with God the father. For the Gospel of Philip it is not

enough to follow Christ and be a Christian. A person must become
Christ and even become God the father. The text announces,

> *In the realm of truth,*
> *you have seen things there and have become those things,*
> *you have seen the spirit and have become spirit,*
> *you have seen Christ and have become Christ,*
> *you have seen the [father] and will become father. (61)*

The sacraments are discussed elsewhere in Valentinian literature,
and in Nag Hammadi Codex XI five liturgical readings for the Valentinian sacraments of chrism, baptism, and the eucharist are appended
to the Valentinian Exposition.[19] It may be that the Valentinian Exposition was meant to give instruction in Valentinian cosmology and
theology in preparation for participation in the sacraments. In the
liturgical reading for the sacrament of chrism, or anointing, the text
cites Luke 10:19 (cf. also Mark 16:18, the longer ending of Mark) as it
gives glory to God for the knowledge and power that come through
the anointing of Jesus Christ:

> *It is fitting [for you] now*
> *to send your son Jesus Christ*
> *to anoint us,*
> *that we may be able*
> *to trample on [snakes]*
> *and [ward off] scorpions*
> *and [all] the power of the devil,*
> *[through] the [supreme] shepherd*
> *Jesus Christ.*
> *Through him have we known you,*
> *and we glorify you.*

> Glory be to you,
> father in the [eternal realm],
> [father] in the son,
> father in the holy church
> and among the holy [angels].
> From [the beginning]
> he abides [forever],
> [in the] harmony of the eternal realms,
> [from] eternity,
> to the boundless eternity
> of the eternal realms.
> Amen. (40)

In the liturgical readings for baptism, two understandings of baptism are distinguished, that of a first baptism for the forgiveness of sins—like the ordinary baptism of the great church—and an additional spiritual understanding of baptism for the transformation and perfection of the spirit. The liturgical reading for this extraordinary spiritual understanding of baptism is fragmentary, but the meaning remains clear. We are transformed, the text declares,

> [from the] world [to the Jordan],
> from [the things] of the world to [the sight] of God,
> from [the carnal] to the spiritual,
> from the physical to the angelic,
> from [creation] to fullness,
> from the world to the eternal realm,
> from [enslavements] to sonship,
> from entanglements to virtue,
> from [wayfaring] to our home,
> from [cold] to warmth,

. . . .

This is how we were brought
from seminal [bodies] into a perfect form.

The cleansing is the symbol
through which Christ has saved us
through the [gift] of his spirit.
He delivered us who are [in him].
From this time forth
souls will become perfect spirits. (42)

Portions of two additional liturgical readings for the eucharist remain, and the sense of the sacramental celebration is captured by the
conclusion of the second reading:

You, lord,
when you die in purity,
you will be pure,
so everyone who receives
food and [drink] from this
[will live].
Glory be to you
forever.
Amen. (44)

THE TREATISE ON RESURRECTION

The Valentinian Treatise on Resurrection is the fourth tractate of Nag
Hammadi Codex I.[20] Most if not all of the other texts in Codex I are
also Valentinian — the Prayer of the Apostle Paul, the Gospel of Truth,
the Tripartite Tractate — and the only text in the codex that may or
may not be Valentinian — the Secret Book of James — may contain
Valentinian elements, so that Nag Hammadi Codex I has sometimes

been considered to be a Valentinian book. The Treatise on Resurrection is written as a letter to a person named Rheginos, and in the body of the letter the author discusses the true meaning of the resurrection. The text vigorously affirms the reality of the resurrection, but the author insists that the true resurrection is spiritual resurrection and the spiritual resurrection has already taken place within the lives of people. The text uses the same threefold Valentinian division into spirit, soul, and flesh noted above when it states, "This is the resurrection of the spirit, which swallows the resurrection of the soul and the resurrection of the flesh" (45–46). This Valentinian affirmation that the resurrection has already happened with the transformation to new spiritual life recalls the position of Hymenaeus and Philetus according to 2 Timothy 2:16–18, where the Paulinist, in heresiological fashion, attacks these two Christian thinkers for having, in his estimation, "strayed from the truth by claiming that the resurrection already happened." 2 Timothy was likely written in the second century, a generation or so after Paul, so that the text addresses a position much like what we encounter in the Treatise on Resurrection. For the Paulinist this position was unpalatable — it does not have the eschatological flavor of a future event — but for the author of the Treatise on Resurrection it affirms the reality of the new life in Christ here and now.

The author of the Treatise on Resurrection begins his argument with the resurrection of Christ himself. Making use of imagery used elsewhere in the text, the author maintains that Christ, as death's destroyer, "swallowed death." "You must know this," Rheginos is told. "When he laid aside the perishable world, he exchanged it for an incorruptible eternal realm. He arose and swallowed the visible through the invisible, and thus he granted us the way to our immortality" (45). As a result, the author continues, we too experience the resurrection of "the living parts that are within"—the spirit, and possibly, some scholars suggest, even a body of spiritual flesh. This resurrection, with all its transforming power, has already occurred and is already a reality

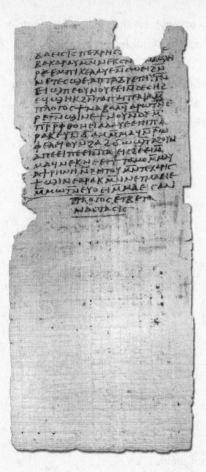

Nag Hammadi Codex I, 50:
the end of the Treatise on
Resurrection, with title

for us. The author refers to the accounts of the transfiguration in the
New Testament gospels and states,

> *What is the resurrection? It is always the disclosure of those who
> have arisen. If you remember reading in the gospel that Elijah
> and Moses appeared with Jesus, do not think that the resurrection
> is an illusion. It is no illusion. It is truth. It is more appropriate to*

say that the world is illusion, rather than the resurrection that
came into being through our lord and savior Jesus Christ. (48)

Overwhelmed by the present bliss and the glorious fullness of the
experience of resurrection, the author of the Treatise on Resurrection adds lines with a more poetic flair to proclaim the life-changing
significance of the resurrection:

What am I telling you?
All at once the living die.
How do they live in illusion?
The rich become poor,
kings are overthrown,
everything changes.
The world is illusion.
Let me not speak so negatively.
The resurrection is different.
It is real,
it stands firm.
It is revelation of what is,
a transformation of things,
a transition into newness.
Incorruptibility [flows] over corruption,
light flows over darkness, swallowing it,
fullness fills what it lacks.
These are symbols and images of resurrection.
This brings goodness. (48–49)

THE VALENTINIAN WORLD OUTSIDE AND WITHIN

As with the Sethians, Valentinian thinkers also are enthusiastic in
their speculation about the world of the *plērōma* of God. For Valen-

tinians, the primal divine being is depth, and depth functions as the unknown God. God's universe above, beyond our world below, is populated with divine couples, and together they make up the glory of God. Sophia plays a key role in the fullness of God, and the Valentinians address issues of theodicy by positing two levels for the drama that ensues. Some things happen inside the divine fullness, some things happen outside, and a boundary — also called the cross — keeps these realms apart. As events unfold, Sophia, the higher wisdom, is restored to the fullness above, but her desire becomes Achamoth, or perhaps Echmoth, lower wisdom. The demiurge is the creator of this world below, but in general Valentinian texts are not as hard on the demiurge as Sethian texts. At times Jesus and wisdom are said to be responsible for the creation of this world, and the demiurge just does the manual labor.

The complexities of the cosmological passages in Sethian and Valentinian texts may present challenges to us, as modern readers whose view of the cosmos is not quite the same as that of those in the world of antiquity and late antiquity. These complexities may be the sort of thing the Paulinist had in mind in referring, in a critical way, to the speculative "myths and endless genealogies" of some people, according to 1 Timothy 1:4. These cosmological and mythological passages reflect ancient and late antique metaphysics and astronomy; they describe the origin, nature, and extent of the cosmos and explain the place of human beings in the whole scheme of things. Among the features of the world outside us and high above us, as portrayed in the texts, are the seven planetary spheres (for the sun, the moon, Mercury, Venus, Mars, Jupiter, and Saturn), the twelve signs of the zodiac, the world of the stars, and powers that correspond to the seven days of the week and the three hundred sixty-five days of the solar year. There are angels and demons without number, and our world is an extremely complex place with countless powers and authorities. Spheres beyond the seven planetary spheres are suggested for the demiurge and his mother, Sophia, and the infinite God is beyond that—hence the eighth, ninth, and at times (as in the Revelation of Paul) even the tenth level of being. Names, often forms of traditional divine names or nicknames or fantastic names, identify the characters in the mythic accounts and add to the exotic mood of the narratives.

These cosmological and mythological passages, I submit, with all their complexities and difficulties, are not fundamentally different from our own contemporary metaphysical and astronomical reflections upon the stars, the universe, and the ultimate limit or limitlessness of things. After the Hubble telescope, the probes to the edge of the universe, and the discovery of cyberspace, we can appreciate more fully the expressions of the Sethian and Valentinian cosmological texts. And as we wonder about finitude and infinity, about big bangs and subatomic particles and the very nature of existence, we can identify with those who have struggled to articulate thoughts and create texts, like the texts in the Nag Hammadi library, in which they write about nonexistent being, the unknown God, and its emanations and manifestations.

Although these gnostic texts are interested in the world outside us, they are also concerned with what is within us, and how what is outside may also be within. In the Gospel of Thomas Jesus says that the kingdom is inside and outside, and in Sethian texts like the Secret Book of John the emanations of the divine One are mental characteristics and capabilities applicable to the world of human psychology. But it is in Valentinian texts in particular that we recognize a deeply mystical interest in focusing upon the inner contemplative life. Thus we have observed that the Gospel of Truth incorporates the terms of the aeons and powers of the universe into a sermon that speaks to the daily lives of Valentinian Christians.

A meditation in the Gospel of Philip on the outer and the inner addresses this issue directly. Based on a saying of Jesus very much like Gospel of Thomas 22, which has Jesus say that the inner is like the

outer and the outer like the inner, the meditation in the Gospel of
Philip suggests that it is more fitting to understand the world of God
as what is within, what is innermost:

> [For this reason] he — Jesus — said, "I have come to make [the
> lower] like the [upper and the] outer like the [inner, and to unite]
> them in that place." [He spoke] here in symbols [and images].
>
> Those who say [there is a heavenly person and] one that is
> higher are wrong, for they call the visible heavenly person "lower"
> and the one to whom the hidden realm belongs "higher." It would
> be better for them to speak of the inner, the outer, and the outer-
> most. For the lord called corruption "the outermost darkness," and
> there is nothing outside it. He said, "My father who is in secret."
> He said, "Go into your room, shut the door behind you, and pray
> to your father who is in secret" — that is, the one who is innermost.
> What is innermost is the fullness, and there is nothing further
> within. And this is what they call uppermost. (67–68)

The world of the *plērōma*, the fullness of God, often thought to be
the divine world above us and outside us, truly is within. For Valentinian mystics, God is not simply the father in heaven; God is within.

6

HERMES, DERDEKEAS, THUNDER, AND MARY

REVEALERS OF WISDOM
IN OTHER NAG HAMMADI TEXTS

I N ADDITION TO Thomas texts and texts from the Sethian and Valentinian schools of thought, there are other gnostic and gnosticizing documents in the Nag Hammadi library. Three tractates represent the Hermetic tradition of Hermes Trismegistos (thrice-greatest Hermes), and other tractates cannot be classified or categorized with any confidence. Like the Thomas texts and Sethian and Valentinian texts, these other tractates also introduce revealers of knowledge and wisdom, and fresh names appear on the pages of the texts: Hermes, Derdekeas, Thunder, Mary. To these texts and these revealers of gnosis we turn in this chapter.

NAG HAMMADI HERMETIC TEXTS

Three texts in the Nag Hammadi library derive from Hermetic religion, one that was not known prior to the Nag Hammadi discoveries and two that were previously known in various editions. The newly discovered Discourse on the Eighth and Ninth is the sixth tractate in Nag Hammadi Codex VI; the Prayer of Thanksgiving is the seventh and the Excerpt from the Perfect Discourse the eighth tractate in the same codex. Together these texts provide a Hermetic account of the revelation of Hermes Trismegistos to a student and the ascent of the student to the higher levels of mystical spirituality.

The Discourse on the Eighth and Ninth describes the teacher Hermes and an unnamed student engaging in a dialogue concerning the stages of spiritual enlightenment called the eighth and the ninth.[1] The Greek god Hermes is the messenger and guide of souls, and in Hermetic texts he is linked to the Egyptian god Thoth. The designation of these stages of enlightenment as the eighth and the ninth assumes that they lie beyond the seven spheres surrounding the earth and housing the sun, moon, and planets — and they also lie within. This Hermetic initiation takes the student beyond the reaches of the solar system. In ancient astronomy the stars are commonly thought to occupy the eighth level of the universe, and beyond that, perhaps, and within, the divine dwells. In the Secret Book of John the demiurge Yaldabaoth is stationed in the eighth realm and his mother, Sophia, is above him in the ninth. In the Discourse on the Eighth and Ninth the gnostic candidate has already studied the sacred books and has advanced through the preliminary stages of spiritual enlightenment, and now he or she is ready for further insight.

The dialogue between Hermes and the student includes prayers and hymns somewhat reminiscent of the Three Steles of Seth. The student utters sounds of spiritual ecstasy and prays, perhaps with the teacher:

> Lord, grant us wisdom — sophia — from your power that
>   reaches us,
> that we may relate to ourselves the vision of the eighth and ninth.
> Already we have advanced to the seventh,

since we are faithful
and abide in your law.
Your will we fulfill always.

. . . .

Accept these spiritual offerings from us,
which we direct to you
with all our heart, soul, and strength.
Save what is within us,
and grant us immortal wisdom. (56–57)

The student sings a hymn in silence and envisions the eighth and ninth, and the souls and angels in the eighth respond in silent song, praising the mind of all that is in the ninth. Hermes himself says, "I am [mind and] I see another mind, one that [moves] the soul" (58). The student declares,

I shall offer up the praise in my heart as I invoke the end of the uni-
verse, and the beginning of the beginning, the goal of the human
quest, the immortal discovery, the producer of light and truth, the
sower of reason, the love of immortal life. No hidden word can
speak of you, lord. My mind wants to sing a song to you every day.
I am the instrument of your spirit, mind is your plectrum, and your
guidance makes music with me. I see myself. I have received power
from you, for your love has reached us. (60–61)

The student has found immortal wisdom and the spirit and mind within.

The Discourse on the Eighth and Ninth ends with directions for preserving the text and an oath for those reading it. The Egyptian context of the Hermetic text is clear. The text is to be inscribed on turquoise steles, in hieroglyphic characters, at the Egyptian temple at Diospolis, either Diospolis Magna (Luxor) or Diospolis Parva (Heou).

The Three Steles of Seth also assumes such engraved tablets. Both of the cities named Diospolis are in Upper Egypt, and Diospolis Parva is particularly close to Nag Hammadi and the very site where the Nag Hammadi codices were discovered. The steles, the text says, are to be protected with images of guardians with animal faces — faces of frogs and cats — as is typical of Egyptian art, and the installation of the steles is to be accomplished at a time that is deemed propitious. Hermes indicates to the student that a time is to be chosen with considerations of astronomy and astrology in mind: "My child, you must do this when I — Hermes, the planet Mercury — am in Virgo, and the sun is in the first half of the day, and fifteen degrees have passed by me." The text is to be used "for wisdom and knowledge" (62), Hermes declares, and an oath must be taken to ensure that the text will be used properly, so that a gnostic candidate "progresses by stages and advances in the way of immortality, and so advances in the understanding of the eighth that reveals the ninth" (63).

Immediately after the Discourse on the Eighth and Ninth, the Hermetic Prayer of Thanksgiving presents a pious meditation, and the sequence of the texts in Nag Hammadi Codex VI would lead a reader to assume that the prayer is offered by Hermes and the student, following the events of the previous tractate.[2] Those offering the prayer give praise to God, who has made them divine through knowledge. The prayer is a good example of Hermetic piety, and it includes heartfelt thanksgiving for the knowledge that transforms:

> The thanksgiving of one approaching you
> is this alone:
> that we know you.
> We have known you,
> light of mind.
> Life of life,
> we have known you.

Womb of every creature,
we have known you.
Womb pregnant with the father's nature,
we have known you.
Eternal constancy of the father who conceives,
so have we worshiped your goodness.
One favor we ask:
we wish to be sustained in knowledge.
One protection we desire:
that we not stumble in this life. (64–65)

After the prayer the worshipers embrace and go to share a sacred vegetarian meal.

The very next tractate, the Excerpt from the Perfect Discourse (also known as the Apocalypse of Asclepius), is the third and final Hermetic text in the Nag Hammadi library, and it presents the portion of the text (21–29) that discusses learning and knowledge and reveals an apocalypse.[3] The teacher is, once more, Hermes Trismegistos, but in this text the student has a name: Asclepius. Hermes begins by comparing the mystery to be discussed with the mystery of sexual intercourse: in both instances participants in the mysteries do what they do in secret, and the participants strengthen each other. Hermes goes on to extol learning (*epistēmē*) and knowledge (*gnōsis*), and he states that learning and knowledge have been given to humankind to restrain passions and vices and bring people to immortality. Created mortal and having become immortal, human beings surpass the gods and goddesses, since human beings are both mortal and immortal and they can create gods and goddesses. In the words of Hermes to Asclepius,

We have begun the discussion of the communion between gods and people. Asclepius, understand what people can do. For just as the

Nag Hammadi Codex VI, 65:
the end of the Hermetic
Prayer of Thanksgiving, a
scribal note, and the opening
of the Excerpt from the
Perfect Discourse

*father, the lord of the universe, creates gods, so too people — mortal,
earthly, living things, who are also like God — create gods. (68)*

Hermes then reveals the future in apocalyptic terms, and things
look grim for Egypt. Egypt, the image of heaven, the temple of the
world, and the school of religion — "our land" (70), says Hermes —
will be abandoned, filled with corpses, and fouled by a bloody Nile
River. The world itself will be despised and godlessness will reign. Yet,

Hermes insists, there is reason for hope, since God will restore the universe:

> *This is the birth of the world. The restoration of the nature of the pious and the good will take place in a period of time without a beginning. For the will of God has no beginning, even as God's nature, which is his will, has no beginning. God's nature is will, and God's will is the good.* (74)

The wicked will be judged and the guilty punished, and they will be thrown to the demons. With terrifying images of the demons, called "stranglers," rolling, whipping, drowning, burning, and torturing the souls of the wicked, the excerpted lines from the Perfect Discourse — and all of the texts of Nag Hammadi Codex VI — come to an end, and the last words of the book are threats of hell that would have satisfied even Jonathan Edwards.

THE PARAPHRASE OF SHEM

The Paraphrase of Shem, the opening tractate of Nag Hammadi Codex VII, is another apocalyptic text, but of a different sort.[4] This text is not about sinners in the hands of an angry God, as with the Perfect Discourse, but rather mortals in the clutches of a lustful universe. The title of the text is related to the incipit, which describes the text as a paraphrase: "The paraphrase about the unconceived spirit — what Derdekeas revealed to me, Shem" (1). Within the text there is also a short paraphrase that explains names used in a litany or testimony or memorial addressed by the revealer Derdekeas to Shem, and among the names are Sophia, Saphaia, and Saphaina. The title of the text is similar to that of another work called the Paraphrase of Seth, described in Hippolytus of Rome as a Sethian text, but the two texts do not seem to be closely related to each other.

According to the Paraphrase of Shem, another prominent figure in
the book of Genesis, Shem, son of Noah and father of the Semitic
people, receives a revelation from the savior and revealer Derdekeas,
whose name may derive from the Aramaic for "male child,"[5] and af-
terward Shem sets it all down in writing. Shem states that his
thoughts ascended to the summit of creation, where all was light, and
there he heard a revelatory voice — the voice of Derdekeas — speaking about the origin of the world. In the beginning, Derdekeas says,
there were three primal powers, the light above, darkness below, and
the spirit in between, and somehow the darkness had control of mind:
"Light was thought full of hearing and word united in one form.
Darkness was wind in the waters, and darkness had a mind wrapped
in restless fire. Between them was spirit, a quiet, humble light" (1–2).
There is no indication of whether mind fell into darkness, and, if so,
how. In the beginning there was peace and harmony, as long as no
one moved. The original peace was an uneasy peace. The darkness,
like the gnostic demiurge in Sethian texts and elsewhere, was un-
aware that there were powers above him. He lurked in the watery
abyss, and, it is said, "as long as he was able to deal with his evil, he remained covered with water" (2).

Then, the Paraphrase of Shem continues, the darkness stirs, the
spirit is surprised by the noise, and the original peace is over. The
light was aware of darkness all along, but now the spirit finds out
about the evil below. The spirit's light shines upon the darkness — as
in the Secret Book of John — and the darkness discovers that there is a
spirit above him. The darkness sees that the spirit is enlightened and
he, in his darkness, is gloomy, and so he lifts up his mind, and his
mind assumes some of the spirit's light. Like Sophia in other gnostic
texts, the darkness tries to imitate the spirit and become equal to the
spirit, but he fails, yet he takes control of a portion of the light. As the
text puts it,

Darkness made his mind take shape partly from the members of the spirit, thinking that by staring at his evil he would be able to equal the spirit. He could not do it; he wanted to do something impossible, and it did not happen. But in order that the mind of darkness, which is the eye of the bitterness of evil, might not remain inactive, since he had been made partially similar to the spirit, he arose and shone with a fiery light upon all of Hades, and in this way the purity of the faultless light was revealed. For the spirit made use of every form of darkness, because he had appeared in his greatness. (3)

In much of the balance of the text Derdekeas narrates the story of how the mind of darkness and the light of the spirit are liberated from the bondage of darkness. The story is wonderfully convoluted, and it is told as a war of the worlds waged with sexual weapons. Themes from ancient philosophy and reflections upon biology and sexuality coalesce as the plot unfolds. Initially, Derdekeas says, he appears as the son of the light in the likeness of the spirit, and this is the first act that will lead, eventually, to the salvation of mind and light. This provokes the creation of the world, which emerges from the water of chaos (cf. Gen. 1:1–2), and part of the water turns into nature, which is a sexual organ, a cosmic womb. Darkness has sex with nature and ejaculates his mind into nature, and nature herself comes to expression with the features of the hymen and placenta. Through it all, mind, with the light of the spirit, is within nature, and while the spirit produces the power of astonishment, Derdekeas actively intervenes to bring about the freedom of mind and light. Derdekeas explains to Shem what he, as savior, is like:

Shem, I have told you these things so that you might understand that my likeness, the son of majesty, is from my infinite thought,

since I am for the majesty a universal likeness that does not lie,
and I am over every truth and the principle of the word. His ap-
pearance is in my beautiful garment of light, which is the voice of
immeasurable thought. We are the unique light that came into
being alone. This light appeared in another root in order that the
power of the spirit might be raised from feeble nature. (11–12)

Derdekeas the savior is light, but he must confront all the sexuality of the darkness, and for this reason he takes off his own garment of light, puts on a garment of fire, and goes down to have sex with nature. Derdekeas prostitutes himself for the salvation of the mind and the light, and he and nature have intercourse. Nature has an orgasm and expels mind, in the form of a fish—reminiscent, perhaps, of the role of the fish in the worship of the Syrian goddess, who sometimes takes the form of a mermaid, or of Aphrodite, who is connected to the sea. Nature then weeps at her loss of mind, and she loses the spirit as well. Derdekeas describes his sexual experience with nature and the outcome of the sexual experience in graphic terms:

My garment of fire, in accordance with the will of the majesty,
went down to the strong one, to the unclean part of nature the
dark power was covering. My garment massaged nature with its
material, and her unclean femaleness grew strong. The passionate
womb came up and dried mind up, in the form of a fish with a
spark of fire and the power of fire. But when nature expelled mind
from herself, she was troubled, and she wept. When she felt hurt
and was in tears, she expelled from herself the power of the spirit.
She remained as quiet as I. I put on the light of the spirit, and I
rested with my garment at the sight of the fish. (18–19)

Nature gives birth to beasts—the zodiac—and Derdekeas puts on the disguise of a beast so that mother nature would think that Derdekeas

Nag Hammadi Codex VII, 1: the opening of the Paraphrase of Shem, with title

is her offspring. The forces of nature are preoccupied with tongue rubbing, copulating, masturbating, and all sorts of sexual activity, and, at one point, through an act of coitus interruptus, the forces of nature ejaculate mind onto the earth. The world of nature is a world of sex, and Derdekeas beats the forces of nature at their own game.

The generation of Shem is produced, according to the Paraphrase of Shem, with a portion of the enlightened thought and mind of the divine within. They are the gnostics, the spiritual people, and nature and darkness conspire to destroy them by means of the great flood, the destruction of Sodom—the people of Sodom are thought to be people of insight and knowledge—and attacks on the savior. Derdekeas reveals, in cryptic language, how he as savior is baptized and later is attacked by nature, and he follows this disclosure with an allegorical account of the beheading of a woman named Rebouel. In the story of nature's attack, Derdekeas describes the death of a certain Soldas:

> That is why I have appeared, without deficiency, because the clouds are not of uniform character, and in order that the wickedness of nature might be brought to completion. For at that time nature wished to seize me. She will nail Soldas, who is a dark flame, who will stand on the [height] ... of error, that he might seize me. She took care of her faith, being vain. (39–40)

Michel Roberge, the leading scholar on the Paraphrase of Shem, understands this revelation about Soldas and Rebouel as referring to Jesus and the Christian church:

> After his baptism, the savior foretells his ascent at the end of his mission on earth. In its anger, nature will try to seize him, but will only manage to crucify Soldas (that is, the terrestrial Jesus). The following allegory which narrates the beheading of Rebouel is intended to explain to the noetics—people of thought and mind—the meaning of the crucifixion: it does not have the effect of purifying the water of baptism, but rather brings out the division between light and darkness. Just as Rebouel is declared blessed in her beheading, so the noetics should not hesitate to separate from the great church, which practices baptism, and enter the community of those who possess gnosis.[6]

The final word for Shem, however, is a word of hope and comfort. Life with nature is difficult, to be sure, but he and the people of his generation — the people of gnosis — will be safe, and they will be able to remember and to know who they are. Derdekeas promises,

> You are blessed, Shem, for your generation has been protected
> from the dark wind with many faces. They will bear witness to the
> universal testimony and the unclean sexuality of <nature>, and
> they will be uplifted through the memorial of light. O Shem, none
> of those who wear the body will be able to complete these things,
> but by remembering they will be able to grasp them, so that when
> their thought separates from the body, then these things may be
> revealed to them. These things have been revealed to your genera-
> tion. (34)

THUNDER

Thunder, entitled Thunder: Perfect Mind in the manuscript, is the self-revelation of a female figure in poetic and frequently paradoxical "I am" statements.[7] The second tractate in Nag Hammadi Codex VI, Thunder is an aretalogical text similar to other aretalogies, especially Isis aretalogies, in which the Egyptian goddess Isis offers disclosures of herself and her acts in "I am" statements.[8] Here another goddess or female figure is the revealer, but precisely who she is remains uncertain. She identifies herself as wisdom, or Sophia, in phrases like those uttered by the Hebrew Hokhmah, and as life, or Zoe, Greek Eve, and even as insight, or Epinoia, one of the heroines of the Secret Book of John. She also identifies herself with knowledge. Several features of Thunder, including her identification with wisdom and knowledge, the apparent concern for divine transcendence articulated through revelatory statements, and the specific reference to insight, may suggest a connection with Sethian thought. In *The Gnostic Scriptures*, Bentley Layton supports such a connection by also pointing to other features of the text: (1) Thunder, like Barbelo in Sethian texts, is sent from the power and comes to be with those who know her; (2) Thunder, like forethought and insight in Sethian texts, continues to call out to all who will hear; and (3) those who respond to Thunder, like gnostics in Sethian texts, will be set free from this world and will ascend to the divine realm, where Thunder is.[9] Layton also notes similarities between Thunder and the Gospel of Eve, which Epiphanius of Salamis says was read among gnostics, that is, Sethians. Epiphanius cites a passage from the Gospel of Eve:

> *I stood on a high mountain.*
> *I saw one person who was tall*
> *and another who was short.*
> *I heard what sounded like the voice of thunder,*
> *and I came closer to listen.*
> *It spoke to me and said,*
> *I am you and you are I.*
> *Wherever you are, I am there.*
> *I am sown in all,*
> *and you gather me from wherever you wish.*
> *But when you gather me,*
> *you gather yourself.*[10]

Thunder opens her revelation by defining her origin, and then she discloses who she is and what she does. Thunder is, she declares, from the divine:

> *I was sent from the power*
> *and have come to those who contemplate me*
> *and am found among those who seek me. (13)*

In striking poetic lines, Thunder employs metaphor and paradox to describe her being:

For I am the first and the last.
I am the honored and the scorned.
I am the whore and the holy.
I am the wife and the virgin.
I am <the mother> and the daughter.
I am the limbs of my mother.
I am a barren woman
who has many children.
I have had many weddings
and have taken no husband.
I am a midwife
and a woman who does not give birth.
I am the solace of my own birth pains.
I am bride and groom,
and my husband conceived me.
I am the mother of my father
and the sister of my husband,
and he is my offspring.
I am the servant of him who fashioned me,
I am the ruler of my offspring.
He [produced me] with a premature birth,
and he is my offspring born on time,
and my strength is from him.
I am the staff of his power in his youth,
and he is the rod of my old age,
and whatever he wishes happens to me.
I am silence that is incomprehensible
and insight whose memory is great.
I am the voice whose sounds are many
and the word whose appearances are many.
I am the utterance of my own name. (13–14)

Thunder is, she insists, both knowledge and ignorance, both tough-
ness and terror, both war and peace. She says,

> *I am the wisdom — sophia — [of the] Greeks*
> *and the knowledge of the barbarians. (16)*

She is thrown down on a dung heap, but she is also honored and
praised. She cries out to those who will listen, and she offers them liberation, life, and rest in her presence:

> *Pay attention, you listeners,*
> *and you also, you angels,*
> *and you who have been sent,*
> *and you spirits who have risen from the dead.*
> *I alone exist,*
> *and I have no one to judge me.*
> *For there are many sorts of seductive sins*
> *and deeds without restraint*
> *and disgraceful desires*
> *and fleeting pleasures that people embrace,*
> *until they become sober*
> *and rise up to their place of rest.*
> *They will find me there,*
> *and they will live and not die again. (21)*

THE GOSPEL OF MARY

The Gospel of Mary is the fragmentary first tractate of the Berlin
Gnostic Codex, and it also survives in Greek fragments as Papyrus
Oxyrhynchus 3525 and Papyrus Rylands 463.[11] In the Coptic version,
which is by far the most complete, six pages are missing at the begin-

ning and four in the middle of the text. In spite of its damaged state, the Gospel of Mary retains a substantial portion of its message, and what is retained is illuminating. The Gospel of Mary is a gnosticizing dialogue between Jesus and his disciples, particularly Mary of Magdala, or Mary Magdalene, and after Jesus leaves the scene Mary and the other disciples continue the conversation. The text seems to display gnostic tendencies, but whether it merits being called a gnostic document is debated by scholars. One of the strongest voices against a gnostic classification of the text is that of Esther A. de Boer, who writes in her book *The Gospel of Mary* that the Gospel of Mary is more Stoic than gnostic. Referring especially to the extant opening section of the text, in which Jesus speaks about matter and nature, de Boer writes,

> *The particular language of the* Gospel of Mary *... belongs to a more specifically Stoic context, in which matter is a thought construct and matter and nature are intertwined. This means that the material world as such is not to be avoided, as would be the case in a gnostic dualistic view, but that one should be careful not to be ruled by the power contrary to nature.*[12]

When the surviving pages of the Gospel of Mary open, Jesus is in the middle of a dialogue with the disciples, including Mary. A question is asked, presumably by one of the disciples, "Will matter be utterly destroyed or not?" Jesus answers that matter will be dissolved into the root of its nature, since every nature is to be restored to its root.

The chief problem in human life is not sin, since, Jesus insists, "There is no such thing as sin." Rather, it is people who create sin by mingling inappropriately with the world—and that is what is referred to as sin (7). In other words, Jesus says, people should not get mixed up in passion, which is contrary to nature, because that is the main source of grief in the lives of people.

Berlin Gnostic Codex 8502, 7: the first extant page of the Gospel of Mary

Jesus goes on to greet the disciples and utter his last words to them. His final message stresses that the child of humankind, or the son of man, is within, and the disciples should follow it — or him — and not lay down rules and regulations:

Peace be with you. Acquire my peace within yourselves. Be on your guard so that no one deceives you by saying, "Look over here" or "Look over there." For the child of humankind exists within

you. Follow it. Those who search for it will find it. Go then, preach
the good news about the kingdom. [Do] not lay down any rule be-
yond what I determined for you, nor promulgate law like the law-
giver, or else you might be dominated by it. (8–9)

The child of humankind that is within may be the presence of Jesus
within a person, or it may be the true humanity that Jesus inspires
and Mary recalls in her comments to her fellow disciples.

After Jesus leaves the disciples, in the Gospel of Mary, Mary con-
soles the disciples and offers words of life. She says, "Do not weep and
be distressed nor let your hearts be irresolute. For his grace will be
with you all and will shelter you. Rather we should praise his greatness, for he has prepared us and made us human beings" (9). She also
recalls a vision of Jesus, and she explains that Jesus told her a person
does not see a vision with the soul, as a purely emotional experience,
or with the spirit, as a purely spiritual experience from outside, but
with the mind, between soul and spirit. A person thinks a vision. Although a large part of Mary's account of the vision is lost, the portion
that remains makes it clear that Mary's vision is of the soul's ascent
through cosmic powers to liberation and rest. The cosmic powers
encountered by the soul in Mary's vision, however, are psychological
forces that may imprison the soul — darkness, desire, ignorance, and
wrath — so that Mary's vision is actually a reflection upon the inner
journey of the soul beyond the passions and powers that may oppress
and enslave it. Freed at last, the soul exclaims,

What binds me has been slain, and what surrounds me has been
destroyed, and my desire has been brought to an end, and igno-
rance has died. In a world I was set loose from a world and in a
type from a type which is above. The chain of forgetfulness is tem-
porary. From this hour on, for the time of the due season of the
age, I will receive rest in silence. (16–17)

As a group, the disciples in the Gospel of Mary admit that Jesus loved Mary more than any other woman and more than the other disciples. In the Gospel of Mary, Mary of Magdala is a beloved disciple, perhaps the beloved disciple, and Andrew does not like any of this. Neither does Peter, and he complains bitterly, with sexist sentiments about Mary's role and her closeness with Jesus, just as he complains at the very end of the Gospel of Thomas. In the Nag Hammadi library and elsewhere—for example, in the Gospel of Philip, the Dialogue of the Savior, Pistis Sophia, and a song from the Psalms of Heracleides in the Manichaean Psalmbook—Mary of Magdala receives similar high praise, but in the New Testament gospels her role is limited and praise of her is muted. Esther de Boer suggests that Mary of Magdala may be the Johannine beloved disciple, but her identity is obscured in the Gospel of John.[13] Elsewhere in the New Testament gospels Mary may be similarly portrayed, through a careful editing of the story of Jesus and his disciples, as a woman whose job is to offer support to Jesus, while the twelve disciples are presented as twelve guys truly involved with Jesus and his work. In the sixth century Pope Gregory the Great completed the work of marginalizing Mary Magdalene by equating Mary with the prostitute of Luke 7, and Mary became the paradigmatic repentant whore thereafter.[14] Mary Magdalene as repentant whore makes a great story and a great subject for works of art, but a whore, even a repentant one, may not be judged an ideal candidate to be a disciple and an apostle of Jesus.

As the years passed, Karen King reminds us in *The Gospel of Mary of Magdala*, Christianity increasingly embraced patriarchal and hierarchical authority, and male bishops founded their authority on apostolic succession going back to the twelve male disciples and Jesus, but this development, she notes, runs counter to the message of the Gospel of Mary:

The Gospel of Mary *directly challenges the validity of such claims, and offers instead a vision of Christian community in*

which authority is based not solely or even primarily upon a suc-
cession of past witnesses, but upon understanding and appropri-
ating the gospel. Authority is vested not in a male hierarchy, but
in the leadership of men and women who have attained strength
of character and spiritual maturity. Prophetic speech and visions
are given a place of primacy as the manifestation of spiritual un-
derstanding and the source of sound teaching. Christian commu-
nity constituted a new humanity, in the image of the true human
within, in which the superficial distinctions of the flesh lacked any
spiritual significance. Women as well as men could assume lead-
ership roles on the basis of their spiritual development. The
Gospel of Mary rejects any view of God as divine ruler and judge
and, hence, repudiates those as proper roles for Christian leader-
ship. The true model for leadership is the savior, the teacher and
mediator of divine wisdom and salvation who cautions his disci-
ples against laying down fixed laws and rules that will come to en-
slave them.[15]

The Gospel of Mary may help to correct a false understanding of
the Christian church, and this gospel and other similar texts may
help to reclaim the image of Mary and restore her to her rightful
place within the history of Judaism and Christianity.

THE MANY REVEALERS IN GNOSTIC TEXTS

In this chapter and the preceding chapters, we have seen that the
message of gnosis is announced by a wide variety of revealers from a
wide variety of religious contexts. There are many different gnostic
saviors who may awaken people to insight and knowledge. For Christian gnostics such as Valentinians, Jesus Christ is the savior and revealer, and for Christian Sethians Jesus is the incarnation of heavenly
Seth. But within gnostic religious traditions Jesus is not the only

savior. For Jewish gnostics great Seth can be the savior and revealer, or the savior can be Derdekeas, the "male child" who speaks to Shem, son of Noah, in the Paraphrase of Shem. In Hermetic literature thrice-greatest Hermes, the Greek counterpart to the Egyptian god Thoth, is the mystagogue who leads a student to understanding. Beyond the texts of the Nag Hammadi library and the Berlin Gnostic Codex, Manichaean sources emphasize the role of Mani, the messenger of light, a Mesopotamian teacher of Iranian descent, and Mani and his followers claim to build on the religious contributions of the prophets Buddha, Jesus, and Zoroaster. Teachers of Islamic gnosis maintain that wisdom may be known through Allah and the Qur'an, and that revealers of truth include the members of the family of Muhammad and Salman, the being of light and word of God.

The gnostics were advocates of religion with a global perspective. Their conviction that religious insight and knowledge may be found in all sorts of religions leads to a multiplicity of saviors and revealers from many different traditions. For gnostics, true gnosis is the wisdom of the world, and universal wisdom may be discovered in the religions of the world.

As portrayed in gnostic texts, the divine figures, saviors, revealers, and teachers of knowledge may be male or female. In gnostic literature there is no thought of a father in heaven who is the great bachelor in the sky. Rather, the divine, and those who represent the divine, may be male or female — or sometimes neither, or sometimes both. In the early Christian movement there are hints of the same concern for gender balance in other sources, and some of the earliest speculation about a divine trinity seems to have suggested that God could be understood through the metaphor of the nuclear family, with God as father, the spirit as mother, and Christ as son of God. (We may recall the repudiation of the traditional story of the virgin birth in the Gospel of Philip on the grounds of the gender of the holy spirit.) The famous Egyptian divine family of father Osiris, mother Isis, and son Horus may have helped to inspire Christian speculation about the trinity as family, and in Semitic sources the gender of the word for "spirit," *ruah* in Hebrew, is feminine, and the divine spirit may be considered, like wisdom, to be female in gender. But the holy spirit became the neuter *pneuma hagion* in Greek and the masculine *spiritus sanctus* in Latin, and masculine images grew dominant. So did the power of men and patriarchal authority, and Christian leaders like Tertullian insisted that only men should provide leadership in the church:

> *It is not permitted for a woman to speak in the church, nor is it permitted for her to teach, nor to baptize, nor to offer the eucharist, nor to claim for herself a share in any masculine function — not to mention any priestly office.*[16]

Meanwhile, among gnostics and in gnostic texts from the Nag Hammadi library and the Berlin Gnostic Codex, the divine is said to come to manifestation as Sophia and a host of other personified beings, many of whom are female, such as forethought, Pronoia, and insight, Epinoia, and Thunder; and the revelation of the divine is communicated by female leaders like Mary of Magdala and the gnostic teacher Marcellina as well as male teachers. Such gnostic texts reflect gnostic practice, which frequently provides equal roles for men and women and allows both men and women to function as prophets, teachers, priests, and possibly even bishops. Tertullian cannot tolerate such gnostic behavior, and he attacks gnostic women: "These heretical women — how audacious they are! They have no modesty; they are bold enough to teach, to engage in argument, to enact exorcisms, to undertake cures, and, it may be, even to baptize!"[17] Gnostic texts often affirm the status of women; the Gospel of Mary maintains that the true understanding of the person and proclamation of Jesus is not found in Peter — the rock upon which Jesus built his church, according to the Gospel of Matthew and the inscription upon the dome of

St. Peter's Basilica in Rome — but in Mary of Magdala, beloved disciple and apostle of Jesus.

The revealer of knowledge in Nag Hammadi texts and other gnostic documents is also considered in more abstract terms. As we have seen in Sethian texts, the gnostic revealer is the insight and wisdom of God that calls out to people. In the "Hymn of the Pearl" in the Acts of Thomas, the call to remember is described as a letter from the king of the east to remember the pearl, and in the hymn the letter becomes voice. In Mandaean literature the revealer is Manda dHayye, "knowledge of life"; and in the Islamic *Umm al-Kitab* the spirit endowed with language and the light of knowledge speaks to one who knows. The call of the insight, wisdom, and knowledge of the gnostic revealer may be understood as coming from outside, but the call of revelation also speaks from within.

Finally, the insight that awakens us is within us, the wisdom that is with God is the wisdom in us, and the knowledge that saves us is self-knowledge. In order to be saved we need to remember, understand, and know our true selves. Zostrianos proclaims in his gnostic sermon, already quoted at length, that those who hearken to the call are to awaken what is divine within them and save themselves, their true selves, so that what is within — the light and life of God — may be saved. That is the gospel of gnosis.

DISCOVERIES AFTER THE NAG HAMMADI LIBRARY

A S WE HAVE SEEN throughout this book, the Nag Hammadi library is providing a remarkable opportunity to reassess religion in the ancient and modern world, and that reassessment is giving us new insights into the quest for knowledge and the wisdom of others and ourselves. The discoveries of the Nag Hammadi library and the Berlin Gnostic Codex are showing that the world of Greco-Roman, Jewish, and Christian antiquity was a world of significant diversity, and gnostic and mystical themes permeated that world. The gnostic discoveries give voice to creative minds and spiritual ideas that have too easily been dismissed in the past, and the result is a fresh opportunity to encounter crucial questions about the nature of God, ways of salvation, and the place of Jesus and other saviors and revealers. These texts of knowledge, wisdom, and insight provide the occasion to reassess the role of spirituality in our own world, and to examine anew, as the Book of Thomas and other texts suggest, who we are, what our existence means, and what will become of us.

Since the uncovering of the Nag Hammadi library, more papyrus and parchment texts have been found in the sands of Egypt, and their impact has yet to be determined.

The Gospel of the Savior is the title given to a document described by its editors, Charles W. Hedrick and Paul A. Mirecki, as "a new ancient gospel."[1] When it was published in 1999, the Gospel of the Savior was received with great enthusiasm by those who hoped that here at last might be a gospel authored by Jesus himself. According to the report of the editors, the Gospel of the Savior was purchased for three hundred deutschmarks and obtained by the Ägyptisches Museum in Berlin in 1967, inventoried as Papyrus Berolinensis 22220. The text consists of an assemblage of parchment fragments, some of which can be arranged to form a more or less coherent text. The Gospel of the Savior includes materials that recall Q, the New Testament synoptic gospels, the Gospel of John, and the Gospel of Peter; and a saying of Jesus in the Gospel of the Savior resembles Gospel of Thomas 82. The Gospel of the Savior reads, "If someone is near me, that person will [burn]. I am the fire that blazes. Whoever is [near me] is near the fire; whoever is far from me is far from life."[2] On the parchment fragments are recorded lines addressed by the savior to his cross, some of which make use of terms and concepts familiar from gnostic texts:

> [A *little longer*], O cross, and that which is lacking is perfected,
>   and that which is diminished is full.
> A *little longer*, O cross, and that which [fell] arises.
> A [little longer], O cross, and all the fullness is perfected.
>
> . . . .
>
> Do not be afraid; I am rich. I will fill you with my wealth. I will
>   mount you, O cross.[3]

The bank of the Nile River near Nag Hammadi

Stephen Emmel has argued that the Gospel of the Savior (called Unbekanntes Berliner Evangelium, the Unknown Berlin Gospel, by Hans-Martin Schenke) is identical with a previously known fragmentary text called the Strasbourg Coptic Gospel, and he calls for a new comparative edition of the fragments.[4] A discussion of the texts is going on among scholars, and it is spirited.

More recently, in July 2004, the Coptologist Rodolphe Kasser announced at the 8ème Congrès International d'Études Coptes in Paris that he has access to a Coptic codex that has been known since the 1980s and includes several texts: the Gospel of Judas, the Letter of Peter to Philip (known from Nag Hammadi Codex VIII), and a Revelation of James.[5] Both Irenaeus of Lyon and Epiphanius of Salamis allude to a Gospel of Judas (that is, Judas Iscariot, the infamous betrayer of Jesus in Christian tradition) that was read by a gnostic group called the Cainites — a group named after Cain, a character from the Jewish scriptures who is no less infamous than Judas. There may be, according to the heresiologists, connections between Cainites and Sethians, who (as we have seen) employed the name Allogenes ("Stranger") in their writings.

Since the 2004 announcement, the story of this Coptic codex and its contents have become clearer. The Maecenas Foundation and the National Geographic Society have collaborated in order to publish the codex, now called Codex Tchacos, and the Gospel of Judas has been made available, initially in an English translation produced by Rodolphe Kasser, Marvin Meyer, and Gregor Wurst, and thereafter in a number of modern foreign language versions. While uncertainties remain about the story of the discovery of Codex Tchacos, it seems that it was found in the 1970s, in Middle Egypt, near al-Minya. Later, Codex Tchacos was moved from place to place and passed from hand to hand, as attempts were made to sell this ancient book. For sixteen years it was hidden away in a safe deposit box in Hicksville, New York, and for a time it was put in deep freeze, apparently in an attempt, misguided as it was, to separate the papyrus pages. Through these years and these unkind manipulations of the papyrus, the codex underwent significant damage. As best we can tell, Codex Tchacos may have been discovered in the context of several other codices (a Greek mathematical text, a Greek edition of Exodus, and a Coptic collection of letters of Paul) in a cave used for burial. The text entitled James within the codex turns out to be a version of the First Revelation of James from Nag Hammadi Codex V, and immediately following the Gospel of Judas there is another fragmentary text, provisionally entitled the Book of the Stranger (or Allogenes), in which Jesus appears as the stranger. Numerous additional fragments of the codex remain, and there may originally have been more Coptic text—perhaps considerably more text—in Codex Tchacos.

Thus far most of the discussion of Codex Tchacos has focused upon the Gospel of Judas. The Gospel of Judas appears to be an early Sethian text in which Judas Iscariot is the favored disciple who confesses, in good Sethian fashion, that Jesus is from the immortal realm (or aeon) of Barbelo. In the gospel, Judas receives a revelation that resembles the revelatory disclosures in such texts as the Secret Book of John and the Holy Book of the Great Invisible Spirit, and at the conclusion of the gospel Jesus announces that Judas will exceed the other followers of Jesus. Judas, Jesus affirms, will sacrifice the human who bears or clothes Jesus, and thus, it is implied, he will liberate the true spiritual person of Jesus. That is the real meaning of the betrayal of Jesus (or, more accurately, the handing over of Jesus) according to the Gospel of Judas.[6]

Again, in February 2005, yet another textual discovery was announced in the Egyptian periodical *Al-Ahram Weekly*.[7] It was reported that a team from the Polish Centre for Mediterranean Archaeology found a collection of papyrus and parchment texts, Coptic ostraca, pottery fragments, and textiles at al-Gurna, near the Valley of the Kings in Upper Egypt. The texts were said to be from the sixth century. According to the article in *Al-Ahram Weekly*, the texts consist of two papyrus codices and a set of parchment pages assembled between two pieces of wood:

The head of the team, Tomaz Gorecki, said the books were well preserved except for the papyri papers, which were exceptionally dry.

The first book has a hard plain cover embellished with Roman text from the inside while the second includes no less than 50 papers coated with a partly deteriorated leather cover bearing

*geometrical drawings. In the middle, a squared cross 32 cm. long
and 26 cm. wide is found.*

*As for the set of parchments, Gorecki said it included 60 papers
with a damaged leather cover and an embellished wooden locker.*

*Immediately after the discovery, restoration was carried out in
order to preserve the books, which will be the subject of extensive
restoration by two Polish experts.*

The head of the Supreme Council of Antiquities in Egypt, Zahi
Hawass, was quoted as comparing the significance of the discovery to
that of the Nag Hammadi library. The only photograph initially available was published in conjunction with the article in *Al-Ahram
Weekly*, and that Coptic page can be identified as coming from a Coptic version of the Acts of Peter. Although an Act of Peter is included
in the Berlin Gnostic Codex and the Acts of Peter and the Twelve
Apostles in the Nag Hammadi library, the page published in *Al-Ahram
Weekly* comes from the text of the Acts of Peter that presents a
polemic against Simon Magus, the figure often associated in heresiological sources with the beginning of gnosis.

So the land of Egypt continues to disclose ancient texts, like the
Nag Hammadi library, that have been hidden away but now may shed
light on our history and our world. The Nag Hammadi library was
hidden near the Jabal al-Tarif probably by Pachomian monks over a
millennium and a half ago and uncovered by Muhammad Ali in our
time. Time will tell what new discoveries may be made in the future
and how they will challenge us anew. We can only hope that with regard to manuscripts buried in Egypt too, the Gospel of Thomas may
prove to be insightful when it states that "there is nothing hidden that
will not be revealed," and the Greek text from Oxyrhynchus adds that
there is "nothing buried that [will not be raised]" (5).

THE TEXTS OF THE NAG HAMMADI LIBRARY AND THE BERLIN GNOSTIC CODEX

I N THIS APPENDIX I survey all the texts of the Nag Hammadi library and the Berlin Gnostic Codex, so as to provide an overview of the texts and their contents. In a brief paragraph I summarize the contents of each document, and select quotations to illustrate its character and style. The texts are listed in the traditional order of arranging the Nag Hammadi codices and the Berlin Gnostic Codex. Each text is introduced with the title that I suggest is to be preferred, an abbreviated reference to the manuscript (Nag Hammadi Codex [NHC] or Berlin Gnostic Codex [BG 8502]), the codex (in Roman numerals) where the text is to be found, and the tractate number within the codex (in italics). Other titles that occur in the manuscripts or are used by scholars are indicated in the notes, as well as the full manuscript reference for each text, with the identification of the codex, the tractate number, and the page and line numbers for the beginning and end of the text. If a given text is known from manuscripts other than the Nag Hammadi codices and the Berlin Gnostic Codex, those manuscripts or versions are also mentioned in the notes.

THE PRAYER OF THE APOSTLE PAUL[1]
NHC I, 1

The Prayer of the Apostle Paul is a short Valentinian prayer attributed to Paul, in which petition is made for mercy, redemption, and apparently healing. In the prayer God is invoked in reverent phrases and graceful lines using terms familiar to gnostics:

[My] redeemer, redeem me,
for [I am] yours;
I have come from [you].
You are [my] mind:
bring me forth.
You are my treasury:
open for me.
You [are] my fullness:
accept me.
You are <my> rest:
give me incomprehensible perfection. (A)

THE SECRET BOOK OF JAMES[2]
NHC I, 2

The Secret Book of James is written in the form of a letter from James the righteous, the brother of Jesus, to a recipient, possibly Cerinthus, who is known in other traditions as an early gnostic teacher, though here the name cannot be recovered with certainty. The text opens with a scene in which the twelve disciples are sitting and composing their books — perhaps their gospels — and James is with them, writing his own book. The body of the text consists of revelatory words, parables, apothegms, and other utterances of the risen Christ in response to the questions and comments of the disciples James and Peter. Thus Jesus says, concerning word and knowledge,

> *The word is like a grain of wheat. When someone sowed it, he had faith in it, and when it sprouted, he loved it, because he saw many grains instead of just one. And after he worked, he was saved because he prepared it as food and he still kept some out to sow.*
>
> *This is also how you can acquire heaven's kingdom for yourselves. Unless you acquire it through knowledge, you will not be able to find it. (8)*

The text, which may contain Valentinian elements, ends with James sending the disciples out to preach. He himself stays in Jerusalem, praying, he says, "that I might acquire a share with the loved ones who are to appear" (16) — the people reading and responding to the message of Jesus in the Secret Book of James.

THE GOSPEL OF TRUTH[3]
NHC I, 3 and XII, 2

The Gospel of Truth is a Valentinian sermon, probably composed by the prominent teacher Valentinus himself, in which knowledge is proclaimed as the way of salvation and Jesus is portrayed as the fruit of knowledge. The gospel, or good news, of truth is said to be joy for those who receive grace from the father and come to know him. At the end of the Gospel of Truth the preacher envisions what it will mean to reside in the place of rest:

*There I shall dwell, to devote myself, constantly, to the father of all
and the true brothers and sisters, upon whom the father's love is
lavished, and in whose midst nothing of him is lacking. They appear in truth, dwelling in true and eternal life, and they speak of
the perfect light filled with the father's seed, which is in his heart
and in the fullness. His spirit rejoices in this and glorifies him in
whom it was. For the father is good, and his children are perfect
and worthy of his name. Children like this the father loves.* (43)

THE TREATISE ON RESURRECTION[4]
NHC I,4

Written in the form of a letter to a person named Rheginos, the Treatise on Resurrection is a Valentinian meditation on the true meaning
of the resurrection. The text announces that the true resurrection of
that which is within a person has already happened (cf. the position
of Hymenaeus and Philetus according to 2 Tim. 2:16–18). As the text
puts it, "This is the resurrection of the spirit, which swallows the resurrection of the soul and the resurrection of the flesh" (45–46). The
resurrection is unlike the world, which is illusion:

The resurrection is different.
It is real,
it stands firm.
It is revelation of what is,
a transformation of things,
a transition into newness. (48)

THE TRIPARTITE TRACTATE[5]
NHC I, 5

The Tripartite Tractate is a long and complex treatise, in three parts,
with a Valentinian view of the divine and the cosmos. In this presentation of Valentinian thought, *logos*, or the word, and not Sophia, or
wisdom, is said to be responsible for the fall from glory, and in the
end both Valentinian and ordinary Christians may be saved. According to the text, the final restoration extends to humans and beyond,
and all happens according to the father's plan. Through the son of
the father, what was deficient attains fullness, and what was in ignorance comes to knowledge. The Tripartite Tractate explains that the
father reveals himself through the son, and in this way the unknowable becomes known:

> In hidden and inscrutable wisdom he guarded the knowledge until
> the end, until all would have labored in their search for God, the
> father, whom no one has found by his own wisdom and power. And
> then he grants them to attain knowledge of this great gift of his by
> means of that superior thought and that method which he has
> given them and which consists in ceaseless thanksgiving to him.
> Out of his immovable counsel, he then reveals himself for eternity
> to the ones who have proved worthy of receiving, by his will, the
> knowledge about the father who is unknowable in his nature. (126)

THE SECRET BOOK OF JOHN[6]
NHC II, 1; III, 1; IV, 1 and BG 8502, 2

The Secret Book of John is a classic Sethian account of the origin, fall,
and salvation of the world. It was composed as a Jewish document,
with Greek philosophical and mythological elements, but was lightly
Christianized, so that the Nag Hammadi and Berlin Gnostic versions

are preserved as revelations of the risen Christ to his disciple John, son of Zebedee. The revelation itself begins with the One, the great invisible spirit, who as the infinite divine mind extends itself in forethought, insight, and wisdom, or Sophia. Sophia errs, but she both saves and is saved, and together with her, people of knowledge are also saved. In the longer version of the Secret Book of John, the text closes with a poetic hymn of the savior, once portrayed as the forethought of God but here presented as Christ in the Christianized version of the text, and the hymn has the savior depict her — or his — acts of descent into this world to bring remembrance of knowledge to those who will hear:

> I am the forethought of pure light,
> I am the thought of the virgin spirit,
> who raises you to a place of honor.
> Arise, remember that you have heard
> and trace your root,
> which is I, the compassionate. (II, 31)

THE GOSPEL OF THOMAS[7]
NHC II, 2

The Gospel of Thomas consists of a collection of sayings of the living Jesus said to be recorded by Judas Thomas, the twin. In general, the sayings of the Gospel of Thomas seem not to be fully gnostic, but reflect gnosticizing ideas. Traditionally numbered by scholars at 114 sayings, the words of Jesus include some that are familiar from the New Testament gospels and other early Christian literature and some that are unfamiliar and new. The gospel proclaims that those who find the interpretation of these sayings "will not taste death" (1). In the text Jesus outlines the way in which the disciples may hear and interact with his sayings, and the result of this interaction is understanding and life:

Jesus said to his disciples, "Compare me to something and tell me what I am like."

Simon Peter said to him, "You are like a righteous messenger."

Matthew said to him, "You are like a wise philosopher."

Thomas said to him, "Teacher, my mouth is utterly unable to say what you are like."

Jesus said, "I am not your teacher. Because you have drunk, you have become intoxicated from the bubbling spring that I have tended."

And he took him, and withdrew, and spoke three sayings to him.

When Thomas came back to his friends, they asked him, "What did Jesus say to you?"

Thomas said to them, "If I tell you one of the sayings he spoke to me, you will pick up rocks and stone me, and fire will come from the rocks and consume you." (13)

THE GREEK GOSPEL OF THOMAS[8]

Versions of the Greek Gospel of Thomas are known only from fragments among the Oxyrhynchus papyri and citations in such church fathers as Hippolytus of Rome. The fragments that survive show that the Gospel of Thomas was known in several versions and that the text could be modified as it was edited and copied. For example, the sayings traditionally numbered 30 and 77 are brought together in one of the Greek fragments of the Gospel of Thomas, and saying 30 has been reconstructed to provide a different reading in Greek:

[Jesus says], "Where there are [three, they are without] God (or, "they are gods"),[9] and where there is only [one], I say, I am with that one. Lift up the stone, and you will find me there. Split the piece of wood, and I am there."

Similarly, saying 36 in another Greek fragment of the Gospel of Thomas expands the saying of Jesus well beyond what we read in the Coptic version:

> [Jesus says, "Do not worry], from morning [to nightfall nor] from evening [to] morning, either [about] your [food], what [you will] eat, [or] about [your robe], what clothing you [will] wear. [You are much] better than the lilies, which do not card or [spin]. And since you have one article of clothing, what ... you ...? (or, according to a previous reading, "what [will you put] on?"). Who might add to your stature? That is the one who will give you your clothing."

THE GOSPEL OF PHILIP[10]
NHC II, 3

The Gospel of Philip is a Valentinian anthology of meditations on a wide variety of themes, including the sacraments and the biblical figures of Adam and Eve. Five sacraments are enumerated in the gospel — baptism, chrism, eucharist, redemption, and bridal chamber — and special emphasis is placed upon the sacrament of the bridal chamber. The story of Adam and Eve is understood in the Gospel of Philip as an account of the separation of humankind into male and female leading to the need for restoration to wholeness and unity. That restoration is realized in the bridal chamber:

> If the female had not separated from the male, the female and the male would not have died. The separation of male and female was the beginning of death. Christ came to heal the separation that was from the beginning and reunite the two, in order to give life to those who died through separation and unite them.
>
> A woman is united with her husband in the bridal chamber, and those united in the bridal chamber will not be separated

again. That is why Eve became separated from Adam, because she had not united with him in the bridal chamber. (70)

THE NATURE OF THE RULERS[11]
NHC II, 4

The Nature of the Rulers offers a Sethian interpretation, with a few Christian elements, of the early chapters of the book of Genesis, part of which is given as a revelation of the angel, or luminary, Eleleth. The text opens with citations from the Pauline letters (Col. 1:13; Eph. 6:12) and explains that the rulers and authorities of this world, as the Pauline texts intimate, are a mean-spirited lot by nature. In spite of the machinations of the rulers of the world and their arrogant leader, however, the text insists that everything happens according to the will of the father of all, and in the end all those who are from the incorruptible realm will realize light and life:

> *Then all the children of the light will know the truth, and their root, and the father of all, and the holy spirit. They will all say with one voice,*
>
> *The father's truth is just,*
> *The child is over all*
> *and with everyone,*
> *forever and ever.*
> *Holy, holy, holy!*
> *Amen. (97)*

ON THE ORIGIN OF THE WORLD[12]
NHC II, 5 and XIII, 2

On the Origin of the World is a gnostic treatise, with a few peripheral Christian themes, that provides interpretations of the origin and destiny of all things and explanations of difficult concepts. Initially the text formulates an argument that something must have existed prior to primordial chaos — something infinite:

> Since everyone, both the gods of the world and people, says that nothing existed before chaos, I shall prove they all are wrong, because they do not know the [origin] of chaos or its root. Here [is the] proof.
>
> Although certainly people in general are [inclined] to say that chaos is darkness, in actuality chaos comes from a shadow, and it is the shadow that has been called darkness. The shadow comes from something that has existed from the beginning, and so it is obvious that something in the beginning existed before chaos came into being, and chaos came after what was in the beginning. (97–98)

From what is infinite everything else came to be, including Sophia, the demiurge Yaldabaoth, the powers of the world, humankind, and all the rest. At this time the world is in ignorance and error, the text maintains, but through the word, Jesus, what was formerly unknown becomes evident, and people come to knowledge. Drawing on perspectives reminiscent of Sethian, Valentinian, and Manichaean traditions, the text has much in common with the tractate just before it in Codex II, the Nature of the Rulers.

EXEGESIS ON THE SOUL[13]
NHC II, 6

The Exegesis on the Soul recounts a gnostic version of the myth of Psyche, the soul, complete with proof texts taken from the Bible and Homer's *Odyssey*. Kurt Rudolph compares this story of the career of the soul with the message of Simon Magus and his companion

Helena, whom he saved, it is said, from a brothel in Tyre. In the Exegesis on the Soul the story tells how the female soul falls into the world of sexual corruption and prostitution, suffers grievously, and is in need of salvation:

> *The soul needs to regenerate herself and become as she formerly was. So the soul stirred, and she received the divine from the father, so that she might be restored and returned to where she was before.*
>
> *This is resurrection from the dead.*
> *This is freedom from captivity.*
> *This is ascent to heaven.*
> *This is the way up to the father.*

At last the soul is saved, born again, renewed, and restored to pure, heavenly love:

> *When the soul is renewed, she will arise and praise the father and her brother, by whom she was rescued. Through rebirth the soul will be saved. This is not because of practical lessons or technical skills or learned books. Rather, it is the grace of the [spirit], it is the gift of the merciful [God], for it is from above.* (134)

THE BOOK OF THOMAS[14]

NHC II, 7

The Book of Thomas is a gnosticizing text that employs sayings of Jesus from the Gospel of Thomas in order to create a dialogue, between the risen savior Jesus and his twin brother Judas Thomas, on the fire of passion and judgment. After heated language that makes use of themes from Plato and other portrayals of hellfire, the text comes

to a close with a monologue of Jesus in which he utters pronounce-
ments of shame and blessing upon people and promises a place in
God's kingdom for the pure and faithful:

> *Watch and pray that you may not remain in the flesh, but that*
> *you may leave the bondage of the bitterness of this life. And when*
> *you pray, you will find rest, for you have left pain and reproach*
> *behind. When you leave the pains and the passions of the body,*
> *you will receive rest from the good one. You will reign with the*
> *king, you united with him and he with you, from now on and for-*
> *ever. (145)*

THE HOLY BOOK OF THE GREAT INVISIBLE SPIRIT[15]
NHC III, 2 and IV, 2

The Holy Book of the Great Invisible Spirit, or the Egyptian Gospel,
is a Sethian baptismal handbook with liturgical instructions for a baptismal ceremony prefaced by an account of the origin of the universe
in Sethian terms. The ritual for baptism includes a hymn with exalted names, ecstatic utterances, chanted vowels, and words of praise
and power:

> *Having known you,*
> *I now have mingled with your constancy.*
> *I have armed myself with the armor of light.*
> *I have become bright.*
> *The mother was there for the lovely beauty of grace.*
> *So I have stretched out my two hands.*
> *I have been formed in the circle of the riches of light in my breast,*
> *giving form to the many beings*
> *produced in light beyond reproach.*
> *In truth I shall declare your glory,*

I have comprehended you:
yours, Jesus;
look,
forever Ō
forever E
O Jesus
O eternal realm, eternal realm,
God of silence,
I honor you completely. (III, 67)

EUGNOSTOS THE BLESSED[16]

NHC III, 3 and V, 1

Eugnostos the Blessed is composed as a letter from Eugnostos to those who are his, and the text presents a Jewish discourse, with Greek influences, on gnostic themes. God is described in the letter as the one who is, who comes to manifestation in imperishable realms, the immortal human, and Sophia, and this description is given in anticipation of the revelation of one who is to come. At the close of the letter, Eugnostos writes of the incomprehensible brilliance of the divine fullness and the coming of a revealer:

All natures, from the immortal one, from the unconceived one to the revelation in chaos, are in the light that shines with no shadow but with ineffable joy and unspeakable praise. They continue to rejoice over their glory that never fades and the state of rest that cannot be measured, which can neither be described nor conceived among all the realms that have come to be, and their powers.

This is enough. I have told you all this so that you might accept it, until one who does not need to be taught appears among you. That one will tell you all these things in joy and pure knowledge. (III, 89–90)

THE WISDOM OF JESUS CHRIST[17]
NHC III, 4 and BG 8502, 3

The Wisdom of Jesus Christ is an expanded and Christianized version of Eugnostos the Blessed. The present text transforms the Jewish discourse of Eugnostos into a gnostic dialogue between the risen Christ and his disciples by means of the insertion of questions and comments within the text, and it adds material about the fall of Sophia and Jesus the savior. The particular interest in Jesus within the Wisdom of Jesus Christ may have been prompted by the reference at the end of Eugnostos the Blessed to the revealer who is to come. In the Wisdom of Jesus Christ, Jesus tells the disciples — and the readers of the text — how they may attain wholeness and rest:

> For this reason I have come here, that these may be united with spirit and breath, and two may become one, as in the beginning. Then you may produce an abundance of fruit and go up to the one who is from the beginning, in ineffable joy and glory and [honor and] grace of [the father of all].
>
> Whoever knows [the father in pure] knowledge [will depart] to the father [and be at rest in] the unconceived [father]. (III, 116–17)

THE DIALOGUE OF THE SAVIOR[18]
NHC III, 5

The Dialogue of the Savior is a dialogue between the master (Jesus) and his disciples, particularly Judas (Judas Thomas), Mary (Mary of Magdala), and Matthew, on a variety of issues important to gnostics. At one point in the dialogue, the disciples ask the master about fullness and deficiency, and he answers, "You are from fullness and you are in a place of deficiency. And look, his light has poured down on me" (139). Matthew follows that with a question about death and life, and the master responds,

> *[You have] asked me about a [true] saying that eye has not seen,*
> *nor have I heard it, except from you. But I say to you, when what*
> *moves a person slips away, that person will be called dead, and*
> *when what is living leaves what is dead, it will be called alive.*

Then he adds, "Whatever is from truth does not die. Whatever is from woman dies" (140). The Dialogue of the Savior, which is significantly damaged, seems to be related to the Gospel of Thomas, as may be seen in the examples just cited, and it may have made use of sayings found in that gospel.

THE REVELATION OF PAUL[19]
NHC V, 2

The Revelation of Paul is a gnostic apocalyptic text that chronicles Paul's trip through the heavens. Paul mentions his heavenly journey in 2 Corinthians 12:2–4, where he claims to have gone up to the third heaven, but in the present text Paul ascends to a much more exalted destination. In the Nag Hammadi apocalypse, a child (Christ) appears to Paul, and Paul proceeds to ascend as high as the tenth heaven. On the way up, Paul passes the gatekeepers of the skies and meets apostles, angels, and spirits. When he gives the gatekeepers the sign he has — his heavenly passport — they open the gates and let him pass. As Paul narrates the culmination of his visionary ascent,

> *Then the <seventh> heaven opened, and we ascended to the*
> *eighth realm. I saw the twelve apostles, and they welcomed me.*
> *We ascended to the ninth heaven, and I greeted all those in the*

ninth heaven. We ascended to the tenth heaven, and I greeted my
fellow spirits. (23–24)

THE FIRST REVELATION OF JAMES[20]
NHC V, 3

The First Revelation of James, an apocalyptic text in name, is a gnostic dialogue between Jesus, the master, and his brother James the righteous concerning the means by which James and others may be liberated from the suffering of this world and may return to their heavenly home. In the text James reflects upon Jesus being opposed by the powers and says to him,

> *You have come with knowledge*
> *to reprove their forgetfulness.*
> *You have come with remembrance*
> *to reprove their ignorance.*
> *I was worried about you.*
> *For you have come down into profound ignorance,*
> *but you were not defiled by any of it.*
> *You have come down into thoughtlessness,*
> *but your memory stayed with you.*
> *You walked in mud,*
> *and your garments did not get dirty.*
> *You were not inundated with their filth,*
> *and they did not apprehend you. (28)*

Jesus in turn says to James, "Cast away from [yourself] the cup, which is bitterness. None of [the rulers will be able] to stand against you, for you [have begun] to understand [their] roots from beginning to end" (40). He adds later, "You have received [the firstfruits] of knowledge, and [you know] now the [place] in [which you will] walk. You will find . . ." (42). Unfortunately, the papyrus of the text is damaged, especially near the end of the revelation.

THE SECOND REVELATION OF JAMES[21]
NHC V,4

The Second Revelation of James is presented as a transcript, prepared by Mareim, of a speech delivered by James the righteous in Jerusalem. The speech focuses upon an appearance of the risen Christ to James (also referred to in 1 Cor. 15:7 and elsewhere), and at the end of the speech there is an account of the martyrdom of James. It is said that those oppressing James threw him down from a high place at the temple, dragged him over the ground, crushed him with a huge rock, and, since he had survived all of this, made him stand up and stoned him. In these dire circumstances, James uttered a prayer as he was dying:

My God and father,
who saved me from this dead hope,
who made me alive through the mystery of your good pleasure,
do not let these days in the world be prolonged for me,
but let the day of your light, in which [no night] remains,
[shine upon me].
[Bring me to where my] salvation is,
and deliver me from this [place of] sojourn.
Let not your grace be squandered on me,
but let your grace be pure.
Save me from an evil death.
Bring me from the tomb alive,
for your grace is alive in me,
the desire to accomplish a work of fullness. (62–63)

THE REVELATION OF ADAM[22]
NHC V, 5

The Revelation of Adam is a Sethian text in which Adam offers revelations to his son Seth just before he dies. A Jewish text with few if any
Christian characteristics, the Revelation of Adam outlines the history
of the gnostic generation of Seth through the hard times of flood and
fire and describes the disputed origin and salvific role of the illumina-
tor of knowledge, the Sethian savior. Thirteen kingdoms of this world
have theories about the origin of the savior, and all thirteen get it
wrong, but the generation without a king — the Sethians — have the
right story of the savior:

> God chose him from all the eternal realms.
> He made knowledge of the undefiled one of truth
> come to be [in] him.
> He said, "The [great] illuminator has come
> [from] foreign air, [from a] great eternal realm."
> And [he] illumined the generation of those people,
> whom he had chosen for himself,
> so that they might illumine the whole eternal realm. (82–83)

THE ACTS OF PETER AND THE TWELVE APOSTLES[23]
NHC VI, 1

The Acts of Peter and the Twelve Apostles represents the genre of literature usually referred to as apocryphal acts of the apostles. In this
case, the text narrates the story of Peter and the other apostles under-
taking a remarkable voyage. At the end of their journey, when they
disembark from their ship, they come to a city and meet a mysterious
stranger named Lithargoel, who is selling pearls. Later this same figure, Lithargoel, appears again, this time looking like a doctor, and the

apostles do not recognize him. He gives Peter and the apostles a medicine case and a bag of medicine, identifies himself as Jesus Christ, and tells the apostles to go heal not only bodies but also hearts of people. As for the costly pearls, Jesus explains, "Do you not know that my name, which you teach, is worth more than all riches, and the wisdom of God is worth more than silver and gold and precious stones?" (10). There are no clear gnostic features in the text, though the image of the pearl is found in other texts like the "Hymn of the Pearl" in the Acts of Thomas.

THUNDER[24]
NHC VI,2

Thunder is a poetic revelation of a female figure who speaks in paradoxical self-predications:

> I am the first and the last.
> I am the honored and the scorned.
> I am the whore and the holy.
> I am the wife and the virgin.
> I am <the mother> and the daughter. (13)

Within the text, Thunder identifies herself as wisdom, life (Zoe), insight, and knowledge, and the text thus illustrates gnostic characteristics. Bentley Layton classifies it as a Sethian text (or, as he terms it, classic gnostic scripture).

AUTHORITATIVE DISCOURSE[25]
NHC VI,3

Authoritative Discourse, a text preserved with a number of lacunae, discusses the descent of the soul, her fate here below, and her return to her home above through the use of images and metaphors. It is said that the word is like food and medicine for the soul. The soul is like a child among stepchildren. A lustful thought in a good person is like chaff mixed with wheat. People are like fish that may be caught in nets. The soul eventually finds shelter in a treasure house. The text concludes with poetic statements about the soul's rest:

> She has found her rising.
> She has come to rest in the one who is at rest.
> She has reclined in the bridal chamber.
> She has eaten of the banquet
> for which she has hungered.
> She has partaken of immortal food.
> She has found what she has sought.
> She has received rest from her labors,
> and the light shining on her does not set.
> To the light belongs the glory
> And the power and the revelation
> forever and ever. (35)

Although Rouel van den Broek suggests that the text may be more Platonic than gnostic, we may be able to identify gnosticizing characteristics in the portrayal of the soul in the text.

THE CONCEPT OF OUR GREAT POWER[26]
NHC VI, 4

The Concept of Our Great Power presents gnostic and apocalyptic views on the destiny of the world, expressed in a series of loosely connected observations and words of reflection. The text employs the terms "thought" and "great power," both names for manifestations of the divine according to the first-century gnostic teacher Simon Magus (cf. Acts 8:9–25), although such terms are also used for the divine in other gnostic traditions. At the beginning of the body of the text, it is said,

> Whoever knows our great power will become invisible. Fire will be unable to consume such a person, but it will purify. And it will destroy all that you possess. For all those in whom my form appears, from seven days old to one hundred twenty years old, will be saved. (36)

At the end, the theme of power is reiterated as the vision of final rest is articulated:

> Then will appear the souls who are holy through the light of the power that is exalted above all powers, the immeasurable, the universal. That is who I am, and all who know me.
>
> They will be in the realm of beauty, of the realm of marriage, and they will be adorned through Sophia.
>
> After praising the one who is in incomprehensible oneness, they behold it on account of its will that is within them.
>
> They all have come to be as reflections in its light. They all have shone; they have found rest in its rest. (47)

EXCERPT FROM PLATO'S REPUBLIC[27]
NHC VI, 5

The Nag Hammadi excerpt from the *Republic* (588A–589B) is a Coptic translation of the portion of Plato's dialogue that discusses the wild beast in relation to the human soul. This excerpt differs somewhat from Plato's version, probably because of problems with the Coptic translation itself as well as gnosticizing interests on the part of ancient interpreters. The excerpt states, for instance, that "the image of a lion is one thing and the image of a human is another" (49). For gnostic interpreters, this sort of reference to the lion and the human could recall the place of the lion in gnostic lore, for instance, in the Gospel of Thomas, where Jesus speaks of the human consuming and being consumed by the lion (7), or in the Secret Book of John, where the demiurge Yaldabaoth looks like a lion.

THE DISCOURSE ON THE EIGHTH AND NINTH[28]
NHC VI, 6

The Discourse on the Eighth and Ninth is a Hermetic dialogue, previously unknown, between the teacher and mystagogue thrice-greatest Hermes and a student about the ascent to exalted realms of spiritual enlightenment. The stages of enlightenment in this text are the higher stages, the eighth and ninth realms, and the mystical vision of the eighth and ninth evokes words of praise and ecstasy from the initiate:

> O grace! After this, I thank you by singing a song to you. You gave
> me life when you made me wise. I praise you. I invoke your name
> hidden in me,
>
> A
> Ō EE
> Ō ĒĒ
> ŌŌŌ III
> ŌŌŌŌ OOOOO
> ŌŌŌŌŌ YYYYY
> ŌŌŌŌŌŌŌŌŌŌŌ
> ŌŌŌŌŌŌŌŌŌŌŌ
> You exist with spirit.
> I sing to you with godliness. (61)

THE PRAYER OF THANKSGIVING[29]

NHC VI, 7

The Prayer of Thanksgiving is a Hermetic prayer, previously known in Greek and Latin versions, in which thanks are given to God for the instruction leading to enlightenment and understanding:

> *If the instruction is sweet and simple,*
> *it grants us mind, word, and knowledge:*
> *mind, that we may understand you,*
> *word, that we may interpret you,*
> *knowledge, that we may know you.*
> *We are happy,*
> *enlightened by your knowledge.*
> *We are happy.*
> *You have taught us about yourself.*
> *We are happy.*
> *While we were in the body*
> *you have made us divine through your knowledge. (64)*

Because this text follows the Discourse on the Eighth and Ninth, it seems to refer back to that Hermetic dialogue. After the prayer, it is said that the teacher and student embrace and share vegetarian food.

EXCERPT FROM THE PERFECT DISCOURSE[30]

NHC VI, 8

The selection from the Perfect Discourse in the Nag Hammadi library presents a portion (21–29) of another Hermetic text, previously known and sometimes referred to as the Apocalypse of Asclepius (or simply Asclepius). Here the teacher, thrice-greatest Hermes, and the student, Asclepius, join together in a dialogue about the experience of the Hermetic mystery, the nature of knowledge, and the end of the world understood in apocalyptic terms. Egypt will suffer a horrible fate, it is predicted, and the wicked will be punished, but the good will be restored by God. All that takes place in the Hermetic mystery is compared to the mystery of sex:

> *If you wish to see the nature of this mystery, consider the marvelous image of sexual intercourse between male and female. For when the male reaches his climax, the semen is ejaculated. At that moment the female receives the strength of the male and the male receives the strength of the female, as the semen does this.*

Both of these mysteries are to be performed in secret: "These are holy mysteries of both words and deeds, because they are neither heard nor seen" (65).

THE PARAPHRASE OF SHEM[31]
NHC VII, 1

The Paraphrase of Shem is written in the form of a long and complicated gnostic revelation provided to Shem by Derdekeas, the son of infinite light. The revelation deals with the interaction among three powers of the universe — light above, darkness below, and spirit in between — and the liberation of the mind and light of the spirit from the clutches of darkness. The story is told in graphically sexual terms, and it includes the great events of the history of salvation: the flood, the destruction of Sodom, and the work of the savior. In the text, Shem is commissioned to speak about all these things to the people of the earth:

> *From now on, O Shem, proceed in grace and remain in faith upon the earth. For all the powers of light and fire will be com-*

pleted by me for your sake. Without you they will not be revealed until you speak of them openly. When you leave the earth, they will be communicated to the worthy. And apart from this revelation, let them speak about you upon the earth, since they will inherit the land, free of care and in harmony. (48–49)

THE SECOND DISCOURSE OF GREAT SETH[32]
NHC VII, 2

The Second Discourse of Great Seth is a speech or message of Jesus — the second such presentation — about saving knowledge and the true meaning of the crucifixion in the face of the theology of the great church. This gnostic text uses the name of Seth in the title, perhaps as an indication that Jesus is the manifestation of heavenly Seth, but little in the text seems indisputably Sethian. In the Second Discourse of Great Seth, Jesus declares that a theology of the cross is illegitimate, and he criticizes those who "proclaim the doctrine of a dead man" (60) — the crucified Christ. In fact, the world rulers tried to kill Jesus, but in their ignorance they were unable to do so:

The death they think I suffered they suffered in their error and blindness. They nailed their man to their death. Their thoughts did not perceive me, since they were deaf and blind. By doing these things they pronounce judgment against themselves. As for me, they saw me and punished me, but someone else, their father, drank the gall and the vinegar; it was not I. They were striking me with a scourge, but someone else, Simon, bore the cross on his shoulder. Someone else wore the crown of thorns. And I was on high, poking fun at all the excesses of the rulers and the fruit of their error and conceit. I was laughing at their ignorance. (55–56)

Instead of preaching a gospel of the cross, Jesus declares, believers should seek mystical union with the divine. Jesus disagrees strongly

with those, like Paul, who maintain that in baptism people die with
Christ. Rather, Jesus affirms in the text, "The scripture regarding the
ineffable water in use among us is this word: I am in you and you are
in me, just as the father is in me <and in> you, with no guile at all"
(49–50).

THE REVELATION OF PETER[33]
NHC VII, 3

The Revelation of Peter is a gnostic apocalypse in which the apostle
Peter has a vision that is interpreted by the savior Jesus. With words
highly critical of the great church — their leaders are "dry canals"
(79) — the revelation gives particular attention to the crucifixion,
here understood in a way comparable to that in the Second Discourse of Great Seth, which is located just before it in Codex VII. In
the Revelation of Peter, Jesus is depicted as laughing at the foolish-
ness of those who are trying in vain to kill him, for he cannot be
grasped by them. The savior looks at the scene of crucifixion and says
to Peter,

> *The one you see smiling and laughing above the cross is the living
> Jesus. The one into whose hands and feet they are driving nails is
> his fleshly part, the substitute for him. They are putting to shame
> the one who came into being in the likeness of the living Jesus.
> Look at him and look at me. (81)*

THE TEACHINGS OF SILVANUS[34]
NHC VII, 4

The Teachings of Silvanus is not a gnostic text. Rather, it consists of a
series of statements of Christian wisdom, typical of expressions of
Alexandrian Christianity, addressed by the author to his "child" or

"son." The advice given in the text emphasizes the use of wisdom, reason, and the mind, so that one may know oneself and become like Christ and like God. In the words of the text, "My child, return to your first father, God, and wisdom, your mother, from whom you came into being from the beginning. Return, that you might fight against all of your enemies, the powers of the adversary" (91). Again, "Do not tire of knocking on the door of the word, and do not cease walking in the way of Christ" (103).

THE THREE STELES OF SETH[35]
NHC VII, 5

The Three Steles of Seth presents three Sethian hymns or prayers for a liturgy of ascent, accompanied by instructions for the proper use of the liturgy. In good Platonizing fashion, the divine is described as existence, life, and mind. There are no clearly Christian elements in the text, and the incipit cites the name of Dositheos, who sometimes is said to be a disciple of John the Baptizer and the predecessor of Simon Magus. The hymns are full of life and light, and they carry spiritual travelers through three stages of ascent to a vision of the divine. Those who are enlightened may then declare,

We rejoice,
we rejoice,
we rejoice.
We have seen,
we have seen,
we have seen what really preexists,
that it really exists
and is the first eternal one.
You unengendered one,
from you are the eternal ones

and the aeons,
the all-perfect ones, who are unified,
and the perfect individuals.
We praise you, nonexistent being,
existence before existences,
first substance before substances,
father of divinity and life,
creator of mind,
supplier of goodness,
supplier of blessedness. (124)

ZOSTRIANOS[36]

NHC VIII, 1

Zostrianos is a long Sethian revelatory text that is preserved in a fragmentary state. Like the Three Steles of Seth, Zostrianos is heavily influenced by Platonic tradition, and a substantial missing portion of
the text can be confidently restored from a parallel passage in *Against
Arius* by the Christian Platonizing author Marius Victorinus. Zostrianos contains only limited references to Christianity. It probably is to
be identified with the Revelation of Zostrianos that was known and
critiqued in the Neoplatonic school of Plotinus in Rome. In the text,
Zostrianos, traditionally thought to be a relative of the Persian sage
Zoroaster, embarks on an ecstatic trip through the heavenly realms as
angels and powers guide him. At the end of the text Zostrianos re-
turns to this world and preaches a sermon to awaken all who will listen and urge them on to enlightenment and salvation:

You who are alive, holy offspring of Seth,
understand this. Do not turn a deaf ear to me.
Awaken your divinity to divinity,
and strengthen your undefiled chosen souls. (130)

THE LETTER OF PETER TO PHILIP[37]
NHC VIII, 2

The Letter of Peter to Philip is called a letter in its title, and the opening of the text is in epistolary form, but the main portion of the text resembles in part a dialogue on gnostic themes between the risen Christ and his disciples and in part acts of apostles similar to the New Testament Acts, especially the first part, which features Peter. In the Nag Hammadi text, too, Peter is the leader of the apostolic group. The savior appears in order to answer the questions of the apostles, and he discourses on the fall of the mother and the emergence of the arrogant world ruler in terms somewhat reminiscent of Sethian thought. In the text, Peter addresses the other apostles in a sermon on suffering — the suffering of Jesus and the suffering of others:

> *My brothers, Jesus is a stranger to this suffering. But we are the ones who have suffered through the mother's transgression. For this reason he did everything symbolically among us. The lord Jesus, child of the father's immeasurable glory, is the author of our life.* (139)

As in the story of Pentecost in the New Testament Acts, the apostles are filled with holy spirit, and they go forth with four words (with four gospels? in four directions?) so that they all might preach.

MELCHIZEDEK[38]
NHC IX, 1

Melchizedek is a Sethian apocalypse that builds upon the Jewish tradition of Melchizedek, king of Salem (Gen. 14:18–20; 2 Enoch; 11QMelch from the Dead Sea Scrolls). In the text, which is in a poor state of preservation, Melchizedek is the recipient of revelation, which he in turn is to communicate to others. Melchizedek is thought to be identified with the savior Jesus Christ in a way that brings to mind Hebrews 7:1–3, and the tangible aspects of the life of Jesus — being born, eating and drinking, being circumcised, being in the flesh, suffering, rising from the dead — are professed. For Jesus, as Melchizedek, the end of all these matters is triumph, and he is told,

> Be [strong, Melchiz]edek, great [high priest] of God [Most High, for the] rulers who [are] your [enemies made] war against you. You have [gained the victory over them, and] they did not prevail over [you. You have] persevered and [destroyed] your enemies . . . [you] will find rest in no other [place except one that is] living and holy. (26)

THE THOUGHT OF NOREA[39]
NHC IX, 2

The Thought of Norea is a short Sethian hymn about the female figure Norea, who is known from the Nature of the Rulers and other texts and is derived from the woman referred to as Naamah in Genesis 4:22. Sometimes Norea is considered the sister and wife of Seth; sometimes she is linked to Noah or Shem. In the present text, Norea is a savior who also needs to be saved, like Sophia in other texts. So, it is said, Norea is to

> speak with words of [life]
> and remain in the [presence] of the exalted one
> by [taking possession] of what she received
> before the world came into being.
> She has the great mind of the invisible one.
> She glorifies their father,
> and she lives among those

who . . . in the fullness,
and she sees the realm of fullness. (28)

THE TESTIMONY OF TRUTH[40]
NHC IX, 3

The Testimony of Truth is a Christian gnostic text, in a fragmentary state of preservation, that Birger Pearson suspects may have been written by Julius Cassianus, an author discussed by Clement of Alexandria as having a strongly ascetical view of life in the world. The text is largely in the form of a sermon on knowledge, ignorance, and renunciation of the world, and the true testimony, it is said, is this: "When a person comes to know himself and God, who is over the truth, that person will be saved and crowned with the unfading crown" (45). Unlike some other Christians, even gnostic Christians, the author proclaims, those who are people of truth and knowledge will forsake the world and the things of the flesh and live a pure spiritual life.

MARSANES[41]
NHC X

The Sethian text Marsanes presents revelations and teachings given by the gnostic prophet Marsanes. Preserved in a fragmentary state, the text is another Sethian work that is heavily influenced by Platonic tradition, and it recalls the gnostic apocalypses said to have been discussed in the Neoplatonic school of Plotinus. Marsanes is the only tractate known from Codex X, and it may have filled the entire book. From what we can read of the text, it offers Marsanes's vision of the cosmos and the realms at various levels of the cosmos; it enumerates thirteen such realms and calls them "seals." As for the thirteenth seal, it is said, "The thirteenth speaks concerning [the unknown] silent one, even the foundation of the indistinguishable one" (4), and at last Marsanes beholds the supreme deity. In the text is included an analysis of the deeper meaning of the letters of the alphabet and numerical configurations in relation to the signs of the zodiac and the nature of the soul.

THE INTERPRETATION OF KNOWLEDGE[42]
NHC XI, 1

The Interpretation of Knowledge is a Valentinian text that reads like a sermon interpreting passages from the Gospel of Matthew and the apostle Paul. The text is written to address a community at odds concerning spiritual gifts and to offer a message of healing and reconciliation. Though the text is preserved imperfectly, it is possible to ascertain that the author or preacher appeals to the Pauline image of the church as the body of Christ in order to plead for a spirit of harmony among Christians with a variety of spiritual gifts. As there is harmony among limbs of the body, so may there be harmony among the limbs or members of the church. The text advises the readers,

> You should [give] thanks on behalf of the limbs and pray that you too may be given the grace that has been given to them. For the word is rich and generous, and it is good. It gives away gifts in this world to its own people without jealousy. (17)

VALENTINIAN EXPOSITION[43]
NHC XI, 2

The Valentinian Exposition provides an account of the origin of the universe, the manifestation of the divine fullness, and the fate of Sophia and of all from a Valentinian point of view. The text gives special attention to the story of Sophia, declaring that Sophia will be saved and restored and, with her, all the eternal realms and beings:

When Sophia, then, receives her partner, and Jesus receives Christ, and the seeds are united with the angels, then the fullness will receive Sophia in joy, and all will be joined together and restored. For then the eternal realms will have received their abundance, for they will have understood that even if they change, they remain unchanging. (39)

To this cosmological account are appended five liturgical readings for rituals of anointing, baptism, and eucharist. One of the readings describes the transformation that takes place in baptism. The person being baptized is brought, it is said,

[from the] world [to the Jordan],
from [the things] of the world to [the sight] of God,
from [the carnal] to the spiritual,
from the physical to the angelic,
from [creation] to fullness,
from the world to the eternal realm. (42)

ALLOGENES THE STRANGER[44]
NHC XI, 3

Allogenes the Stranger is a Sethian revelation, and yet another Sethian text that was influenced by Platonic tradition and debated in the Neoplatonic school of Plotinus. Portions of the text also closely parallel the Secret Book of John, including the description, in negative theological terms, of the transcendent One. The text has the stranger Allogenes — probably Seth — give account of his ascent to the realms above and the visions he saw in the heavenly realms. The stranger claims to have been guided on his heavenly journey by the female power Youel, and while above the stranger is invited to envision his own true self and the being of God:

O great power! O name that has come to be in the world! O stranger, behold your blessedness, how silently it abides, by which you know your proper self, and, seeking yourself, ascend to the life that you will see moving.

And even if you cannot stand, fear not. But if you wish to stand, ascend to existence, and you will find it standing and still after the likeness of the One who is truly still and embraces all these silently and without activity. (59)

When the foreigner returned, it is said, he wrote everything down for his "son" Messos, so that he in turn might proclaim it to others.

HYPSIPHRONE[45]
NHC XI, 4

The text Hypsiphrone, perhaps a Sethian document, is represented in its incipit as "the book [concerning the things] seen [by] Hypsiphrone when they were [revealed] in the place of [her] virginity" (69). In this short and fragmentary text, Hypsiphrone, whose name means "woman of high mind," is a female revealer who records how she came down to this world and what transpired thereafter. Phainops, "bright-eyed one," and a wellspring of blood are also involved. The role of Hypsiphrone may be compared with that of the luminary Eleleth or even Sophia in other Sethian texts.

THE SENTENCES OF SEXTUS[46]
NHC XII, 1

The Nag Hammadi Sentences of Sextus is a Coptic translation of a collection of words of wisdom that were composed in Greek, translated into several languages, and studied by many Christians. Only a portion of the text in the Nag Hammadi library survives. Among the surviving sentences are the following:

> *That person is [faithful] who takes the lead in all [that is good].*
> *Wisdom guides [the soul] to the place of [God].*
> *[There is no one] of the household of [truth except] wisdom.*
> *A [believing] nature cannot [be enamored of] lying.*
> *A fearful [and enslaved] nature cannot share in faith.*
> *When you are [faithful,] saying what is right [is no greater than] listening.*
> *When you [are] with believers, be more inclined [to listen than] to speak.*
> *A [hedonist] is good [for nothing].*
> *Only if you have no [sin may you speak] of whatever is from [God].*
> *The sins of the [ignorant are] the shame of [their teachers].*
> (15–16)

Two other fragments of Codex XII also survive, but it is difficult to judge meaningfully what their contents may have been. The rest of Codex XII may have been lost when the mother of Muhammad Ali burned pages from the Nag Hammadi library in the oven at her home in al-Qasr.

THREE FORMS OF FIRST THOUGHT[47]

NHC XIII, 1

The Sethian text entitled Three Forms of First Thought narrates, in the first-person singular, a revelation of the three descents of the female heavenly figure Protennoia (first thought) as voice, speech, and word. With "I am" statements, first thought describes her trips down to the world below in a manner like that of the final hymn of the savior (Pronoia [forethought] or Christ) in the longer version of the Secret Book of John. In Three Forms of First Thought, the third descent as *logos* (or word) closely resembles the hymn to the word in John 1. The Nag Hammadi text has first thought explain how she, as word, revealed herself to human beings, and particularly to those who are hers:

> *The third time I revealed myself to them in their tents as the word,*
> *and I revealed myself in the likeness of their shape.*
> *I wore everyone's garment.*
> *I hid in them,*
> *and [they] did not know who empowers me.*
> *For I am in all sovereignties and powers*
> *and in angels and every movement in all matter.*
> *I hid in them*
> *until I revealed myself to my brothers and sisters.* (47)

THE GOSPEL OF MARY[48]
BG 8502,1

The Gospel of Mary, which survives with six pages missing at the beginning and four in the middle, is a gnosticizing dialogue between Jesus and his disciples, especially Mary of Magdala. Whether the text is specifically gnostic is debated among scholars. Mary of Magdala occupies the position of most-loved disciple in the Gospel of Mary, as elsewhere, and after Jesus tells the disciples to follow the child of humankind within and then leaves them, Mary ministers to them and comforts them: "Do not weep and be distressed nor let your hearts be irresolute. For his grace will be with you all and will shelter you. Rather we should praise his greatness, for he has prepared us and made us human beings" (9). Mary also recalls a vision — neither of the soul nor of the spirit, but rather of the mind — of the soul's ascent. Peter and Andrew use harsh and sexist words to express their doubt about Mary's authority, but Levi speaks on her behalf, and the disciples go out to teach and preach.

THE ACT OF PETER[49]
BG 8502,4

The Act of Peter, in the tradition of acts of apostles, tells the story of a single "act": a miracle of healing — and nonhealing — performed by Peter. According to the text, Peter the miracle worker is confronted by someone who asks why Peter does not heal his own disabled daughter, and so Peter proceeds to heal her — and then he does something no one expects:

> *Peter said to his daughter, "Now go back to your place, lie down, and become an invalid again, for this is better for both of us." The girl returned, lay down in her place, and became as she was before. The whole crowd wept and begged Peter to make her well.* (130–131)

Peter explains that when his daughter was younger and was about to be defiled sexually, she was suddenly stricken with paralysis to protect her. Ptolemy, the man who wanted to have sex with Peter's daughter, then responds to a vision and hurries to Peter's house, and in his will he donates a parcel of land in the name of the daughter. This text has no discernible gnostic features, but it does speak to two concerns that have frequently dominated life in the church ever since: protecting purity and raising money.

NOTES

INTRODUCTION : GNOSTIC WISDOM ANCIENT AND MODERN

1. On the texts of the Nag Hammadi library in general, see Marvin Meyer, ed., *The Nag Hammadi Scriptures*; James M. Robinson, ed., *The Nag Hammadi Library in English*; Hans-Martin Schenke, Hans-Gebhard Bethge, and Ursula Ulrike Kaiser, eds., *Nag Hammadi Deutsch*; Jean-Pierre Mahé and Paul-Hubert Poirier, eds., *Écrits gnostiques*.

2. For a fine general introduction to gnosis, see Kurt Rudolph, *Gnosis*.

3. For English translations of many of the heresiological passages relating to gnostic religion, see Werner Foerster, ed., *Gnosis*, vol. 1; Bentley Layton, *The Gnostic Scriptures*.

4. For English translations of the Naassene Sermon, the Book of Baruch, the "Hymn of the Pearl," and the "Round Dance of the Cross," see Willis Barnstone and Marvin Meyer, eds., *The Gnostic Bible*, 119–33, 351–55, 386–94, 482–94; Marvin Meyer, *The Gnostic Gospels of Jesus*, 261–86.

5. Carl Schmidt and Violet MacDermot, eds., *Pistis Sophia*; *The Books of Jeu and the Untitled Text in the Bruce Codex*.

6. For selections from Hermetic, Mandaean, and Manichaean texts, see Willis Barnstone and Marvin Meyer, eds., *The Gnostic Bible*, 495–654.

7. On the gnostic gems, see Campbell Bonner, *Studies in Magical Amulets, Chiefly Graeco-Egyptian*; Erwin R. Goodenough, *Jewish Symbols of the Greco-Roman Period*; Birger A. Pearson, *Gnosticism and Christianity in Roman and Coptic Egypt*, 249–67.

8. Hans Jonas, *The Gnostic Religion*, 101.

9. Jonas, *The Gnostic Religion*, 237.

10. Jonas, *The Gnostic Religion*, 338.

11. Jonas, *The Gnostic Religion*, 290–319.

12. I discuss the discoveries of the Nag Hammadi library, the Berlin Gnostic Codex, and the Oxyrhynchus papyri in Chapter 1 and the discovery of the Gospel of Judas in the Epilogue.

13. Robert M. Grant's comment is on the cover of Pagels, *The Gnostic Gospels.*

14. Elaine H. Pagels, *The Gnostic Gospels*, 150.

15. Elaine H. Pagels, *Beyond Belief*, 73.

16. Michael Baigent, Richard Leigh, and Henry Lincoln, *Holy Blood, Holy Grail.*

17. Dan Brown, *The Da Vinci Code*, 247–48.

CHAPTER 1: FERTILIZER, BLOOD VENGEANCE, AND CODICES: THE DISCOVERY OF THE NAG HAMMADI LIBRARY

1. On Christianity in Egypt, see Birger A. Pearson, *Gnosticism and Christianity in Roman and Coptic Egypt.*

2. For the story of the discovery of the Nag Hammadi codices, see James M. Robinson, "From the Cliff to Cairo: The Story of the Discoverers and Middlemen of the Nag Hammadi Codices"; "Nag Hammadi: The First Fifty Years."

3. Robinson, "Nag Hammadi: The First Fifty Years," 80 (slightly modified, in consultation with the author).

4. On the breaking of the monopoly, see Robinson, "Nag Hammadi: The First Fifty Years," 83–99; "The Jung Codex: The Rise and Fall of a Monopoly."

5. For the story of the discovery of the Berlin Gnostic Codex, see Karen L. King, *The Gospel of Mary of Magdala*, 7–12; Michael Waldstein and Frederik Wisse, eds., *The Apocryphon of John*, 2–3.

6. Bernard P. Grenfell, Arthur S. Hunt, et al., eds., *The Oxyrhynchus Papyri.*

7. Stephen Emmel, "A Fragment of Nag Hammadi Codex III in the Beinecke Library: Yale inv. 1784."

8. Marius Victorinus, *Against Arius* 1.49, 9–40; see Michel Tardieu, "Recherches sur la formation de l'Apocalypse de Zostrien et les sources de Marius Victorinus"; Catherine Barry, Wolf-Peter Funk, Paul-Hubert Poirier, and John D. Turner, eds., *Zostrien*, 32–225, 483–662.

9. On the Nag Hammadi archeological excavations, see Fernand Debono, "La basilique et le monastère de St. Pachôme"; *Biblical Archeologist* 42 (1979); Peter Grossmann and Gary Lease, "Faw Qibli — 1989 Excavation Report (= Sixth Season)"; Gary Lease, "Traces of Early Egyptian Monasticism: The Faw Qibli Excavations."

10. Lease, "Traces of Early Egyptian Monasticism," 6–8.

11. Arnold Van Lantschoot, "Allocution de Timothée d'Alexandrie prononcée à l'occasion de la dédicace de l'église de Pachôme à Pboou."

12. Bastiaan Van Elderen and James M. Robinson, "The First Season of the Nag Hammadi Excavation: 27 November–19 December 1975."

13. On the Wadi Sheikh Ali, see Marvin Meyer, "Archaeological Survey of the Wadi Sheikh Ali: December 1980."

14. Meyer, "Archaeological Survey of the Wadi Sheikh Ali," 78–79.

15. Meyer, "Archaeological Survey of the Wadi Sheikh Ali," 79–80.

16. On the codicology of the Nag Hammadi library, see James M. Robinson, "Introduction," 1–102, in *The Facsimile Edition of the Nag Hammadi Codices: Introduction* (1984).

17. John W. B. Barns, Gerald M. Browne, and John C. Shelton, eds., *Nag Hammadi Codices: Greek and Coptic Papyri from the Cartonnage of the Covers*, 61–76, 137–38, 142–44; cf. 39–41.

18. James M. Robinson, "Introduction," 21, in James M. Robinson, ed., *The Nag Hammadi Library in English*.

19. Wilhelm Schneemelcher, ed., *New Testament Apocrypha*, 1.50.

CHAPTER 2: COPTIC TEXTS FROM THE SANDS OF EGYPT: THE NAG HAMMADI LIBRARY AND THE BERLIN GNOSTIC CODEX

1. On the cryptogram at the end of Zostrianos, see Jean Doresse, "Les apocalypses de Zoroastre, de Zostrien, de Nicothée"; John H. Sieber, ed., *Nag Hammadi Codex VIII*, 224–25.

2. On the Coptic language, see Bentley Layton, *A Coptic Grammar*; "Coptic Language."

3. For a valiant attempt to determine the place and date of composition of the texts in the Nag Hammadi library and the Berlin Gnostic Codex, see Birger A. Pearson, *Gnosticism and Christianity in Roman and Coptic Egypt*, 11–81.

4. On gnostic texts and Platonic literature, see John D. Turner, *Sethian Gnosticism and the Platonic Tradition*.

5. Michael A. Williams, *Rethinking "Gnosticism,"* 263.

6. Williams, *Rethinking "Gnosticism,"* 51.

7. Karen L. King, *What Is Gnosticism?* 15.

8. King, *What Is Gnosticism?* 189.

9. King, *What Is Gnosticism?* 235–36.

10. For a fuller discussion of the nature of gnosis, see Bentley Layton, "Prolegomena to the Study of Ancient Gnosticism"; Marvin Meyer, *The Gnostic Gospels of Jesus*, x–xiii; "Gnosticism, Gnostics, and *The Gnostic Bible*," 1–19, in Willis Barnstone and Marvin Meyer, eds., *The Gnostic Bible*; Birger A. Pearson, *Gnosticism and Christianity in Roman and Coptic Egypt*, 201–23.

11. Cf. Meyer, *The Gnostic Gospels of Jesus*, xiii.

12. James M. Robinson, "Introduction," 14–16, in James M. Robinson, ed., *The Nag Hammadi Library in English*; "Introduction," 1–102, in *The Facsimile Edition of the Nag Hammadi Codices: Introduction* (1984).

13. Robinson, "Introduction," 15, in Robinson, ed., *The Nag Hammadi Library in English*.

14. Marvin Meyer, *The Letter of Peter to Philip*, 4–5.

15. Williams, *Rethinking "Gnosticism*," 235–62.

16. Williams, *Rethinking "Gnosticism*," 261.

17. On the Thomas tradition, see Bentley Layton, *The Gnostic Scriptures*, 357–409; James M. Robinson and Helmut Koester, *Trajectories Through Early Christianity*, 290–306.

18. On the sayings gospel Q, see John S. Kloppenborg, *Excavating Q; The Formation of Q*; Burton L. Mack, *The Lost Gospel*; James M. Robinson, Paul Hoffmann, and John S. Kloppenborg, eds., *The Critical Edition of Q*; James M. Robinson, *The Gospel of Jesus*.

19. On the Sethian school of thought, see Hans-Martin Schenke, "Das sethianische System nach Nag-Hammadi-Handschriften"; "The Phenomenon and Significance of Sethian Gnosticism"; John D. Turner, "Sethian Gnosticism: A Literary History"; *Sethian Gnosticism and the Platonic Tradition*; Michael A. Williams, "Sethianism."

20. On the Valentinian school of thought, see Layton, *The Gnostic Scriptures*, 215–353; Elaine H. Pagels, *The Gnostic Paul; The Johannine Gospel in Gnostic Exegesis*; François Sagnard, *La gnose valentinienne et le témoignage de Saint Irénée*; Einar Thomassen, *The Spiritual Seed*.

21. On the Hermetic religious heritage, see André-Jean Festugière, *La Révélation d'Hermès Trismégiste*; Arthur Darby Nock and André-Jean Festugière, eds., *Corpus Hermeticum*.

22. On *Poimandres*, see Barnstone and Meyer, eds., *The Gnostic Bible*, 502–11; Layton, *The Gnostic Scriptures*, 449–59.

CHAPTER 3: "THEY WILL NOT TASTE DEATH": THE WISDOM OF THE
LIVING JESUS IN THE GOSPEL OF THOMAS AND THOMAS TEXTS

1. On the development of the wisdom tradition in the ancient world, see John S. Kloppenborg, *The Formation of Q*.

2. James B. Pritchard, ed., *Ancient Near Eastern Texts*, 412.

3. Pritchard, ed., *Ancient Near Eastern Texts*, 596.

4. On the *progymnasmata* and the *chreiai*, see Ronald F. Hock and Edward N. O'Neil, eds., *The Chreia in Ancient Rhetoric*.

5. James M. Robinson, Paul Hoffmann, and John S. Kloppenborg, eds., *The Critical Edition of Q*.

6. On the Gospel of Thomas, see April D. DeConick, *The Original Gospel of Thomas; Recovering the Original Gospel of Thomas*; Helmut Koester, Bentley Layton, Thomas O. Lambdin, and Harold W. Attridge, "The Gospel According to Thomas";

Marvin Meyer, *The Gospel of Thomas; Secret Gospels;* Elaine H. Pagels, *Beyond Belief;* Stephen J. Patterson, *The Gospel of Thomas and Jesus;* Stephen J. Patterson, James M. Robinson, and Hans-Gebhard Bethge, *The Fifth Gospel;* Gregory J. Riley, *Resurrection Reconsidered;* Jens Schröter and Hans-Gebhard Bethge, "Das Evangelium nach Thomas"; Risto Uro, ed., *Thomas at the Crossroads;* Richard Valantasis, *The Gospel of Thomas.*

7. Albert Schweitzer, *Reverence for Life,* 65.

8. Søren Giversen, "The Palaeography of Oxyrhynchus Papyri 1 and 654–655."

9. Stephen J. Patterson, "Understanding the Gospel of Thomas Today," 43, in Stephen J. Patterson, James M. Robinson, and Hans-Gebhard Bethge, *The Fifth Gospel.*

10. Valantasis, *The Gospel of Thomas,* 7.

11. Valantasis, *The Gospel of Thomas,* 196.

12. Hans-Martin Schenke, Hans-Gebhard Bethge, and Ursula Ulrike Kaiser, eds., *Nag Hammadi Deutsch,* 1.151–81; Kurt Aland, ed., *Synopsis Quattuor Evangeliorum,* 517–46.

13. Cf. Marvin Meyer, "'Be Passersby': *Gospel of Thomas* Saying 42, Jesus Traditions, and Islamic Literature."

14. On sayings of Jesus in Islamic sources, see Marvin Meyer, *The Unknown Sayings of Jesus,* 144–56; Tarif Khalidi, *The Muslim Jesus.*

15. Meyer, *The Unknown Sayings of Jesus,* 148.

16. Bentley Layton, *The Gnostic Scriptures,* 376.

17. For a fuller discussion of saying 114, see Marvin Meyer, "Making Mary Male: The Categories 'Male' and 'Female' in the *Gospel of Thomas*"; "*Gospel of Thomas* Logion 114 Revisited."

18. On the Book of Thomas, see Raymond Kuntzmann, *Le Livre de Thomas;* Marvin Meyer, *The Gnostic Gospels of Jesus,* 203–23; Hans-Martin Schenke, "Das Buch des Thomas"; *Das Thomas-Buch;* Hans-Martin Schenke and Einar Thomassen, "The Book of Thomas"; John D. Turner, *The Book of Thomas the Contender;* "The Book of Thomas the Contender"; John D. Turner and Bentley Layton, "The Book of Thomas the Contender Writing to the Perfect."

19. Cf. Turner, "The Book of Thomas the Contender," 200–201.

20. Schenke, "Das Buch des Thomas," 281–82.

21. On the Dialogue of the Savior, see Beate Blatz and Einar Thomassen, "The Dialogue of the Savior"; Stephen Emmel, ed., *Nag Hammadi Codex III,5;* Julian V. Hills, "The Dialogue of the Savior"; Helmut Koester and Elaine H. Pagels, "Introduction," in Stephen Emmel, ed., *Nag Hammadi Codex III,5;* Pierre Létourneau, *Le Dialogue du Sauveur;* Meyer, *The Gnostic Gospels of Jesus,* 219–39; Silke Peterson and Hans-Gebhard Bethge, "Der Dialog des Erlösers."

22. Koester and Pagels, "Introduction," 1–17, in Stephen Emmel, ed., *Nag Hammadi Codex III,5.*

23. Compare also the place of Mary of Magdala in the Gospel of Philip, discussed in Chapter 5, and the Gospel of Mary, discussed in Chapter 6.

CHAPTER 4: THE WISDOM OF INSIGHT: THE FALL AND RESTORATION OF SOPHIA IN THE SECRET BOOK OF JOHN AND SETHIAN TEXTS

1. James H. Charlesworth, ed., *The Old Testament Pseudepigrapha*, 1.33.

2. Stanley Lombardo and Robert Lamberton, eds., *Hesiod: Works and Days, and Theogony*, 85–87.

3. Kurt Rudolph, *Gnosis*, 109–11, 255. On the Exegesis on the Soul, see also Christina-Maria Franke, "Die Erzählung über die Seele"; Bentley Layton and William C. Robinson Jr., "The Expository Treatise on the Soul"; William C. Robinson Jr. and Madeleine Scopello, "The Exegesis on the Soul"; Madeleine Scopello, *L'Exégèse de l'Âme*.

4. On the Secret Book of John, see Karen L. King, "The Apocryphon of John: Part II of the Gospel of John?"; "Sophia and Christ in the Apocryphon of John"; Bentley Layton, *The Gnostic Scriptures*, 23–51; Marvin Meyer, *The Gnostic Gospels of Jesus*, 143–83; Elaine H. Pagels, *Beyond Belief*, 114–85; Michel Tardieu, *Écrits gnostiques*; Michael Waldstein, "Das Apocryphon des Johannes"; Michael Waldstein and Frederik Wisse, eds., *The Apocryphon of John*.

5. On Three Forms of First Thought (or Trimorphic Protennoia), see Yvonne Janssens, *La Prôtennoia trimorphe*; Gesine Schenke Robinson, "Die dreigestaltige Protennoia"; John D. Turner, "Trimorphic Protennoia."

6. See Meyer, *The Gnostic Gospels of Jesus*, 312–13.

7. Cf., for example, Birger A. Pearson, *Gnosticism and Christianity in Roman and Coptic Egypt*, 258–59.

8. Plotinus's work *Against the Gnostics* is discussed in Kurt Rudolph, *Gnosis*, 61.

9. Cf. the discussion of Augustine in Rudolph, *Gnosis*, 367–76.

10. Rudolph, *Gnosis*, 370.

11. Birger A. Pearson, *Gnosticism, Judaism, and Egyptian Christianity*, 58–59.

12. Pagels, *Beyond Belief*, 164.

13. Walter E. Crum, "A Gnostic Fragment"; Paul E. Kahle, *Bala'izah*, 1.473–77.

14. On Theodore bar Konai, see Addai Scher, ed., *Theodore bar Konai, Liber Scholiorum*, 319,29–330,26.

15. On the *Umm al-kitab* and the *ghulat*, see Willis Barnstone and Marvin Meyer, eds., *The Gnostic Bible*, 655–725; Heinz Halm, *Die islamische Gnosis*.

16. Willis Barnstone and Marvin Meyer, eds., *The Gnostic Bible*, 724.

17. Régine Charron, *Concordance des textes de Nag Hammadi: Le Codex III*, and a personal communication.

18. On the Holy Book of the Great Invisible Spirit, see Alexander Böhlig and Frederik Wisse, eds., *Nag Hammadi Codices III, 2 and IV, 2*; Layton, *The Gnostic*

Scriptures, 101–20; Meyer, *The Gnostic Gospels of Jesus*, 113–42; Uwe-Karsten Plisch, "Das heilige Buch des großen unsichtbaren Geistes"; John D. Turner, *Sethian Gnosticism and the Platonic Tradition*.

19. Josephus, *Antiquities of the Jews* 1.67–71. On the Three Steles of Seth and the Discourse on the Eighth and Ninth, see below.

20. Turner, *Sethian Gnosticism and the Platonic Tradition*, 105; cf. also Jean-Marie Sevrin, *Le dossier baptismal séthian*.

21. On the Elkesaites, the Mandaeans, and the Manichaeans, see Barnstone and Meyer, eds., *The Gnostic Bible*, 525–654.

22. On the Three Steles of Seth, see Paul Claude, *Les Trois Stèles des Seth*; James E. Goehring and James M. Robinson, "The Three Steles of Seth"; Hans-Martin Schenke, "Die drei Stelen des Seth." The quotations from the Three Steles of Seth are translated by John D. Turner.

CHAPTER 5 : VALENTINUS THE CHRISTIAN MYSTIC: SALVATION THROUGH KNOWLEDGE IN THE GOSPEL OF TRUTH AND VALENTINIAN TEXTS

1. Irenaeus of Lyon, *Against Heresies* 1.11.1, cited in Bentley Layton, *The Gnostic Scriptures*, 225, and discussed on 217–220.

2. For translations of Ptolemy's *Letter to Flora* and Heracleon's *Commentary on the Gospel of John*, see Willis Barnstone and Marvin Meyer, eds., *The Gnostic Bible*, 299–331.

3. On the life and thought of Valentinus, see Ismo Dunderberg, "The School of Valentinus"; Layton, *The Gnostic Scriptures*, 215–64; Christoph Markschies, *Valentinus Gnosticus?*

4. Layton, *The Gnostic Scriptures*, 217–220.

5. Tertullian, *Against the Valentinians* 4.1–2, briefly discussed in Dunderberg, "The School of Valentinus," 72, and Kurt Rudolph, *Gnosis*, 318.

6. Hippolytus of Rome, *Refutation of All Heresies* 6.37.7; translation by Marvin Meyer in Barnstone and Meyer, eds., *The Gnostic Bible*, 112–13.

7. On the Gospel of Truth, see Harold W. Attridge and George W. MacRae, "The Gospel of Truth"; Kendrick Grobel, *The Gospel of Truth*; Layton, *The Gnostic Scriptures*, 250–64; Jacques-É. Ménard, *L'Évangile de Vérité*; Marvin Meyer, *The Gnostic Gospels of Jesus*, 89–112; Hans-Martin Schenke, "Evangelium Veritatis"; *Die Herkunft des sogenannten Evangelium Veritatis*.

8. Layton, *The Gnostic Scriptures*, 251.

9. On opening the eyes of the blind, cf. Matt. 11:5; Luke 7:21–22; John 9:10–11; 11:37.

10. On the parable of the lost sheep, cf. Matt. 18:12–14; Luke 15:4–7; Gospel of Thomas 107.

11. On true sabbath observance, cf. Gospel of Thomas 27, cited in Chapter 3.

12. Cf. Irenaeus of Lyon, *Against Heresies* 1.11.1.

13. Einar Thomassen, notes to his translation of the Valentinian Exposition. Cf. Thomassen, *The Spiritual Seed*.

14. On the Gospel of Philip, see April D. DeConick, "The Great Mystery of Marriage"; Wesley W. Isenberg and Bentley Layton, "The Gospel According to Philip"; Layton, *The Gnostic Scriptures*, 325–53; Jacques-É. Ménard, *L'Évangile selon Philippe*; Meyer, *The Gnostic Gospels of Jesus*, 43–87; Hans-Martin Schenke, "Das Evangelium nach Philippus"; "The Gospel of Philip."

15. Layton, *The Gnostic Scriptures*, 325.

16. Cf. Matt. 27:46; Mark 15:34; Ps. 22:1.

17. Layton, *The Gnostic Scriptures*, 336.

18. DeConick, "The Great Mystery of Marriage," 342.

19. On the Valentinian liturgical readings, see Wolf-Peter Funk, "Valentinianische Abhandlung"; Jacques-É. Ménard, *L'Exposé valentinien*; Elaine H. Pagels and John D. Turner, "A Valentinian Exposition, with On the Anointing, On Baptism A and B, and On the Eucharist A and B."

20. On the Treatise on Resurrection, see Bentley Layton, *The Gnostic Treatise on Resurrection from Nag Hammadi*; Jacques-É. Ménard, *Le Traité sur la Résurrection*; Malcolm L. Peel, "The Treatise on the Resurrection"; Hans-Martin Schenke, "Der Brief an Rheginus."

CHAPTER 6: HERMES, DERDEKEAS, THUNDER, AND MARY: REVEALERS OF WISDOM IN OTHER NAG HAMMADI TEXTS

1. On the Discourse on the Eighth and Ninth, see Peter A. Dirkse, James Brashler, and Douglas M. Parrott, "The Discourse on the Eighth and Ninth"; Jean-Pierre Mahé, *Hermès en Haute-Égypte*; Karl-Wolfgang Tröger, "Über die Achtheit und Neunheit."

2. On the Prayer of Thanksgiving, see Peter A. Dirkse and James Brashler, "The Prayer of Thanksgiving"; Mahé, *Hermès en Haute-Égypte*; Karl-Wolfgang Tröger, "Ein (hermetisches) Dankgebet."

3. On the Perfect Discourse, see Peter A. Dirkse and Douglas M. Parrott, "Asclepius 21–29"; Jens Holzhausen, "Asklepios"; Jean-Pierre Mahé, *Hermès en Haute-Égypte*.

4. On the Paraphrase of Shem, see Michel Roberge, *La Paraphrase de Sem*; Michel Roberge and Frederik Wisse, "The Paraphrase of Shem"; Hans-Martin Schenke, "Die Paraphrase des Sêem"; Frederik Wisse, "The Paraphrase of Shem." The quotations from the Paraphrase of Shem are translated by Michel Roberge.

5. Cf. Gedaliahu A. G. Stroumsa, *Another Seed*, 79; Wisse, "The Paraphrase of Shem," 16.

6. In Roberge and Wisse, "The Paraphrase of Shem," 341.

7. On Thunder, see George W. MacRae, "The Thunder: Perfect Mind"; Uwe-Karsten Plisch, "Die Brontê — Vollkommener Verstand"; Paul-Hubert Poirier, *Le Tonnerre, intellect parfait.*

8. Cf., for example, the Isis aretalogy from Cyme, discussed in Marvin Meyer, ed., *The Ancient Mysteries,* 172–74.

9. Bentley Layton, *The Gnostic Scriptures,* 77.

10. Epiphanius of Salamis, *Panarion* 26.2.6. See the discussion in Wilhelm Schneemelcher, ed., *New Testament Apocrypha,* 1.358–60.

11. On the Gospel of Mary, see Esther de Boer, *The Gospel of Mary; Mary Magdalene: Beyond the Myth;* Karen L. King, *The Gospel of Mary of Magdala;* Marvin Meyer, *The Gospels of Mary;* Anne Pasquier, *L'Évangile selon Marie.* The quotations from the Gospel of Mary are translated by Karen L. King.

12. De Boer, *The Gospel of Mary.*

13. Esther A. de Boer, "Mary Magdalene and the Disciple Jesus Loved."

14. Cf. Meyer, *The Gospels of Mary,* xv–xvi.

15. King, *The Gospel of Mary of Magdala,* 189.

16. Tertullian of Carthage, *On the Veiling of Virgins* 9, cited in Elaine H. Pagels, *The Gnostic Gospels,* 60.

17. Tertullian of Carthage, *Prescription Against Heretics* 41, cited in Pagels, *The Gnostic Gospels,* 60.

EPILOGUE : DISCOVERIES AFTER
THE NAG HAMMADI LIBRARY

1. Charles W. Hedrick and Paul A. Mirecki, *Gospel of the Savior: A New Ancient Gospel.*

2. Gospel of the Savior 12:7–9 (*Gospel of the Savior,* 40–41).

3. Gospel of the Savior fragment 5 (*Gospel of the Savior,* 54–57).

4. Stephen Emmel, "The Recently Published *Gospel of the Savior*"; Stephen Emmel, "Unbekanntes Berliner Evangelium = the Strasbourg Coptic Gospel"; note also the response by Charles W. Hedrick, "Caveats to a 'Righted Order' of the *Gospel of the Savior.*"

5. Rodolphe Kasser, "Un nouvel apocryphe copte."

6. Cf. Rodolphe Kasser, Marvin Meyer, and Gregor Wurst, *The Gospel of Judas* (Washington, D.C.: National Geographic, 2006); Herbert Krosney, *The Lost Gospel: The Quest for the Gospel of Judas Iscariot* (Washington, D.C.: National Geographic, 2006); James M. Robinson, *The Secrets of Judas: The Story of the Misunderstood Disciple and His Lost Gospel* (San Francisco: HarperSanFrancisco, 2006); Bart D. Ehrman, *The Lost Gospel of Judas Iscariot: A New Look at Betrayer and Betrayed* (Oxford: New

York and Oxford: Oxford University Press, 2006). The Gospel of Judas and the Book of the Stranger are also included in Marvin Meyer, ed., *The Nag Hammadi Scriptures: The International Edition* (San Francisco: HarperSanFrancisco, 2007 [in press]).

7. *Al-Ahram Weekly* (http://weekly.ahram.org.eg/2005/730/he1.htm), February 17–23, 2005.

APPENDIX: THE TEXTS OF THE NAG HAMMADI LIBRARY AND THE BERLIN GNOSTIC CODEX

1. Nag Hammadi Codex I,1: A,1–B,10 (front flyleaf).

2. The title is construed from the contents of the text; the text may also be entitled the Apocryphon of James, the Letter of James, or the Apocryphal Letter of James. Nag Hammadi Codex I,2: 1,1–16,30.

3. The title comes from the incipit. Nag Hammadi Codex I,3: 16,31–43,24; XII,2: 53,1–54,28; 57,1–60,30 (fragments).

4. The text is sometimes referred to as the Epistle to Rheginos. Nag Hammadi Codex I,4: 43,25–50,18.

5. The title is construed from the contents of the text. Nag Hammadi Codex I,5: 51,1–138,27. The quotation is translated by Einar Thomassen.

6. Or the Apocryphon of John. Nag Hammadi Codex II,1: 1,1–32,9; III,1: 1,1–40,11; IV,1: 1,1–49,28; Berlin Gnostic Codex 8502,2: 19,6–77,7; Irenaeus of Lyon provides a summary of part of the Secret Book of John in *Against Heresies* 1.29.1–4.

7. Or the Hidden Sayings of Jesus, from the incipit. Nag Hammadi Codex II,2: 32,10–51,28; fragments of the Greek Gospel of Thomas are found in Papyrus Oxyrhynchus 1; 654; 655; Hippolytus of Rome, *Refutation of All Heresies* 5.7.20; 5.8.32.

8. Papyrus Oxyrhynchus 1; 654; 655; Hippolytus of Rome, *Refutation of All Heresies* 5.7.20; 5.8.32.

9. The reading "they are gods" is based on a new collation of the text by April D. DeConick and is discussed in her book *The Original Gospel of Thomas*.

10. Nag Hammadi Codex II,3: 51,29–86,19.

11. Or the Hypostasis of the Archons, or the Reality of the Rulers. Nag Hammadi Codex II,4: 86,20–97,23.

12. The title is construed from the contents of the text; the text is also "entitled" by scholars the Treatise Without a Title. Nag Hammadi Codex II,5: 97,24–127,17; XIII,2: 50,25–34 (fragment); British Library Oriental Manuscript 4926(1) (fragments).

13. Or the Expository Treatise on the Soul. Nag Hammadi Codex II,6: 127,18–137,27.

14. Or the Contender Writing to the Perfect, a secondary title in the manuscript; the text sometimes is referred to, erroneously, as the Book of Thomas the Contender. Nag Hammadi Codex II,7: 138,1–145,19; 145,20–23 (scribal note).

15. Or the Egyptian Gospel, a secondary title in the manuscript; the text sometimes is referred to, erroneously, as the Gospel of the Egyptians. This text is not to be confused with the Gospel of the Egyptians known from patristic sources. Nag Hammadi Codex III,2: 40,12–69,20; IV,2: 50,1–81,2 (the conclusion is lost).

16. Nag Hammadi Codex III,3: 70,1–90,12; V,1: 1,1–17,18.

17. Or the Sophia of Jesus Christ. Nag Hammadi Codex III,4: 90,14–119,18; Berlin Gnostic Codex 8502,3: 77,8–127,12; Papyrus Oxyrhynchus 1081 (fragment).

18. Nag Hammadi Codex III,5: 120,1–147,23; Yale Inventory 1784.

19. Or the Apocalypse of Paul. Nag Hammadi Codex V,2: 17,19–24,9.

20. Or the First Apocalypse of James, or the Revelation of James (the word "first" is not in the title in the manuscript). Nag Hammadi Codex V,3: 24,10–44,10. The quotation is translated by Wolf-Peter Funk. Stephen Emmel, Rodolphe Kasser, and Charles W. Hedrick report that there is a revelation of James in an unpublished Coptic codex.

21. Or the Second Apocalypse of James, or the Revelation of James (the word "second" is not in the title in the manuscript). Nag Hammadi Codex V,4: 44,11–63,32. The quotation is translated by Wolf-Peter Funk.

22. Or the Apocalypse of Adam. Nag Hammadi Codex V,5: 64,1–85,32.

23. Nag Hammadi Codex VI,1: 1,1–12,22.

24. Or Thunder: Perfect Mind (the full title in the manuscript). Nag Hammadi Codex VI,2: 13,1–21,32.

25. Or Authentikos Logos. Nag Hammadi Codex VI,3: 22,1–35,24.

26. This is the title at the end of the text. Other titles are the Thought of Our Great Power and Intellectual Perception: The Concept of the Great Power (the title at the opening of the text). Nag Hammadi Codex VI,4: 36,1–48,15.

27. Nag Hammadi Codex VI,5: 48,16–51,23.

28. The title is construed from the contents of the text. Nag Hammadi Codex VI,6: 52,1–63,32.

29. The title is construed from the contents of the text. Nag Hammadi Codex VI,7: 63,33–65,7; 65,8–14 (scribal note); Papyrus Mimaut 591–611; Latin *Asclepius* 41.

30. Or Asclepius 21–29. The Perfect Discourse is the original Greek title. Nag Hammadi Codex VI,8: 65,15–78,43; Latin *Asclepius* 21–29.

31. Or the Paraphrase of Seem (the spelling of the name in the manuscript). Nag Hammadi Codex VII,1: 1,1–49,9. The quotation is translated by Michel Roberge. Another text with a similar title, the Paraphrase of Seth, is known from the writings of Hippolytus of Rome, but it seems to have been a different work.

32. Or the Second Treatise of the Great Seth, or the Second Logos of the Great Seth. Nag Hammadi Codex VII,2: 49,10–70,12.

33. Or the Apocalypse of Peter. This text is not to be confused with the Ethiopic or Arabic Revelations or Apocalypses of Peter. Nag Hammadi Codex VII,3: 70,13–84,14.

34. Nag Hammadi Codex VII,4: 84,15–118,7; 118,8–9 (colophon). The quotations are translated by Birger A. Pearson. Compare also texts associated with the desert father S. Antony.

35. Or the Three Tablets of Seth, or Dositheos's Revelation of the Three Steles of Seth (the incipit). Nag Hammadi Codex VII,5: 118,10–127,27; 127,28–32 (scribal note). The quotation is translated by John D. Turner.

36. Nag Hammadi Codex VIII,1: 1,1–132,9. At the end of the text, after the title, there is a cryptogram that may be resolved to read "Words of truth of Zostrianos. God of truth. Words of Zoroaster."

37. Or the Letter of Peter Which He Sent to Philip (the title in the manuscript). Nag Hammadi Codex VIII,2: 132,10–140,27. Stephen Emmel, Rodolphe Kasser, and Charles W. Hedrick report that there is another version of the Letter of Peter to Philip in an unpublished Coptic codex.

38. Nag Hammadi Codex IX,1: 1,1–27,10. The quotation is translated by Birger A. Pearson.

39. The title is construed from the contents of the text. The text is sometimes also entitled the Ode on Norea. Nag Hammadi Codex IX,2: 27,11–29,5.

40. The title is construed from the contents of the text. Nag Hammadi Codex IX,3: 29,6–74,30. The quotation is translated by Birger A. Pearson.

41. Nag Hammadi Codex X: 1,1–68,18. The quotation is translated by John D. Turner.

42. Nag Hammadi Codex XI,1: 1,1–21,35. The quotation is translated by Einar Thomassen.

43. The title is construed from the contents of the text. Nag Hammadi Codex XI,2: 22,1–39,39. The quotation is translated by Einar Thomassen. The liturgical readings are on pages 40, 1–44, 37.

44. Nag Hammadi Codex XI,3: 45,1–69,20. The quotation is translated by John D. Turner.

45. Nag Hammadi Codex XI,4: 69,21–72,33.

46. Nag Hammadi Codex XII,1: 15,1–34,28 (pp. 17–26 are missing). The Sentences of Sextus is also known in Greek, Latin, Syriac, Armenian, and Georgian versions.

47. Or Trimorphic Protennoia. Nag Hammadi Codex XIII,1: 35,1–50,24. The quotation is translated by John D. Turner.

48. Berlin Gnostic Codex 8502,1: 7,1–19,5 (pp. 11–14 are missing); Papyrus Oxyrhynchus 3525; Papyrus Rylands 463 (both are fragments). The quotation is translated by Karen L. King.

49. Berlin Gnostic Codex 8502,4: 128,1–141,7 (pp. 133–34 are missing).

BIBLIOGRAPHY

Al-Ahram Weekly. February 17–23, 2005. http://weekly.ahram.org.eg.

Aland, Kurt, ed. *Synopsis Quattuor Evangeliorum: Locis parallelis evangeliorum apocryphorum et partum adhibitis.* 15th rev. ed. Stuttgart: Deutsche Bibelge-sellschaft, 1996. Corrected printing. With an Appendix by the Berliner Arbeit-skreis für koptisch-gnostische Schriften, "Das Thomas-Evangelium / The Gospel According to Thomas," 517–46.

Asgeirsson, Jon Ma., Kristin De Troyer, and Marvin W. Meyer, eds. *From Quest to Q: Festschrift James M. Robinson.* Bibliotheca Ephemeridum Theologicarum Lovaniensium 146. Louvain: Presses Universitaires de Louvain; Peeters, 2000.

Attridge, Harold W. "The Greek Fragments." In *Nag Hammadi Codex II, 2–7,* edited by Bentley Layton, 1.95–128.

——, ed. *Nag Hammadi Codex I (The Jung Codex).* 2 vols. Nag Hammadi Studies 22–23. Leiden: Brill, 1985.

Attridge, Harold W., and George W. MacRae. "The Gospel of Truth." In *Nag Hammadi Codex I,* edited by Harold W. Attridge, 1.55–122. Also Harold W. Attridge and George W. MacRae, "The Gospel of Truth," in *The Nag Hammadi Library in English,* edited by James M. Robinson, 38–51.

Baigent, Michael, Richard Leigh, and Henry Lincoln. *Holy Blood, Holy Grail.* New York: Dell, 1983.

Barns, John W. B., Gerald M. Browne, and John C. Sheldon, eds. *Nag Hammadi Codices: Greek and Coptic Papyri from the Cartonnage of the Covers.* Nag Hammadi Studies 16. Leiden: Brill, 1981.

Barnstone, Willis, ed. *The Other Bible.* Rev. ed. San Francisco: HarperSanFrancisco, 2005.

Barnstone, Willis, and Marvin Meyer, eds. *The Gnostic Bible.* Boston: Shambhala, 2003.

Barry, Catherine, Wolf-Peter Funk, Paul-Hubert Poirier, and John D. Turner, eds. *Zostrien (NH VIII,1).* Bibliothèque copte de Nag Hammadi, Section "Textes" 24. Québec: Les Presses de l'Université Laval; Louvain and Paris: Peeters, 1999.

Bauer, Walter. *Orthodoxy and Heresy in Earliest Christianity.* 2d ed. Philadelphia: Fortress, 1971.

Bethge, Hans-Gebhard, Stephen Emmel, Karen L. King, and Imke Schletterer, eds. *For the Children, Perfect Instruction: Studies in Honor of Hans-Martin Schenke on the Occasion of the Berliner Arbeitskreis für koptisch-gnostische Schriften's Thirtieth Year.* Nag Hammadi and Manichaean Studies 54. Leiden: Brill, 2002.

Bianchi, Ugo, ed. *Le Origini dello Gnosticismo: Colloquia di Messina, 13–18 Aprile 1966.* Studies in the History of Religions (Supplements to *Numen*) 12. Leiden: Brill, 1970.

Biblical Archeologist 42 (1979). Issue devoted to the Nag Hammadi discovery.

Blake, William. *The Four Zoas.* In *The Complete Poetry and Prose of William Blake*, edited by David V. Erdman, commentary by Harold Bloom. New York: Doubleday, 1988.

Blatz, Beate. "The Coptic Gospel of Thomas." In *New Testament Apocrypha*, edited by Wilhelm Schneemelcher, 1.110–33.

Blatz, Beate, and Einar Thomassen. "The Dialogue of the Savior." In *New Testament Apocrypha*, edited by Wilhelm Schneemelcher, 1.300–12.

Bloom, Harold. *The Flight to Lucifer: A Gnostic Fantasy.* New York: Vintage Books, 1980.

Böhlig, Alexander, and Frederik Wisse, eds. *Nag Hammadi Codices III,2 and IV,2: The Gospel of the Egyptians.* Nag Hammadi Studies 4. Leiden: Brill, 1975. Also Alexander Böhlig and Frederik Wisse, "The Gospel of the Egyptians," in *The Nag Hammadi Library in English*, edited by James M. Robinson, 208–19.

Bonner, Campbell. *Studies in Magical Amulets, Chiefly Graeco-Egyptian.* Ann Arbor: University of Michigan Press, 1950.

Bowe, Barbara E. "Dancing into the Divine: The Hymn of the Dance in the *Acts of John*." *Journal of Early Christian Studies* 7 (1999): 83–104.

Brown, Dan. *The Da Vinci Code: A Novel.* New York: Doubleday, 2003.

Buckley, Jorunn Jacobsen. *Female Fault and Fulfillment in Gnosticism.* Studies in Religion. Chapel Hill and London: University of North Carolina Press, 1986.

Bullard, Roger A., and Joseph A. Gibbons. "The Second Treatise of the Great Seth." In *The Nag Hammadi Library in English*, edited by James M. Robinson, 362–71.

Bultmann, Rudolf. *The Gospel of John: A Commentary.* Translated by G. R. Beasley-Murray. Philadelphia: Westminster, 1971.

Cameron, Ron. *Sayings Traditions in the Apocryphon of James.* Harvard Theological Studies 34. Philadelphia: Fortress, 1984.

Charlesworth, James H., ed. *The Old Testament Pseudepigrapha.* 2 vols. New York: Doubleday, 1983, 1985.

Charron, Régine. *Concordance des textes de Nag Hammadi: Le Codex III.* Bibliothèque copte de Nag Hammadi, Section "Concordances" 3. Québec, Louvain, and Paris: Les Presses de l'Université Laval, 1995.

Claude, Paul. *Les Trois stéles des Seth: Hymne gnostique à la Triade (NH VII,5)*. Bibliothèque copte de Nag Hammadi, Section "Textes" 8. Québec: Les Presses de l'Université Laval, 1983.

Crossan, John Dominic. *The Cross That Spoke: The Origins of the Passion Narrative*. San Francisco: Harper & Row, 1988.

———. *Four Other Gospels: Shadows on the Contours of Canon*. Minneapolis: Winston (Seabury), 1985.

Crum, Walter E. "A Gnostic Fragment." *Journal of Theological Studies* 44 (1943): 176–79.

Culianu, Ioan. "The Gnostic Revenge: Gnosticism and Romantic Literature." In *Religionstheorie und Politische Theologie, Band 2: Gnosis und Politik*, edited by Jacob Taubes, 290–306. Munich, Paderborn, Vienna, and Zurich: Wilhelm Fink/Ferdinand Schöningh, 1984.

———. *The Tree of Gnosis: Gnostic Mythology from Early Christianity to Modern Nihilism*. Translated by H. S. Wiesner. San Francisco: HarperSanFrancisco, 1992.

Davies, Stevan. *The Gospel of Thomas and Christian Wisdom*. New York: Seabury, 1983.

de Boer, Esther A. *The Gospel of Mary: Beyond a Gnostic and a Biblical Mary Magdalene*. New York and London: Clark International, 2004.

———. *Mary Magdalene: Beyond the Myth*. Translated by John Bowden. Harrisburg, PA: Trinity Press International, 1997.

———. "Mary Magdalene and the Disciple Jesus Loved." *Lectio Difficilior* 1 (2000). http://www.lectio.unibe.ch.

Debono, Fernand. "La basilique et le monastère de St. Pachôme." *Bulletin de l'Institut français d'archéologie orientale* 70 (1971): 191–220.

DeConick, April D. "The Great Mystery of Marriage: Sex and Conception in Ancient Valentinian Traditions." *Vigiliae Christianae* 57 (2003): 307–42.

———. *The Original Gospel of Thomas in Translation, with Commentary and New English Translation of the Complete Gospel*. Journal for the Study of the New Testament, Supplement Series. London: Clark, 2006 (forthcoming).

———. *Recovering the Original Gospel of Thomas: A History of the Gospel and Its Growth*. Early Christianity in Context. New York and London: Clark International, 2005.

Denzey, Nicola F. "Genesis Exegetical Traditions in the *Trimorphic Protennoia*." *Vigiliae Christianae* 55 (2001): 20–44.

Dick, Philip K. *Valis*. New York: Vintage Books, 1991.

Dirkse, Peter A., and James Brashler. "The Prayer of Thanksgiving." In *Nag Hammadi Codices V, 2–5 and VI*, edited by Douglas M. Parrott, 375–87. Also James Brashler, Peter A. Dirkse, and Douglas M. Parrott, "The Prayer of Thanksgiving," in *The Nag Hammadi Library in English*, edited by James M. Robinson, 328–29.

Dirkse, Peter A., James Brashler, and Douglas M. Parrott. "The Discourse on the Eighth and Ninth." In *Nag Hammadi Codices V, 2–5 and VI*, edited by Douglas M. Parrott, 341–73. Also James Brashler, Peter A. Dirkse, and Douglas M. Parrott, "The Discourse on the Eighth and Ninth," in *The Nag Hammadi Library in English*, edited by James M. Robinson, 321–27.

Dirkse, Peter A., and Douglas M. Parrott. "Asclepius 21–29." In *Nag Hammadi Codices V, 2–5 and VI*, edited by Douglas M. Parrott, 395–451. Also James Brashler, Peter A. Dirkse, and Douglas M. Parrott, "Asclepius 21–29," in *The Nag Hammadi Library in English*, edited by James M. Robinson, 330–38.

Doresse, Jean. "Les apocalypses de Zoroastre, de Zostrien, de Nicothée … (Porphyre, *Vie de Plotin*, §16)." In *Coptic Studies in Honor of Walter Ewing Crum*, edited by Michel Malinine, 255–63. Bulletin of the Byzantine Institute 2. Boston: Byzantine Institute, 1950.

———. *The Secret Books of the Egyptian Gnostics: An Introduction to the Gnostic Coptic Manuscripts Discovered at Chenoboskion*. Translated by Philip Mairet. London: Hollis & Carter, 1960.

Dunderberg, Ismo. "The School of Valentinus." In *A Companion to Second-Century Christian "Heretics,"* edited by Antti Marjanen and Petri Luomanen, 64–99.

Ehrman, Bart. *Lost Christianities: The Battle for Scripture and the Faiths We Never Knew*. New York and Oxford: Oxford University Press, 2003.

———. *Lost Scriptures: Books That Did Not Make It into the New Testament*. New York and Oxford: Oxford University Press, 2005.

Emmel, Stephen. "A Fragment of Nag Hammadi Codex III in the Beinecke Library: Yale inv. 1784." *Bulletin of the American Society of Papyrologists* 17 (1980): 53–60.

———. "The Recently Published *Gospel of the Savior* ('Unbekanntes Berliner Evangelium'): Righting the Order of Pages and Events." *Harvard Theological Review* 95 (2002): 45–72.

———. "Unbekanntes Berliner Evangelium = the Strasbourg Coptic Gospel: Prolegomena to a New Edition of the Strasbourg Fragments." In *For the Children, Perfect Instruction*, edited by Hans-Gebhard Bethge, Stephen Emmel, Karen L. King, and Imke Schletterer, 353–74.

———, ed. *Nag Hammadi Codex III,5: The Dialogue of the Savior*. Nag Hammadi Studies 26. Leiden: Brill, 1984. Also Helmut Koester, Elaine H. Pagels, and Stephen Emmel, "The Dialogue of the Savior," in *The Nag Hammadi Library in English*, edited by James M. Robinson, 244–55.

The Facsimile Edition of the Nag Hammadi Codices. Published under the auspices of the Department of Antiquities of the Arab Republic of Egypt in conjunction with the United Nations Educational, Scientific and Cultural Organization. 12 vols. Leiden: Brill, 1972–84.

Fallon, Francis T. *The Enthronement of Sabaoth: Jewish Elements in Gnostic Creation Myths.* Nag Hammadi Studies 10. Leiden: Brill, 1978.

Festugière, André-Jean. *La Révelation d'Hermès Trimégiste.* 4 vols. Paris: Gabalda, 1949–54.

Foerster, Werner, ed. *Gnosis: A Selection of Texts.* Translated by Robert McLachlan Wilson. 2 vols. Oxford: Clarendon Press, 1974.

Franke, Christina-Maria. "Die Erzählung über die Seele." In *Nag Hammadi Deutsch,* edited by Hans-Martin Schenke, Hans-Gebhard Bethge, and Ursula Ulrike Kaiser, 1.263–78.

Frankfurter, David. *Religion in Roman Egypt: Assimilation and Resistance.* Princeton, NJ: Princeton University Press, 1998.

Funk, Wolf-Peter. "Valentinianische Abhandlung." In *Nag Hammadi Deutsch,* edited by Hans-Martin Schenke, Hans-Gebhard Bethge, and Ursula Ulrike Kaiser, 2.747–62.

Giversen, Søren. "The Palaeography of Oxyrhynchus Papyri 1 and 654–655." Paper presented at the Society of Biblical Literature Annual Meeting, Boston, November 1999.

Goehring, James E., and James M. Robinson. "The Three Steles of Seth." In *Nag Hammadi Codex VII,* edited by Birger A. Pearson, 371–421. Also James E. Goehring and James M. Robinson, "The Three Steles of Seth," in *The Nag Hammadi Library in English,* edited by James M. Robinson, 396–401.

Goodenough, Erwin R. *Jewish Symbols in the Greco-Roman Period.* 13 vols. Princeton, NJ: Princeton University Press, 1953–68.

Grant, Robert M. *Gnosticism and Early Christianity.* 2d ed. New York: Columbia University Press, 1966

——, ed. *Gnosticism: An Anthology.* New York: Harper, 1961.

Grenfell, Bernard P., Arthur S. Hunt, et al., eds. *The Oxyrhynchus Papyri.* London: Egypt Exploration Fund, 1898–.

Grobel, Kendrick. *The Gospel of Truth: A Valentinian Meditation on the Gospel, Translation from the Coptic and Commentary.* Nashville and New York: Abingdon, 1960.

Grossmann, Peter, and Gary Lease. "Faw Qibli — 1989 Excavation Report (= Sixth Season)." *Göttingen Miszellen* 114 (1990): 9–16.

Haardt, Robert, ed. *Gnosis: Character and Testimony.* Leiden: Brill, 1971.

Halm, Heinz. *Die islamische Gnosis: Die extreme Schia und die 'Alawiten.* Die Bibliothek des Morgenlandes. Zurich: Artemis Verlag, 1982.

Hartenstein, Judith. "Das Evangelium nach Maria." In *Nag Hammadi Deutsch,* edited by Hans-Martin Schenke, Hans-Gebhard Bethge, and Ursula Ulrike Kaiser, 2.833–44.

Hartenstein, Judith, and Uwe-Karsten Plisch. "Der Brief des Jacobus." In *Nag Ham-madi Deutsch*, edited by Hans-Martin Schenke, Hans-Gebhard Bethge, and Ur-sula Ulrike Kaiser, 1.11–26.

Hedrick, Charles W. "Caveats to a 'Righted Order' of the *Gospel of the Savior*." *Har-vard Theological Review* 96 (2003): 229–38.

———, ed. *Nag Hammadi Codices XI, XII, XIII*. Nag Hammadi Studies 28. Leiden: Brill, 1990.

Hedrick, Charles W., and Robert Hodgson, Jr., eds. *Nag Hammadi, Gnosticism, and Early Christianity*. Peabody, MA: Hendrickson, 1986.

Hedrick, Charles W., and Paul A. Mirecki. *Gospel of the Savior: A New Ancient Gospel*. California Classical Library. Santa Rosa, CA: Polebridge Press, 1999.

Hills, Julian V. "The Dialogue of the Savior." In *The Complete Gospels: Annotated Scholars Version*, edited by Robert J. Miller, 336–50.

Hock, Ronald F., and Edward N. O'Neil, eds. *The Chreia in Ancient Rhetoric*. Vol. 1. Atlanta: Scholars, 1986.

Holzhausen, Jens. "Asklepios." In *Nag Hammadi Deutsch*, edited by Hans-Martin Schenke, Hans-Gebhard Bethge, and Ursula Ulrike Kaiser, 2.527–41.

Isenberg, Wesley W., and Bentley Layton. "The Gospel According to Philip." In *Nag Hammadi Codex II,2–7*, edited by Bentley Layton, 1.129–217. Also Wesley W. Isenberg, "The Gospel According to Philip," in *The Nag Hammadi Library in English*, edited by James M. Robinson, 139–60.

Janssens, Yvonne. *La Prôtennoia trimorphe (NH XIII,1)*. Bibliothèque copte de Nag Hammadi, Section "Textes" 4. Québec: Les Presses de l'Université Laval, 1978.

Jeremias, Joachim. *Unknown Sayings of Jesus*. 2d ed. Translated by Reginald H. Fuller. London: S.P.C.K., 1964.

Jonas, Hans. *The Gnostic Religion: The Message of the Alien God and the Beginnings of Christianity*. 2d ed. Boston: Beacon, 1963.

———. *Gnosis und spätantiker Geist. I. Die mythologische Gnosis*. 3d ed. Forschun-gen zur Religion und Literatur des Alten und Neuen Testaments 51. Göttingen: Vandenhoeck & Ruprecht, 1964.

Jones, F. Stanley, ed. *Which Mary? The Marys of Early Christian Tradition*. Sympo-sium 19. Atlanta: Society of Biblical Literature, 2002.

Jung, Carl G. *The Seven Sermons to the Dead (Septem Sermones ad Mortuos)*. In *The Collected Works of C. G. Jung*, edited by Herbert Read, Michael Fordham, and Gerard Adler. 20 vols. London: Routledge & Kegan Paul; Princeton, NJ: Prince-ton University Press, 1953–79.

Kahle, Paul E. *Bala'izah: Coptic Texts from Deir el-Bala'izah in Upper Egypt*. 2 vols. Oxford: Oxford University Press, 1954.

Kasser, Rodolphe. "Un nouvel apocryphe copte." Paper presented at the 8ème Con-grès International d'Études Coptes, Paris, July 2004.

Khalidi, Tarif. *The Muslim Jesus: Sayings and Stories in Islamic Literature*. Cambridge, MA, and London: Harvard University Press, 2001.

King, Karen L. "The Apocryphon of John: Part II of the Gospel of John?" Paper presented at the Society of Biblical Literature Annual Meeting, Denver, CO, November 2001.

———. "The Gospel of Mary." In *The Complete Gospels*, edited by Robert J. Miller, 351–60.

———. *The Gospel of Mary of Magdala: Jesus and the First Woman Apostle*. Santa Rosa, CA: Polebridge Press, 2003.

———. *Revelation of the Unknowable God: With Text, Translation, and Notes to NHC XI,3, Allogenes*. Santa Rosa, CA: Polebridge Press, 1995.

———. "Sophia and Christ in the Apocryphon of John." In *Images of the Feminine in Gnosticism*, edited by Karen L. King, 158–76.

———. *What Is Gnosticism?* Cambridge, MA: Belknap Press/Harvard University Press, 2003.

———. "Why All the Controversy? Mary in the *Gospel of Mary*." In *Which Mary?* edited by F. Stanley Jones, 53–74.

———, ed. *Images of the Feminine in Gnosticism*. Studies in Antiquity and Christianity. Philadelphia: Fortress, 1988.

King, Karen L., George W. MacRae, Robert McLachlan Wilson, and Douglas M. Parrott. "The Gospel of Mary." In *The Nag Hammadi Library in English*, edited by James M. Robinson, 523–27.

Kirchner, Dankwart. *Epistula Jacobi Apocrypha: Die zweite Schrift aus Nag-Hammadi-Codex I*. Texte und Untersuchungen 136. Berlin: Akademie Verlag, 1989.

Kirchner, Dankwart, and Einar Thomassen. "The Apocryphon of James." In *New Testament Apocrypha*, edited by Wilhelm Schneemelcher, 1.285–99.

Klijn, A. F. J. *Seth in Jewish, Christian, and Gnostic Literature*. Leiden: Brill, 1977.

Kloppenborg, John S. *Excavating Q: The History and Setting of the Sayings Gospel*. Minneapolis: Fortress, 2000.

———. *The Formation of Q: Trajectories in Ancient Wisdom Collections*. Philadelphia: Fortress, 1987.

———. *Q Parallels: Synopsis, Critical Notes and Concordance*. Sonoma, CA: Polebridge Press, 1988.

Kloppenborg, John S., Marvin W. Meyer, Stephen J. Patterson, and Michael G. Steinhauser. *Q–Thomas Reader*. Sonoma, CA: Polebridge Press, 1990.

Koester, Helmut. *Ancient Christian Gospels: Their History and Development*. Philadelphia: Trinity; London: SCM, 1990.

Koester, Helmut, Bentley Layton, Thomas O. Lambdin, and Harold W. Attridge. "The Gospel According to Thomas." In *Nag Hammadi Codex II,2–7*, edited by Bentley Layton, 1.37–128. Also Helmut Koester and Thomas O. Lambdin, "The

Gospel of Thomas," in *The Nag Hammadi Library in English*, edited by James M. Robinson, 126–38.

Koester, Helmut, and Elaine H. Pagels. "Introduction." In *Nag Hammadi Codex III,5: The Dialogue of the Savior*, edited by Stephen Emmel, 1–17.

Kuntzmann, Raymond. *Le Livre de Thomas (NH II,7)*. Bibliothèque copte de Nag Hammadi, Section "Textes" 16. Québec: Les Presses de l'Université Laval, 1986.

Layton, Bentley. *A Coptic Grammar, with Chrestomathy and Glossary (Sahidic Dialect)*. 2d ed. Porta Linguarum Orientalium, Neue Serie 20. Wiesbaden: Harrassowitz, 2004.

———. "Coptic Language." In *The Interpreter's Dictionary of the Bible: Supplementary Volume*, edited by Keith Crim, 174–79. Nashville, TN: Abingdon, 1976.

———. *The Gnostic Scriptures: A New Translation with Annotations and Introductions*. Garden City, NY: Doubleday, 1987.

———. *The Gnostic Treatise on Resurrection from Nag Hammadi: Edited with Translation and Commentary*. Harvard Dissertations in Religion 12. Missoula, MT: Scholars, 1979.

———. "Prolegomena to the Study of Ancient Gnosticism." In *The Social World of the First Christians: Essays in Honor of Wayne A. Meeks*, edited by L. Michael White and O. Larry Yarbrough, 334–50. Minneapolis: Fortress, 1995.

———, ed. *Nag Hammadi Codex II,2–7, Together with XIII,2*, Brit. Lib. Or. 4926(1), and P. Oxy. 1, 654, 655*. 2 vols. Nag Hammadi Studies 20–21. Leiden: Brill, 1989.

———, ed. *The Rediscovery of Gnosticism: Proceedings of the International Conference on Gnosticism at Yale, New Haven, Connecticut, March 28–31, 1978*. 2 vols. Studies in the History of Religions (Supplements to *Numen*) 41. Leiden: Brill, 1980–81.

Layton, Bentley, and William C. Robinson, Jr. "The Expository Treatise on the Soul." In *Nag Hammadi Codex II,2–7*, edited by Bentley Layton, 2.135–69.

Lease, Gary. "Traces of Early Egyptian Monasticism: The Faw Qibli Excavations." Occasional Papers of the Institute for Antiquity and Christianity 22. Claremont, CA: Institute for Antiquity and Christianity, 1991.

Létourneau, Pierre. *Le Dialogue du Sauveur (NH III,5)*. Bibliothèque copte de Nag Hammadi, Section "Textes" 29. Québec: Les Presses de l'Université Laval; Louvain and Paris: Peeters, 2003.

Lombardo, Stanley, and Robert Lamberton, eds. *Hesiod: Works and Days, and Theogony*. Indianapolis, IN: Hackett, 1993.

Lüdemann, Gerd, and Martina Janssen. *Bibel der Haretiker: Die gnostischen Schriften aus Nag Hammadi*. Stuttgart: Radius, 1997.

Luttikhiuzen, Gerard P., ed. *Eve's Children: The Biblical Stories Retold and Interpreted in Jewish and Christian Traditions*. Themes in Biblical Narrative 5. Leiden: Brill, 2003.

———, ed. *Paradise Interpreted: Representations of Biblical Paradise in Judaism and Christianity*. Themes in Biblical Narrative 2. Leiden: Brill, 1999.

Mack, Burton L. *Logos und Sophia: Untersuchungen zur Weisheitstheologie im hellenistischen Judentum*. Göttingen: Vandenhoeck & Ruprecht, 1973.

———. *The Lost Gospel: The Book of Q and Christian Origins*. San Francisco: HarperSanFrancisco, 1993.

MacRae, George W. "The Thunder: Perfect Mind." In *Nag Hammadi Codices V, 2–5 and VI*, edited by Douglas M. Parrott, 231–55. Also George W. MacRae and Douglas M. Parrott, "The Thunder: Perfect Mind," in *The Nag Hammadi Library in English*, edited by James M. Robinson, 295–303.

MacRae, George W., and Robert McLachlan Wilson. "The Gospel of Mary." In *Nag Hammadi Codices V, 2–5 and VI*, edited by Douglas M. Parrott, 453–71.

Mahé, Jean-Pierre. *Hermès en Haute-Égypte (Tome I): Les textes hermétiques de Nag Hammadi et leurs parallèles grecs et latins*. Bibliothèque copte de Nag Hammadi, Section "Textes" 3. Québec: Les Presses de l'Université Laval, 1978.

———. *Hermès en Haute-Égypte (Tome II): Le Fragment du Discours Parfait et les Définitions hermétiques arméniennes*. Bibliothèque copte de Nag Hammadi, Section "Textes" 7. Québec: Les Presses de l'Université Laval, 1982.

Mahé, Jean-Pierre, and Paul-Hubert Poirier, eds. *Écrits gnostiques*. Bibliothèque de la Pléiade. Paris: Gallimard, 2007 (forthcoming).

Marjanen, Antti. *The Woman Jesus Loved: Mary Magdalene in the Nag Hammadi Library and Related Documents*. Nag Hammadi and Manichaean Studies 40. Leiden, New York, and Köln: Brill, 1996.

Marjanen, Antti, and Petri Luomanen, eds. *A Companion to Second-Century Christian "Heretics."* Supplements to *Vigiliae Christianae* 76. Leiden and Boston: Brill, 2005.

Markschies, Christoph. *Valentinus Gnosticus? Untersuchungen zur valentinianischen Gnosis mit einem Kommentar zu den Fragmenten Valentins*. Tübingen: J. C. B. Mohr (Paul Siebeck), 1992.

McGuire, Anne. "Conversion and Gnosis in the *Gospel of Truth*." *Novum Testamentum* 28 (1986): 338–55.

———. "Women, Gender, and Gnosis in Gnostic Texts and Traditions." In *Women and Christian Origins*, edited by Ross Shepard Kraemer and Mary Rose D'Angelo, 257–99. New York and Oxford: Oxford University Press, 1999.

Ménard, Jacques-É. *L'Évangile de Vérité: Rétroversion grecque et commentaire*. Paris: Letouzey & Ané, 1962.

———. *L'Évangile selon Philippe: Introduction, texte, traduction, commentaire*. Strasbourg and Paris: Letouzey & Ané, 1967.

———. *L'Évangile selon Thomas*. Nag Hammadi Studies 5. Leiden: Brill, 1975.

———. *L'Exposé valentinien; Les Fragments sur le baptême et sur l'eucharistie (NH XI, 2)*. Bibliothèque copte de Nag Hammadi, Section "Textes" 14. Québec: Les Presses de l'Université Laval, 1985.

———. *Le Traité sur la résurrection (NH I, 4)*. Bibliothèque copte de Nag Hammadi, Section "Textes" 12. Québec: Les Presses de l'Université Laval, 1983.

Meyer, Marvin. "Archaeological Survey of the Wadi Sheikh Ali: December 1980." *Göttingen Miszellen* 64 (1983): 77–82.

———. "'Be Passersby': *Gospel of Thomas* Saying 42, Jesus Traditions, and Islamic Literature." In Marvin Meyer, *Secret Gospels*, 59–75.

———. "*Gnōsis, Mageia,* and the Holy Book of the Great Invisible Spirit." In *The Wisdom of Egypt: Jewish, Early Christian, and Gnostic Essays in Honour of Gerard P. Luttikhuizen,* edited by Anthony Hilhorst and George H. van Kooten. Arbeiten zur Geschichte des Antiken Judentums und des Urchristentums 59. Leiden: Brill, 2005.

———. *The Gnostic Gospels of Jesus: The Definitive Collection of Mystical Gospels and Secret Books About Jesus of Nazareth*. San Francisco: HarperSanFrancisco, 2005.

———. *The Gospel of Thomas: The Hidden Sayings of Jesus*. San Francisco: HarperSanFrancisco, 1992.

———. "*Gospel of Thomas* Logion 114 Revisited." In *For the Children, Perfect Instruction,* edited by Hans-Gebhard Bethge, Stephen Emmel, Karen L. King, and Imke Schletterer, 101–11. Also in Marvin Meyer, *Secret Gospels*, 96–106.

———. *The Gospels of Mary: The Secret Tradition of Mary Magdalene, the Companion of Jesus*. San Francisco: HarperSanFrancisco, 2004.

———. *The Letter of Peter to Philip: Text, Translation, and Commentary*. Society of Biblical Literature Dissertation Series 53. Atlanta: Scholars, 1981.

———. "Making Mary Male: The Categories 'Male' and 'Female' in the *Gospel of Thomas*." *New Testament Studies* 31 (1985): 544–70. Also in Marvin Meyer, *Secret Gospels*, 76–95.

———. Review of Karen L. King, *What Is Gnosticism? Review of Biblical Literature* (2004). http://www.bookreviews.org.

———. "The Round Dance of the Cross." In *The Gnostic Bible,* edited by Willis Barnstone and Marvin Meyer, 351–55.

———. *Secret Gospels: Essays on Thomas and the Secret Gospel of Mark*. Harrisburg, New York, and London: Trinity Press International/Continuum, 2003.

———. *The Unknown Sayings of Jesus*. Boston: Shambhala, 2005.

———, ed. *The Ancient Mysteries: A Sourcebook of Sacred Texts*. Philadelphia: University of Pennsylvania Press, 1999.

———, ed. *The Nag Hammadi Scriptures: The International Edition*. San Francisco: HarperSanFrancisco, 2006 (forthcoming).

Meyer, Marvin, and Charles Hughes, eds. *Jesus Then and Now: Images of Jesus in History and Christology*. Harrisburg, New York, and London: Trinity Press International/Continuum, 2001.

Meyer, Marvin, and Richard Smith, eds. *Ancient Christian Magic: Coptic Texts of Ritual Power*. Mythos. Princeton, NJ: Princeton University Press, 1999.

Miller, Robert J., ed., *The Complete Gospels: Annotated Scholars Version*. Santa Rosa, CA: Polebridge Press, 1994.

Nock, Arthur Darby, and André-Jean Festugière, eds. *Corpus Hermeticum*. 4 vols. Paris: Société d'édition "Les Belles lettres," 1945–54.

Orbe, Antonio. *Estudios Valentinianos*. Analecta Gregoriana 99. Rome: Pontificia Università Gregoriana, 1958.

Pagels, Elaine H. *Beyond Belief: The Secret Gospel of Thomas*. New York: Random House, 2003.

———. *The Gnostic Gospels*. New York: Random House, 1979.

———. *The Gnostic Paul: Gnostic Exegesis of the Pauline Letters*. Philadelphia: Fortress, 1975.

———. *The Johannine Gospel in Gnostic Exegesis: Heracleon's Commentary on John*. Society of Biblical Literature Monograph Series 17. Nashville, TN: Abingdon, 1973.

Pagels, Elaine H., and John D. Turner. "A Valentinian Exposition, with On the Anointing, On Baptism A and B, and On the Eucharist A and B." In *Nag Hammadi Codices XI, XII, XIII*, edited by Charles W. Hedrick, 89–172. Also Elaine H. Pagels and John D. Turner, "A Valentinian Exposition, with On the Anointing, On Baptism A and B, and On the Eucharist A and B," in *The Nag Hammadi Library in English*, edited by James M. Robinson, 481–89.

Painchaud, Louis. *Le Deuxième Traité du Grand Seth (NH VII,2)*. Bibliothèque copte de Nag Hammadi, Section "Textes" 6. Québec: Les Presses de l'Université Laval, 1982.

Parrinder, Geoffrey. *Jesus in the Qur'an*. New York: Oxford University Press, 1965.

Parrott, Douglas M, ed. *Nag Hammadi Codices V, 2–5 and VI with Papyrus Berolinensis 8502,1 and 4*. Nag Hammadi Studies 11. Leiden: Brill, 1979.

Pasquier, Anne. *L'Évangile selon Marie (BG 1)*. Bibliothèque copte de Nag Hammadi, Section "Textes" 10. Québec: Les Presses de l'Université Laval, 1983.

Patterson, Stephen J. *The Gospel of Thomas and Jesus*. Foundations and Facets. Santa Rosa, CA: Polebridge, 1993.

———. "Understanding the Gospel of Thomas Today." In *The Fifth Gospel*, edited by Stephen J. Patterson, James M. Robinson, and Hans-Gebhard Bethge, 33–75.

Patterson, Stephen J., James M. Robinson, and Hans-Gebhard Bethge. *The Fifth Gospel: The Gospel of Thomas Comes of Age*. Harrisburg, PA: Trinity Press International, 1998.

Pearson, Birger A. *Gnosticism and Christianity in Roman and Coptic Egypt*. Studies in Antiquity and Christianity. New York and London: Clark International, 2004.

———. *Gnosticism, Judaism, and Egyptian Christianity*. Studies in Antiquity and Christianity. Minneapolis: Fortress, 1990.

———, ed. *Nag Hammadi Codex VII*. Nag Hammadi and Manichaean Studies 30. Leiden: Brill, 1996.

Peel, Malcolm L. "The Treatise on the Resurrection." In *Nag Hammadi Codex I*, edited by Harold W. Attridge, 1.123–57. Also Malcolm L. Peel, "The Treatise on the Resurrection," in *The Nag Hammadi Library in English*, edited by James M. Robinson, 52–57.

Perkins, Pheme. *Gnosticism and the New Testament*. Minneapolis: Fortress, 1993.

Petersen, Silke, and Hans-Gebhard Bethge. "Der Dialog des Erlösers." In *Nag Hammadi Deutsch*, edited by Hans-Martin Schenke, Hans-Gebhard Bethge, and Ursula Ulrike Kaiser, 1.381–97.

Plisch, Uwe-Karsten. "Die Brontê — Vollkommener Verstand." In *Nag Hammadi Deutsch*, edited by Hans-Martin Schenke, Hans-Gebhard Bethge, and Ursula Ulrike Kaiser, 2.455–66.

———. "Das heilige Buch des großen unsichtbaren Geistes." In *Nag Hammadi Deutsch*, edited by Hans-Martin Schenke, Hans-Gebhard Bethge, and Ursula Ulrike Kaiser, 1.293–321.

Poirier, Paul-Hubert. *Le Tonnerre, intellect parfait (NH VI,2)*. Bibliothèque copte de Nag Hammadi, Section "Textes" 22. Québec: Les Presses de l'Université Laval; Louvain and Paris: Peeters, 1995.

Pritchard, James B., ed. *Ancient Near Eastern Texts Relating to the Old Testament*. 3d ed. Princeton, NJ: Princeton University Press, 1969.

Riley, Gregory J. *Resurrection Reconsidered: Thomas and John in Controversy*. Minneapolis: Fortress, 1995.

———. "Second Treatise of the Great Seth." In *Nag Hammadi Codex VII*, edited by Birger A. Pearson, 129–99.

Roberge, Michel. *La Paraphrase de Sem (NH VII,1)*. Bibliothèque copte de Nag Hammadi, Section "Textes" 25. Québec: Les Presses de l'Université Laval; Louvain and Paris: Peeters, 1999.

Roberge, Michel, and Frederik Wisse. "The Paraphrase of Shem." In *The Nag Hammadi Library in English*, edited by James M. Robinson, 339–61.

Robinson, Gesine Schenke. "Die dreigestaltige Protennoia." In *Nag Hammadi Deutsch*, edited by Hans-Martin Schenke, Hans-Gebhard Bethge, and Ursula Ulrike Kaiser, 2.807–31.

Robinson, James M. "From the Cliff to Cairo: The Story of the Discoverers and Middlemen of the Nag Hammadi Codices." In *Colloque international sur les texts de Nag Hammadi (Québec, 22–25 août 1978)*, edited by Bernard Barc, 21–58. Bibliothèque copte de Nag Hammadi, Section "Études" 1. Québec: Les Presses de l'Université Laval, 1981.

———. "From the Nag Hammadi Codices to the Gospels of Mary and Judas." *Watani International*, July 10, 2005. http://www.wataninet.com.

———. *The Gospel of Jesus: In Search of the Original Good News*. San Francisco: HarperSanFrancisco, 2005.

———. "The Jung Codex: The Rise and Fall of a Monopoly." *Religious Studies Review* 3 (1977): 17–30.

———. "Nag Hammadi: The First Fifty Years." In Stephen J. Patterson, James M. Robinson, and Hans-Gebhard Bethge, *The Fifth Gospel*, 77–110.

——. "The Pachomian Monastic Library at the Chester Beatty Library and the Bibliothèque Bodmer." Occasional Papers of the Institute for Antiquity and Christianity 19. Claremont, CA: Institute for Antiquity and Christianity, 1990.

——. "Sethians and Johannine Thought: The Trimorphic Protennoia and the Prologue of the Gospel of John." In *The Rediscovery of Gnosticism*, edited by Bentley Layton, 643–62.

——. "A Written Greek Sayings Cluster Older Than Q: A Vestige." *Harvard Theological Review* 92 (1999): 61–77.

——, ed. *The Nag Hammadi Library in English*. 3d ed. San Francisco: HarperSanFrancisco, 1988.

Robinson, James M., Paul Hoffmann, and John S. Kloppenborg, eds. *The Critical Edition of Q : Synopsis Including the Gospels of Matthew and Luke, Mark, and Thomas with English, German, and French Translations of Q and Thomas*. Louvain: Peeters, 2000.

Robinson, James M., and Helmut Koester. *Trajectories Through Early Christianity*. Philadelphia: Fortress, 1971.

Robinson, William C., Jr., and Madeleine Scopello. "The Exegesis on the Soul." In *The Nag Hammadi Library in English*, edited by James M. Robinson, 190–98.

Rouleau, Donald. *L'Épître apocryphe de Jacques (NH I,2)*, with L. Roy, *L'Acte de Pierre (BG 4)*. Bibliothèque copte de Nag Hammadi, Section "Textes" 18. Québec: Les Presses de l'Université Laval, 1987.

Rudolph, Kurt. *Gnosis: The Nature and History of Gnosticism*. English translation edited by Robert McLachlan Wilson. San Francisco: HarperSanFrancisco, 1987.

Sagnard, François. *La gnose valentinienne et le témoignage de Saint Irénée*. Paris: Vrin, 1947.

Schenke, Hans-Martin. "Der Brief an Rheginus (Die Abhandlung über die Auferstehung)." In *Nag Hammadi Deutsch*, edited by Hans-Martin Schenke, Hans-Gebhard Bethge, and Ursula Ulrike Kaiser, 1.45–52.

——. "Das Buch des Thomas." In *Nag Hammadi Deutsch*, edited by Hans-Martin Schenke, Hans-Gebhard Bethge, and Ursula Ulrike Kaiser, 1.279–91.

——. "Die drei Stelen des Seth." In *Nag Hammadi Deutsch*, edited by Hans-Martin Schenke, Hans-Gebhard Bethge, and Ursula Ulrike Kaiser, 2.625–32.

——. "Das Evangelium nach Philippus." In *Nag Hammadi Deutsch*, edited by Hans-Martin Schenke, Hans-Gebhard Bethge, and Ursula Ulrike Kaiser, 1.183–312.

——. "Evangelium Veritatis." In *Nag Hammadi Deutsch*, edited by Hans-Martin Schenke, Hans-Gebhard Bethge, and Ursula Ulrike Kaiser, 1.27–44.

——. "The Gospel of Philip." In *New Testament Apocrypha*, edited by Wilhelm Schneemelcher, 1.179–208.

——. *Die Herkunft des sogennanten Evangelium Veritatis*. Berlin: Evangelischer Verlag, 1958.

——. "Die Paraphrase des Sêem." In *Nag Hammadi Deutsch*, edited by Hans-Martin Schenke, Hans-Gebhard Bethge, and Ursula Ulrike Kaiser, 2.543–68.

———. "The Phenomenon and Significance of Sethian Gnosticism." In *The Redis-covery of Gnosticism*, edited by Bentley Layton, 2.588–616.

———. "The Problem of Gnosis." *Second Century* 3 (1983): 78–87.

———. "Das sethianische System nach Nag-Hammadi-Handschriften." In *Studia Coptica*, edited by Peter Nagel, 165–72. Berlin: Akademie Verlag, 1974.

———. *Das Thomas-Buch (Nag-Hammadi-Codex II,7)*. Texte und Untersuchungen 138. Berlin: Akademie Verlag, 1989.

Schenke, Hans-Martin, Hans-Gebhard Bethge, and Ursula Ulrike Kaiser, eds. *Nag Hammadi Deutsch*. 2 vols. Die Griechischen Christlichen Schriftsteller der er-sten Jahrhunderte, Neue Folge, 8, 12. Berlin and New York: Walter de Gruyter, 2001, 2003.

Schenke, Hans-Martin, and Einar Thomassen. "The Book of Thomas." In *New Tes-tament Apocrypha*, edited by Wilhelm Schneemelcher, 1.232–40.

Scher, Addai, ed. *Theodore bar Konai, Liber Scholiorum*. Corpus Scriptorum Chris-tianorum Orientalium 69. Paris and Louvain: Peeters, 1912.

Schmidt, Carl, and Violet MacDermot, eds. *The Books of Jeu and the Untitled Text in the Bruce Codex*. Nag Hammadi Studies 13. Leiden: Brill, 1978.

———, eds. *Pistis Sophia*. Nag Hammadi Studies 9. Leiden: Brill, 1978.

Schmithals, Walter. *Gnosticism in Corinth: An Investigation of the Letters to the Corinthians*. Translated by John E. Steely. Nashville, TN: Abingdon Press, 1971.

Schneemelcher, Wilhelm, ed. *New Testament Apocrypha*. English translation edited by Robert McLachlan Wilson. 2 vols. Cambridge: James Clarke; Louisville: Westminster/John Knox, 1991–92.

Scholem, Gershom. *Jewish Gnosticism, Merkabah Mysticism, and Talmudic Tradi-tion*. New York: Jewish Theological Seminary of America, 1960.

Scholer, David M. *Nag Hammadi Bibliography 1948–1969*. Nag Hammadi Studies 1. Leiden: Brill, 1971.

———. *Nag Hammadi Bibliography 1970–1994*. Nag Hammadi and Manichaean Studies 32. Leiden: Brill, 1997.

Schröter, Jens, and Hans-Gebhard Bethge. "Das Evangelium nach Thomas." In *Nag Hammadi Deutsch*, edited by Hans-Martin Schenke, Hans-Gebhard Bethge, and Ursula Ulrike Kaiser, 1.151–81.

Schweitzer, Albert. *The Quest of the Historical Jesus: A Critical Study of Its Progress from Reimarus to Wrede*. Translated by William Montgomery. New York: Macmillan, 1968; Baltimore: Johns Hopkins University Press, 1998.

———. *Reverence for Life*. Translated by Reginald H. Fuller. New York: Irvington/Harper & Row, 1969.

Scopello, Madeleine. *L'Exégèse de l'Âme: Nag Hammadi Codex II, 6*. Nag Ham-madi Studies 25. Leiden: Brill, 1985.

Segal, Alan F. *Two Powers in Heaven: Early Rabbinic Reports About Christianity and Gnosticism*. Studies in Judaism and Late Antquity 25. Leiden: Brill, 1977.

Sevrin, Jean-Marie. *Le dossier baptismal séthien: Études sur la sacramentaire gnostique*. Bibliothèque copte de Nag Hammadi, Section "Études" 2. Québec: Les Presses de l'Université Laval, 1986.

Sieber, John H. "The Barbelo Aeon as Sophia in Zostrianos and Related Tractates." In *The Rediscovery of Gnosticism*, edited by Bentley Layton, 2.788–95.

———, ed. *Nag Hammadi Codex VIII*. Nag Hammadi Studies 31. Leiden: Brill, 1991.

Smith, Jonathan Z. *Drudgery Divine: On the Comparison of Early Christianities and the Religions of Late Antiquity*. Chicago: University of Chicago Press, 1990.

Stead, G. C. "The Valentinian Myth of Sophia." *Journal of Theological Studies* 20 (1969): 75–104.

Stroumsa, Gedaliahu A. G. *Another Seed: Studies in Gnostic Mythology*. Leiden: Brill, 1984.

Tardieu, Michel. *Écrits gnostiques: Codex de Berlin*. Sources gnostiques et manichéennes 1. Paris: Cerf, 1984.

———. "Recherches sur la formation de l'Apocalypse de Zostrien et les sources de Marius Victorinus." In *Res Orientales IX*, 7–114. Bures-sur-Yvette: Groupe pour l'Étude de la Civilisation du Moyen-Orient, 1996.

———. *Trois mythes gnostiques: Adam, Éros et les animaux d'Égypte dans un écrit de Nag Hammadi (II,5)*. Paris: Études augustinennes, 1974.

Tardieu, Michel, and Jean-Daniel Dubois. *Introduction à la Littérature Gnostique*. Paris: Cerf, 1986.

Thomassen, Einar. *The Spiritual Seed: The Church of the "Valentinians."* Nag Hammadi and Manichaean Studies 60. Leiden: Brill, 2006.

———. "The Valentinianism of the Valentinian Exposition (NHC XI,2)." *Le Muséon* 102 (1989): 225–36.

Till, Walter C. *Das Evangelium nach Philippos*. Patristische Texte und Studien 2. Berlin: Walter de Gruyter, 1963.

Till, Walter C., and Hans-Martin Schenke. *Die gnostischen Schriften des koptischen Papyrus Berolinensis 8502*. 2d ed. Texte und Untersuchungen 60. Berlin: Akademie Verlag, 1972.

Torjesen, Karen Jo. *When Women Were Priests: Women's Leadership in the Early Church and the Scandal of Their Subordination in the Rise of Christianity*. San Francisco: HarperSanFrancisco, 1993.

Tröger, Karl-Wolfgang. "Ein (hermetisches) Dankgebet." In *Nag Hammadi Deutsch*, edited by Hans-Martin Schenke, Hans-Gebhard Bethge, and Ursula Ulrike Kaiser, 2.519–25.

———. "Über die Achtheit und Neunheit." In *Nag Hammadi Deutsch*, edited by Hans-Martin Schenke, Hans-Gebhard Bethge, and Ursula Ulrike Kaiser, 2.499–518.

Turner, John D. "The Book of Thomas the Contender." In *The Nag Hammadi Library in English*, edited by James M. Robinson, 199–207.

——. *The Book of Thomas the Contender from Codex II of the Cairo Gnostic Library from Nag Hammadi (CG II,7): The Coptic Text with Translation, Introduction and Commentary.* Society of Biblical Literature Dissertation Series 23. Missoula, MT: Scholars, 1975.

——. "Sethian Gnosticism: A Literary History." In *Nag Hammadi, Gnosticism, and Early Christianity,* edited by Charles W. Hedrick and Robert Hodgson, Jr., 55–86.

——. *Sethian Gnosticism and the Platonic Tradition.* Bibliothèque copte de Nag Hammadi, Section "Études" 6. Sainte-Foy, Québec: Les Presses de l'Université Laval; Louvain: Peeters, 2001.

——. "Trimorphic Protennoia." In *Nag Hammadi Codices XI, XII, XIII,* edited by Charles W. Hedrick, 371–454. Also John D. Turner, "Trimorphic Protennoia," in *The Nag Hammadi Library in English,* edited by James M. Robinson, 511–22.

Turner, John D., and Bentley Layton. "The Book of Thomas the Contender Writing to the Perfect." In *Nag Hammadi Codex II,2–7,* edited by Bentley Layton, 2.171–205.

Uro, Risto, ed. *Thomas at the Crossroads: Essays on the Gospel of Thomas.* Edinburgh: Clark, 1998.

Valantasis, Richard. *The Gospel of Thomas.* New Testament Readings. London and New York: Routledge, 1997.

Van Elderen, Bastiaan, and James M. Robinson. "The First Season of the Nag Hammadi Excavation: 27 November–19 December 1975." *Göttingen Miszellen* 22 (1976): 71–79; *American Research Center in Egypt Newsletter* 96 (1976): 18–24.

Van Lantschoot, Arnold. "Allocution de Timothée d'Alexandrie prononcée à la occasion de la dédicace de l'église de Pachôme à Pboou." *Le Muséon* 47 (1934): 13–56.

von Harnack, Adolf. *History of Dogma.* 7 vols. Translated by Neil Buchanan. New York: Dover, 1961.

——. *Marcion: The Gospel of the Alien God.* Translated by John E. Steely and Lyle D. Bierma. Durham, NC: Labyrinth Press, 1990.

Waldstein, Michael. "Das Apokryphon des Johannes." In *Nag Hammadi Deutsch,* edited by Hans-Martin Schenke, Hans-Gebhard Bethge, and Ursula Ulrike Kaiser, 1.95–150.

Waldstein, Michael, and Frederik Wisse, eds. *The Apocryphon of John: Synopsis of Nag Hammadi Codices II,1; III,1; and IV,1 with BG 8502,2.* Nag Hammadi and Manichaean Studies 33. Leiden: Brill, 1985.

Williams, Francis E. "The Apocryphon of James." In *Nag Hammadi Codex I,* edited by Harold W. Attridge, 1.13–53, 2.7–37. Also Francis E. Williams, "The Apocryphon of James," in *The Nag Hammadi Library in English,* edited by James M. Robinson, 29–37.

Williams, Michael A. *The Immovable Race: A Gnostic Designation and the Theme of Stability in Late Antiquity.* Nag Hammadi Studies 29. Leiden: Brill, 1985.

———. *Rethinking "Gnosticism": An Argument for Dismantling a Dubious Category.* Princeton, NJ: Princeton University Press, 1996.

———. "Sethianism." In *A Companion to Second-Century Christian "Heretics,"* edited by Antti Marjanen and Petri Luomanen, 32–63.

Wilson, Robert McLachlan. *The Gospel of Philip: Translated from the Coptic Text with an Introduction and Commentary.* New York and Evanston, IL: Harper and Row, 1962.

Wilson, Robert McLachlan, and George W. MacRae. "The Gospel According to Mary." In *Nag Hammadi Codices V, 2–5 and VI with Papyrus Berolinensis 8502,1 and 4,* edited by Douglas M. Parrott, 453–71.

Wisse, Frederik. "The Apocryphon of John." In *The Nag Hammadi Library in English,* edited by James M. Robinson, 104–23.

———. "The Paraphrase of Shem." In *Nag Hammadi Codex VII,* edited by Birger A. Pearson, 15–127.